Burnchurch Castle, Kilkenny

THE CASTLES
OF LEINSTER

Mike Salter

FOLLY PUBLICATIONS

ACKNOWLEDGEMENTS

The illustrations in this book are mostly the product of the author's own site surveys since 1971. Plans redrawn from his field notebooks are mostly reproduced to scales of 1:400 for keeps, tower houses, gatehouses and stronghouses, and 1:800 for courtyard castles and bawns, whilst a few large sites and earthworks are shown at 1:2000. Thanks are due to Eamon Cody and the staff of the National Monuments Record section of the Department of the Environment, Heritage and Local Government in Dublin for allowing access to the archaeological records and providing much help, information and advice. About a dozen of the drawings are at least partly based on material contained in their records. Thanks are also due to: Max Barfield for driving on the 1992 field-trip, Ian Rennie and Jeremy Morfey who each drove on one trip in 2003 (Jeremy also took the picture of Newtown), Keith Mears for a few plans, Helen Thomas for checking the text, Ken McLeod for information and many pictures, including those used here of Togher, Leap and Doon and that of Trim used on the back of the cover, and to the staff of the Bodleian Library at Oxford.

AUTHOR'S NOTES

This book is the fourth in a series of five volumes superseding the author's previous work Castles and Stronghouses of Ireland, published in 1993 and now out of print. It is part of a series of books about castles and fortified houses throughout Britain and Ireland, all in a similar style with plans on a set of common scales, allowing useful comparisons of sizes, wall thicknesses, etc. It is recommended that visitors use the Ordnance Survey 1:50,000 scale maps to locate the monuments, grid references being given in the gazetteers, along with codes indicating which castles can be visited or viewed from public rights of way (see page 17). The book is intended as a portable field guide giving as much information and illustrative material as possible in a book of modest size, weight and price, and especially providing material about buildings not properly described elsewhere in print. The aim has been to give some basic information about owners or tenants of castles, but no attempt has been made to provide detailed genealogical histories. Ghost stories, myths and legends are not normally included, and personalities later than the 1690s are generally only mentioned if of importance to an understanding of a building's architectural development or its current state of ruination such as deliberate dismantling to obtain building materials.

All dimensions are given in metres and usually refer to the size of the building at or near ground level. Most towers will be smaller than the quoted dimensions higher up because of the external batter of the walls. The majority of the measurements quoted were personally taken by the author. On plans original work is shown black, post 1700 work is shown stippled, and alterations and additions of intermediate periods are shown hatched. Each level is called a storey, lofts tucked under vaults being treated as full storeys, and the basement being the first or lowest storey with its floor at or near ground level unless mentioned as otherwise. An attic room entirely within the height of a gabled roof is usually mentioned as an extra level additional to the number of storeys given.

ABOUT THE AUTHOR

Mike Salter is 50 and has been a professional writer and publisher since 1988. He is particularly interested in the planning and layout of medieval buildings and has a huge collection of plans of castles and churches he has measured during tours (mostly by bicycle and motorcycle) throughout all parts of the British Isles since 1968. Wolverhampton born and bred, Mike now lives in an old cottage beside the Malvern Hills. His other interests include walking, maps, railways, board games, morris dancing and playing percussion instruments and calling folk dances with an occasional folk group.

First published February 2004. Copyright Mike Salter 2004.
Folly Publications, Folly Cottage, 151 West Malvern Rd, Malvern, Worcs WR14 4AY
Printed by Aspect Design, 89 Newtown Rd, Malvern, Worcs WR14 2PD.

Maynooth Castle, Kildare

CONTENTS

BRIEF HISTORICAL INTRODUCTION

Castles as the Normans knew them were almost unknown in Ireland prior to the invasion of Richard de Clare (Strongbow) in 1170 in support of Dermot, King of Leinster, whose daughter and heiress he married. King Henry II of England arrived in Ireland in 1171 and forced de Clare to hold Leinster as a fief of the English Crown. Most of the Irish leaders submitted to King Henry, who then made Hugh de Lacy his Justiciar of Ireland, giving him a huge lordship formed from the former kingdom of Meath. In 1177 King Henry's youngest son John was created Lord of Ireland, and in 1210 John, by then King of England, campaigned in Ireland in an effort to reduce the power of the de Lacy and de Braose families. By this time the Normans ruled over all of what eventually became the twelve counties of the province of Leinster.

The Gaelic-speaking native Irish, however, remained in the majority, having generally been left the poorer uplands. They only nominally submitted to English rule and rebelled whenever there was an opportunity, such as when Edward Bruce, brother of Robert Bruce, King of Scots, campaigned in Ireland in 1315-17. To encourage the Norman magnates to resist the rebels Edward II in 1316 created an earldom of Carrick for Edmund Butler and an earldom of Kildare for Thomas FitzGerald. However, by 1327 the MacMurroughs of Wicklow were strong enough to call themselves kings of Leinster again and before long other Irish families such as the O'Mores of Laois and the O'Connors of Ely had re-established themselves in positions of power. In 1328 Edward III created an additional earldom of Ormond for James Butler, Earl of Carrick.

Athlumney: plan.

Tremblestown Castle, Meath

Holdensrath, Kilkenny

Castle Columb, Kilkenny

Cloncourse Castle, Laois

By 1394 Art og MacMurrough, King of Leinster was so powerful that Richard II came over with a huge English army to try and bring him to terms. However, as soon as Richard returned to England there was turmoil again in Ireland, and three years later the rebels defeated and killed the Lord Lieutenant, Roger Mortimer, Earl of March and claimant of the earldom of Ulster and the lordships of Connacht, Meath, Laois and Ossory. A second campaign by King Richard failed to achieve anything before he was forced to return to England, where he was deposed and eventually murdered. In the 15th century the earls of Ormond and Kildare functioned almost as independent princes and by the end of that period the English Crown only had control over a few scattered towns and an area known as the English Pale comprising Dublin and the adjoining parts of Kildare, Meath and Louth.

The earls of Kildare supported the Yorkist faction during the Wars of the Roses and in 1470 the then earl was made Lord Deputy of Ireland by the Irish Parliament. Apart from being held by Sir Edward Poynings in 1494-6 and by the Earl of Surrey in 1520-22, the all-powerful office of Lord Deputy of Ireland remained with the earls of Kildare until Henry VIII destroyed them in 1534 after the 9th Earl was imprisoned in London and his son "Silken" Thomas was goaded into rebellion. King Henry adopted the title King of Ireland in 1541. In 1556 his daughter Queen Mary made the territories of Laois and Offaly into the shires of Queen's County and King's County. Much of the land there was given to English and Welsh families, the O'Carrolls and O'Connors of Offaly being dispossessed for their part in the 1534 rebellion. The Gaelic-speaking native Irish remained in the majority, however, and when the Desmond FitzGeralds rebelled in 1579 the O'Byrnes of Wicklow and the O'Connors of Offaly soon joined in, although without much success.

Only after the northern Earls of Tyrone and Tyrconnell fled to Spain in 1607 was there peace in Ireland. It lasted until the oppressed Catholics rebelled in 1641, and then in 1649 Cromwell invaded Ireland, capturing many fortresses. After he had finally established a peace again many of the Catholic families were transplanted to western Ireland and their estates given to English families and former Cromwellian army officers. Only a few of the Catholics managed to recover their lands after Charles II was restored to the thrones of England and Scotland in 1660. They naturally supported the exiled Catholic James II in his unsuccessful campaign in Ireland in 1689-90. This was the last occasion when town defences and private castles were seriously defended in Ireland. By the 18th century a few castles had been adapted as country houses but the majority were abandoned ruins.

ARCHITECTURAL INTRODUCTION

Forts with earth ramparts with a hedge or wooden palisade on top or with walls of limestone blocks laid without mortar were common in Ireland in the Dark Ages. There is evidence of a feudalism of a sort and a very limited amount of castle-building in Ireland in the early 12th century, but castles were essentially a Norman idea introduced by them in the 1170s along with the feudal system of land being held in return for military service (often later changed to some form of rent). By the early 13th century the invading Normans had built about three hundred castles in what later became the twelve counties of the province of Leinster. Only a few major castles had stone buildings and the most of the others took the form of a timber house or tower within a small palisaded court set upon a motte, a wholly or partly man-made flat-topped mound raised from material taken out of a surrounding ditch. Sometimes there was an accompanying enclosure or bailey containing wooden buildings and defended by a palisade on an earth rampart with a ditch in front. Alternatively the mound might take a larger but lower form known as a ringwork and combine the functions of both motte and bailey. In some cases natural features such as drumlins or promontories were adapted to form castles of this type. These castles vary considerably in size and strength according to the needs and the resources of those who built them, but few have mounds or ramparts higher than 8m. Most ringworks are between 20m and 30m across on top, while mottes rarely have summits more than 15m across. Some of them are quite modest in size and the majority are now overgrown, sometimes to the point where little can be seen of the earthworks. This book is essentially about stone castles, tower houses being the author's particular subject of interest, and since few of the mottes and ringworks have been properly surveyed or excavated, most of them are merely listed in this book. The only earthworks described in the gazetteers and their supplementary lists are those which had stone defences, plus a few that have been excavated, or whose construction by the Norman invaders or destruction by the Irish is recorded by contemporary chroniclers. There are also a large number of manor-house sites in Leinster taking the form of a square or rectangular platform up to 30 or 40m across surrounded by remains of a water-filled moat. Such moats provided some protection against malefactors and wild animals, safely secured the domestic animals, and were also status symbols. For a more detailed discussion of mottes, ringworks and moated sites see the early chapters of Medieval Ireland by Tadhg O'Keefe, and the references given there.

The keep at Carlow

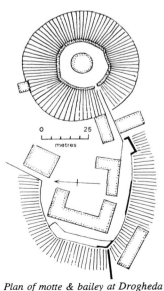

Plan of motte & bailey at Drogheda

Motte at Drogheda, Louth

Rathmore, Co Kildare

Castlering, Co Louth

Mount Temple, Co Westmeath

Motte at Rathmore, Co Kildare

Lea Castle, Laois   *Kilkenny Castle*

Very few castles in Leinster retain stone buildings of the last three decades of the 12th century. The cruciform keep at the chief de Lacy seat at Trim in Meath is thought to have been begun c1174 but was probably not completed until the early 13th century. It now has four storeys but originally contained just a hall and private chamber side-by-side. An even larger but more ruinous keep at Dunamase in Laois contained a hall and chamber end to end, and excavations have recently revealed an early gatehouse. A keep at Maynooth in Kildare probably begun in the 1190s had a hall and chamber raised over dark cellars. All these castles have spacious courts, although that at Maynooth is mostly or entirely of the later medieval period. Trim has a gatehouse with the outer corners chamfered off at the top, similar to towers in the late 11th century de Lacy castle of Ludlow in Shopshire. This feature also appears on a flanking tower of the small court on a rock at another de Lacy castle at Carlingford. It also has remains of a gatehouse with a passage between two rectangular towers, a plan recalling that of the gatehouses of the inner ward of the 1180s at Dover in Kent, but not found elsewhere in Britain at such an early date.

The castle built by William Marshal at Kilkenny in 1207-12 was of a more advanced type with circular towers of differing sizes at the four corners of a quadrangular court. A royal castle of a similar type was begun at Dublin in 1213. Of these castles there remain three towers at Kilkenny and two (very altered) at Dublin. They are usually described as keepless castles although in fact each had at least one huge tower as big as any of the circular keeps existing elsewhere in Ireland. A three storey circular keep of c1200 remains in use as a lighthouse at Hook in Wexford and a later and more altered example lies on a mound at Low's Castle in Westmeath. Athlone has a much altered polygonal tower keep standing in the middle of an also heavily rebuilt 13th century court with round corner towers, and there is a fragment of another polygonal keep on a motte at Castle Knock, near Dublin. Nothing remains of a gatehouse with a passageway between twin U-shaped towers at Dublin itself, nor anything of a similar gatehouse thought to have existed at Kilkenny. At about this period the bailey at Trim was given a new south curtain wall with a series of small open-backed D-shaped towers and a second gatehouse on a circular plan (unique in the British Isles) with a barbican extending in front of it.

Ballymoon Castle, Carlow

William Marshal's castle at Carlow took a different form, being a rectangular keep with circular corner towers. It contained a public hall over a cellar and a private chamber on top, with other private rooms in the towers. Later in the 13th century a similar keep was built at Lea in Laois. The castle at Ferns in Wexford represents a further development of this form, being so large that it seems to have had ranges with timber-framed inner walls towards a tiny central court. One rib-vaulted room in a corner tower was a chapel, a rare instance of such a room surviving in an Irish secular building. There are impressive remains of these keeps, although none of them is now anything like complete. That at Lea was fairly closely surrounded by a thinly-walled court, arcading being necessary to give enough width for a wall-walk and parapet. This castle also has a large outer court to which a gatehouse with twin U-shaped towers was added in the 1290s, the most complete example of its type in Ireland. Another gatehouse of that period at Newcastle in Wicklow has been much altered, losing the round outer fronts of its towers. Dunamase has a smaller gatehouse of this type probably of c1230 with narrower towers with square ends. The outer part remains of another twin-towered gatehouse at Roche, where the curtain wall remains unusually complete (despite the loss of the only flanking tower), as does a block which contained an unusually wide hall over a basement below courtyard level.

Also of the 13th century are a series of rectangular buildings known either as hall-keeps if they have substantial outer defences, or hall-houses if they stand alone. The finest of them is a building at Grenan in Kilkenny which probably contained a hall and private chamber end to end over cellars given vaults in the later medieval period. The fragmentary keep at Clonmacnoise had pilaster buttresses clasping the corners carried up at turrets. This building was accompanied by a small court lying within massive earthworks. A hall-block at Carbury in Kildare has been much altered and ruined, but another at Carlingford in Louth is relatively complete. Only the lowest levels remain of other hall-houses at Corrool in Longford and Castle Lost in Westmeath, the latter being vaulted. Although much altered later in the medieval period, the building at Woodstock in Kildare may have originally been a 13th century hall-house. Another at Kindlestown in Wicklow may be as late as the 14th century.

Trim: west gateway

Dunamase Castle, Laois

Swords Castle, Dublin

Dating from the late 13th and early 14th centuries are a very ruined aisled hall and adjacent chamber tower on the river front at Trim and a series of three castles in County Carlow all with square courts up to 40m across. One, at Clonmore, has a series of domestic ranges built in several campaigns to eventually extend along one side of the court and rectangular towers at three of the corners. The second, Ballymoon, had four ranges of two storey domestic buildings set around a central court, a layout with several English parallels but not otherwise found in Ireland. There are no towers, just turrets containing latrines for the upper rooms, whose inner walls have vanished. The third, Ballyloughan, has rectangular towers at two diagonally opposite corners and a square gatehouse with circular towers on the corners facing the field. The only other medieval gatehouse similar to this remaining in Ireland is the barbican known as the St Laurence Gate on the town walls of Drogheda. Probably dating from c1375-80 is a square court at Granagh on the southern edge of Co Kilkenny with a hall and chamber tower facing to landward and circular towers on the corners facing the river. The bawn has quite thick walls but if defence against overland assaults was a priority one would expect the plan to be reversed, with domestic buildings against the river and flanking towers to landward.

Apart from those mentioned above, secular buildings known to date with certainty from the 14th century are not common in Ireland. A few of the tower houses about to be discussed could be of c1370-1400 and represent a development from the earlier hall-houses, whilst the fortified churches at Clonmines and Killesk in Wexford may be of the late 14th century. The tower at the archbishop of Dublin's 14th century castle at Swords could be regarded as an early tower house, standing alone across the large irregularly planned court from domestic ranges around the gateway, and it has been suggested that a small group of fragmentary towers in Co Carlow are also late 14th century.

Nearly all of the castles built in Ireland during the 15th and 16th centuries were of the type now known as a tower house. They are widespread also in Scotland and the northern parts of England and seem to have been generally regarded as a suitable form of residence for lesser landholders needing a measure of defensibility and security at night within strife-torn areas where raiding was endemic. In England only a few of the later medieval lordly residences (fortified or not) away from the border regions featured a tower house, but in Ireland the type was almost universally adopted, regardless of rank, although the great lords naturally tended to build larger and more massive towers. They were often built to impress the local inhabitants after an estate or district changed hands, whether by marriage, purchase, inheritance, an exchange of lands or military conquest. For the defence of the Pale around Dublin the Irish government under Henry VI in 1429 encouraged the erection of small towers by offering cash grants. Small towers such as those at Newcastle in Co Dublin may be typical of the so-called "£10 castles" then built, although the slightly larger example with round corners and a circular stair turret at one corner at Donore in Meath is often quoted as an example. Commonly these towers contained two levels forming a cellar and loft under a vault, and two storeys of single living rooms above the vault, at which level slightly larger windows could be provided.

Old sketch of Castleknock

Clonony Castle, Offaly

Old Print of Dunmoe Castle

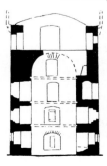

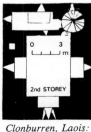

Clonburren, Laois:
plan & section

Bartizan at Toberdaly, Offaly

Circular tower house at Grantstown, Laois   *Lismaine Castle, Kilkenny*

Since the same architectural features remained in fashion up until the 1640s and reliable records of construction only survive for a very few towers, individual examples are quite hard to date, although, as will be discussed later, certain features introduced during the 16th century suggest a later date for some them. Timber joists which appear to be original in the tower at Tyrrelspass in Westmeath have been dendrochronologically dated to c1410, but the majority of the towers are thought to date from the period 1450 to 1550. They vary quite a lot in size, those of the English Pale being generally quite small and thinly walled, often having projecting turrets to contain staircases and latrines. Towers built by the native Irish and by English families outside the Pale (many of whom gradually adopted Gaelic speech and customs) tend to be larger. Apart from a few circular examples of the late 16th century they are mostly plain rectangles since their thicker walls were able to accommodate stairs, latrines and mural chambers without needing projections.

Towers known or assumed to have been built by English-speaking families, and also those built in towns by merchants and the clergy tend to conform to the normal tower house layout found in England and Scotland with a public hall immediately over a vault over the storage areas and then more private rooms further up. The larger towers further inland often have a different layout with the private rooms halfway up and a main hall formed in the topmost storey where a considerable thinning of the walls, often above a vault, allowed a much larger chamber than anywhere lower down. It appears that Gaelic-speaking land-owners (whether native Irish or Gaelicised Anglo-Norman) may have been less concerned about their personal security and privacy than their English-speaking counterparts. It should be noted, however, that allegiances in Ireland were constantly shifting and many families were neither purely Irish nor purely English in their speech, customs and allegiances, and the political and social position became even more complicated with the effects of the Reformation of the 1540s further dividing loyalties.

Window at Donore, Co Westmeath

Dundrum, Co Dublin

Knocklyon, Co Dublin

Many of the tower houses have graceful batter to the external wall-faces but others rise vertically above a battered base. The Leinster towers usually have entrances at ground level leading into a lobby covered by a murder-hole from a chamber or embrasure higher up and sometimes there is an external machicolation as well. Where original battlements survive they are of the normal late medieval Irish type with stepped merlons, the origin of which is unknown as they do not occur on buildings in England, Wales or Scotland. Entrances were always closed by a wooden door opening inwards and secured with a drawbar sliding in slots in the jambs, but there was also sometimes a hinged iron grill called a yett opening outwards, a hole in the door jamb being used to secure the yet with a chain. Tower houses rarely had portcullises but there are grooves for them in a few towers in Co Wexford. From the entrance lobby there is usually access to either a spiral staircase in an adjacent corner to the lowest of several flights of straight steps.

The smaller towers usually had up to four habitable levels with one vault but a few of the larger and taller buildings in the western parts of Leinster had five storeys with a vault below the topmost level, and sometimes also a second vault lower down. In this book each level is called a storey even if it was no more than a storage loft or sleeping space for servants lighted by a single loop in an end wall and squeezed in under a vault. The vaults may be round arched, segmental or pointed, and where there are two they may be of different forms, or even orientated differently. Later medieval vaults in Ireland were usually laid over mats of wickerwork supported upon wooden frames and often show clear traces of these mats, which were left in position and plastered over. They contrast sharply with the plank-centred vaulting found in 13th century buildings such as in the staircase of the keep at Clonmacnoise.

flanker at Sierkernan, Offaly

Moygaddy Castle

Many of the towers built by English-speaking landowners in the counties of Dublin, Meath and Louth, plus a few in Westmeath, have projecting corner turrets. There are four rectangular turrets of differing sizes and degrees of projection on the towers at Athlumney, Castletown, Dunsoghly and Killeen, and three at Athcarne, Balregan, the Court House at Ardee, and on the oldest of the two buildings at Liscartan. The large buildings at Dunmoe and Delvin, and a much smaller building at Heynestown all had four circular turrets. More common, however, was the provision of two turrets, one for the staircase (usually with the entrance beside it) and the other (which is sometimes smaller) for latrines. At Dunmahon they are square and lie at adjacent corners, but a more usual arrangement was for them to lie at diagonally opposite corners, as in the round pairs at Killincoole and Milltown, and the square pair at Roodstown, all of these being in Louth. Several towers in Dublin have just one turret for the stair, as at Ashtown, Athgoe, Corr and Newcastle. They served no military purpose since they do not have firing loops and do not generally flank all the sides of the building. In fact gunloops are not often found in the English areas.

About twenty of the inland towers adopt a plan form more common in Connacht and Munster with a tier of mural chambers above the entrance passage in an end wall. Sometimes there are other rooms and passages in the upper walls and some of these are squeezed into the haunches of upper vaults, which would otherwise be too heavy if they were entirely solid. Loops piercing the corners of the building are quite common too, this feature being another Irish speciality not found in England, Wales or Scotland. Several towers in Kilkenny have one or both ends of the tower raised up above the main wall-walk, as at Burnchurch. A number of towers in Tipperary also share this feature.

Windows in Irish towers tend to be narrow. On the upper levels the lights are often paired and on the topmost level they are sometimes tall enough to justify the use of a transom. For the sake of brevity in the gazetteers only those windows with ogival heads, hoodmoulds or other decorative features such as carved or sunk spandrels beside ogival heads are mentioned specifically, and other windows not fully described will have square-headed (or occasionally round-headed) lights. These tall narrow windows were usually provided with internal full-length shutters rather than glass panes. Here and there a stone hanging eye for mounting the upper pivots of a window shutter or door still survives, although most have been broken when the wood was salvaged for burning or re-use elsewhere. The embrasures of upper room windows sometimes have stone seats. The rere-arches are often semi-circular or segmental, although lintels were often used, especially for the narrower embrasures of loops in mural chambers and passages.

Ballybrittain Castle, Offaly

Baldwinstown, Wexford

Aghaviller, Kilkenny: church converted into stronghouse   *Boherquill Castle, Longford*

All the arrangements and features of tower houses described so far can occur at any period from the early 15th century to the early 17th century. There are, however certain features that seem to have begun to be used more commonly from about the 1540s. Large Gunports for cannon mounted on carriages are rare in medieval towers and bawns in Ireland, but small circular or square gunloops for the discharge of hackbuts and pistols are common enough in towers of the period 1540 to 1640. Portable firearms existed in Ireland in the late 15th century but they were not in general use until later. They are found in the inland towers and bawns built by Gaelic-speaking families and their allies, or by nervous English families that replaced Gaelic-speakers under resettlement schemes. Sometimes a window or loop will have gunloops opening either side of it from the same embrasure. Many of the towers within the Pale probably predate the common useage of firearms, and gunloops are rare in towers and bawns in counties Dublin, Louth and Wexford.

Towers with gunloops also have fireplaces in their upper rooms and consequently have chimney stacks on the end gables. Other stacks on the sidewalls partly or entirely impede access round the wall-walk. Some of the later towers did not have full circuits of wall-walks. Annaghs in Kilkenny had an unusual four-gabled cross-shaped roof with open fighting tops on the corners only. Towers in English areas have small fireplaces that are probably original but further inland 15th century towers seem to have originally been without fireplaces, the only heating being a central hearth or brazier on the stone floor of the topmost hall, with a louvre in the roof to allow the smoke to escape. There are several instances of large upper fireplaces (often with joggled lintels and side brackets to take the thrust of the walling above) bearing initials of owners and dates, but these can be misleading, since they may refer to minor later alterations and not the original period of construction. Many 15th century towers were modernised in the late 16th and early 17th centuries with inserted fireplaces, gunloops and one or two large new mullioned windows of the flat-headed type then in fashion with somewhat wider lights than beforehand.

Early 17th century towers may occasionally have the lowest storey subdivided into two cellars or provided with a fireplace for use as a kitchen. Both these features are rare in Irish tower houses, although 16th and 17th century Scottish castellated buildings often have basement kitchens together with separate cellars for food and wine. Donadea in Kildare and Shrule in Laois, both towers bearing datestones (another late feature), have their lowest levels subdivided, the crosswall at Shrule clearly being in insertion.

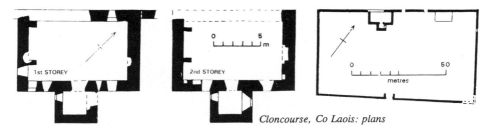

Cloncourse, Co Laois: plans

Towers in Dublin, Kildare, Meath, Louth and Wexford often have non-projecting top turrets raised above those corners not already having projecting turrets rising from ground level. Circular bartizans with machicolations between their corbels also occur, especially in Wexford, are more common further inland. A few late 16th century bartizans on towers in Offaly and Laois (circular at Ballinlough but square elsewhere, as at Srah) contain gunloops and are set below the wallhead so that they contain small roofed chambers. Corbels carrying bartizans and box-machicolations in Leinster are usually of the double-stepped curved bracket type also used in England, but there are a few instances in the province of the tall inverted-pyramid type more usual in Connacht and Munster.

About a sixth of the towers have or had a court known as a bawn. Although they can be of any shape and size, bawns are usually rectangular and of modest size (rarely more than 45m long). They can have walls up to 1.6m thick and 6m high but the later examples, which are more numerous, tend to have walls up to about 1.1m thick and 4m high. Well preserved bawns are rare in the English Pale, but there are two fine examples with wall-walks and bartizans at Killiane and Rathmacknee in Wexford, and larger examples in Kilkenny at Clonmanagh, Foulksrath and Ballyragget, the last of these having circular corner flankers. A large and massive 15th century tower at Cullahill in Laois is very closely surrounded by a 16th century chemise bawn with gunloops both in the low and thin bawn wall and in the tiny casemate-type slab-roofed corner flankers. There is also a spacious outer bawn without flankers. Although a few bawns had proper gatehouses, as at Drimnagh and Monkstown in Co Dublin, most bawns had modest gateways closed simply by two-leaved doors secured with drawbars. None of them had portcullises, and few had drawbridges, since they rarely had moats. A moat does survive at Drimnagh, although it encloses a larger area than that enclosed by the bawn. Domestic buildings in the bawns remain at Dunsoghly and Drimnagh, both in Co Dublin, but they rarely survive otherwise, although traces of their former presence can sometimes be seen on the outer walls. There are several instances of substantial later wings being added to tower houses in Meath, and also at Rathcline in Longford, and Killeenbrack in Westmeath.

Rathcline Castle, Longford

A few 15th and 16th century castles in Leinster deviate from the standard tower house type with or without a bawn. Rathumney in Wexford is a rather domestic looking building with two storey blocks at either end of a single storey hall. Also in Wexford are several castles with a long main block containing a hall and chamber end-to-end over cellars and then a third storey above, the levels being linked by a staircase in a taller service tower at one end which also contains the entrance and latrines, as at Bargy and Coolhull. Fethard is an earlier variant of this with a lofty circular corner tower and an added gatehouse and kitchen range. Kilkea in Kildare has been much altered and extended but appears to have had two ranges at right angles allowing a hall and principal private chamber on the same level. Boherquill in Longford has a tower-like block at one end of a very ruined building which presumably contained an upper-floor hall, perhaps with another chamber block at the far end. Trimblestown in Meath has a main block containing a hall and perhaps also a private chamber over a vault over two lower levels whilst a projecting wing provided extra chambers. A late building at Kilbreedy in Laois seems to have contained just one large upper room with large windows over a vault over two poorly lighted lower levels.

In the medieval period walls were often harled (or rendered) on the outside, whilst whitewashing the internal walls made the best of the limited light admitted through the narrow windows. The living rooms sometimes had wall-paintings of biblical, allegorical or heroic scenes, or tapestries or other hangings with similar motifs. Carpets were only introduced in the late 16th century, before which those floors not formed of planks laid on massive beams were made of rammed earth or clay. All the floors were covered with rushes changed occasionally as thought necessary.

Since those few towers which are not ruins have mostly been heavily remodelled and re-roofed at some point during the 18th and 19th centuries, medieval roofs rarely survive in Ireland. There is one on the tower at Dunsoghly in Dublin, and another which appears to be ancient has recently been exposed again to view at Foulksrath in Kilkenny. As already mentioned, a tower at Tyrrelspass has 15th century joists surviving, and a few also remain at Clara. Other old woodwork has rarely survived, although a rather ruinous tower at Kilrush in Kilkenny retains a studded entrance door which may be 16th century.

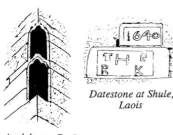

Angleloop, Coole,
Co Offaly

Datestone at Shule,
Laois

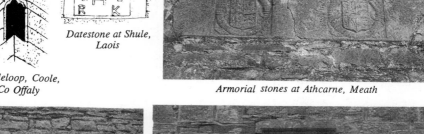

Armorial stones at Athcarne, Meath

Latrine chutes, Castle Rea, Longford

Armorial panel at Talbot's Castle, Trim, Meath

The sort of privacy we now all take for granted hardly existed in a medieval castle. Even nobles often had attendants sleeping in the same room or in a passage outside, although the lordly bed would be screened or curtained off. However, many of the towers were owned or occupied as tenants by those of much lower rank. Furniture was sparse and of the simplest kind until the 17th century. Only the owner (or tenant) and his immediate family were likely to have individual chairs, but the main public room would contain tables and benches. Also suitable for seating were the chests within which clothes, plate and other valuables were kept. A notable feature of the tower houses, especially the thicker walled towers of Kilkenny, Laois and Offaly, is the number of lockers within the walls, nearly every window embrasure having one in some towers.

The confiscation of lands held by Catholics and their redistribution to English-speaking Protestants occurred at about the time when some families, both the native Irish and the new Protestant settlers, began building stronghouses or fortified houses. Generally larger than tower houses, these are mansions with mullion-and-transom windows like the Tudor and Stuart manor houses in England but with ground level windows kept small and provided with iron stanchions, and defensive features such as bartizans, gunloops and entrances with yetts, enabling them to be defended against attacks of short duration by belligerent neighbours, landless marauders, or unruly tenants. In Leinster such buildings tend either to be attached to older towers, as at Slade in Wexford, and Rathcline in Longford, or to take a form not unlike that of the tower houses, except for their generally longer and lower outline (often with lofty or projecting chimney stacks), as at Tinnahinch in Carlow, Deeps, Enniscorthy and Rathshillane in Wexford, Cloncourse in Laois, and Ballycowen, Castle Armstrong and Curralanty in Offaly. Enniscorthy and Curralanty have circular corner towers, whilst stair-wings at Tinnahinch, Ballycowen and Cloncourse result in L-planned or T-planned buildings. Of these only Ballycowen has vaulted cellars.

In Wexford the abbeys of Tintern and Dunbrody were converted into embattled houses, although another house with a towered bawn was later built close by at Dunbrody. At Timahoe in Laois a wide-naved medieval church was converted into a tower and bawn. Buildings of a more domestic nature are Tullomoy in Laois, Rathfarnham near Dublin and, in Meath, Fennor and the house added to an older tower at Athlumney. In a few cases the house itself was a modest building or has become very ruinous and more striking now is its bawn wall and flankers, as at Carlanstown in Westmeath, where the circular flankers are quite lofty towers, and Newtown in Offaly. Also in Offaly are Birr, with a much altered gatehouse and substantial earthen artillery ramparts of the 1620s, and Kilcolgan, which has circular flankers with triangular prows on the outermost part, which would otherwise be dead ground not covered by gunloops in the next flanker. At Rush Hall in Laois the flankers are polygonal, not a common form for structures of any period in Ireland. These were the last privately owned defensible buildings built in Leinster. After the restoration of Charles II in 1660 the Irish gentry lived in undefended country houses, the tower houses either been abandoned, or, in a few cases, adapted and extended as country houses, whilst only the government erected and maintained fortifications, mostly to defend the shores and waterways.

Dowth Castle, Co Meath

Robertstown Castle, Co Meath

Dunboyne: plans

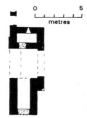

Sheep Gate, Trim

Tullomoy, Laois

ACCESS TO THE CASTLES

The majority of the 650 buildings described in this book are uncared-for ruins mouldering away in fields or farmyards. Only about thirty ruins and a few roofed buildings are maintained by the state as monuments regularly open to the public, and access without permission is only possible in a few other instances. Fifty buildings remain occupied as private dwellings and one or two others remain roofed but are not in use as dwellings. These can generally only be viewed at a distance, if at all.

The following codes appear after the Ordnance Survey grid references in the gazetteers. They give only an indication since access arrangement may change from time to time, as may the amount of vegetation obscuring distant views, whilst some monuments may only be open during the summer months. Sites not given a code lie on private land and can only be seen by obtaining prior permission from landowners. Only occasionally will a courteous request for access by those with a genuine interest in ancient buildings be refused outright. Some owners may be reluctant to allow visitors to ascend the staircases of ruins considered precarious or may only allow access to the exterior. Visitors should in all cases close any gates that they need to open, ensure that their dogs do not cause any kind of nuisance to the farmers or their animals, and generally follow the maxim of taking away only photographs and leaving behind nothing but footprints.

A - Free access on foot to the whole site at any time. Mostly sites in state care.
B - Free access on foot at any time to the exterior only. Mostly sites in state care.
C - Private, but clearly visible from public road, path, or other public open space.
D - Private, but distant view usually possible from road, path, or other open space.
E - Open to the public (fee usually payable) during certain hours in summer at least.
G - Private, unmaintained, but fairly easy courtesy access currently normally possible.
H - Buildings in use as hotels, shops, museums, etc. Exterior access usually possible.

DEFENSIBLE ECCLESIASTICAL BUILDINGS

In Leinster late medieval ecclesiastical buildings were often embattled and capable of defence against raids of short duration. Windows in the local churches and abbeys are generally small except a few high above the ground, and they were generally protected with iron stanchions, whilst doorways are usually fitted with drawbar slots. The abbeys of Bective in Meath and Fore in Westmeath, plus Slane college in Meath incorporate defensible towers in their layout. Most abbeys had semi-defensible precinct walls, Kells in Kilkenny being the most spectacular example with several tower houses flanking the precinct wall (which has no wall-walk) and two others amongst the claustral buildings, whilst an abbey at Clonmines in Wexford has a gatehouse with a portcullis groove. Irish parish churches are usually plain single chambers but a few churches in Leinster had towers which not only served as campaniles but also as defensible residences for clergy, with a couple of living rooms over a vaulted basement, as at Kilfane and Threecastles in Kilkenny, and Newcastle in Co Dublin. Killesk in Wexford and Templecross in Westmeath are buildings with similar layouts in which the west end of a small single chamber is vaulted over and the walls thickened to provide a solid floor for a single living room above that end of the building. Taghmon in Westmeath has a rather larger single chamber which is entirely vaulted with an embattled parapet above. This church has a four storey west tower, also embattled, providing the clergy with a secure and impressive residence. Clonmines in Wexford has a rectangular building with two corner turrets and a machicolation over the main entrance which is variously described as a fortified church or ecclesiastic court house, the single chamber being vaulted throughout, although the east end has ribs on the vault. See the separate entries for Bective (p111), Clonmines (p168), Kilfane (p76), Slane (p119), St Johns (p125) Threecastles (p77), & Timahoe (p91).

Fortified church at Clonmines, Wexford

Bective Abbey

Templecross, Westmeath: plan

Killesk, Wexford, plan of church

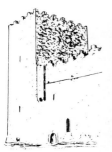

Taghmon Church

*Tower at St Johns,
Co Meath*

Slane College

Taghmon, Westmeath: plan of church

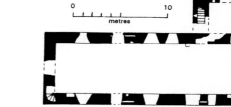

Plan of Kilfane Church, Co Kilkenny

Killesk Church, Wexford

Tower by church at Donabate, Dublin

A GLOSSARY OF ARCHITECTURAL TERMS

BAILEY - Defensible space enclosed by a stone wall or a palisade and ditch. BARTIZAN - Turret corbelled out from a corner. BASTION - Flanking projection of about the same height as a wall, not rising above it as a tower ot turret would. BAWN - An enclosure, usually modest in size, surrounded by a wall. CASEMATE - A small vaulted chamber providing flanking fire along a wall. CORBEL - A projecting bracket supporting other stonework or timber beams. FLANKER - A bastion or turret at the corner of a bawn. Usually provided with gunloops. GUNPORT - An opening, usually with an embrasure splayed both internally and externally, for the mounting of cannon. GUNLOOP - A small hole suitable for the discharge of a musket or hand-pistol. HALL-HOUSE - A two storey building containing a hall or chamber over a cellar. HARLING or ROUGHCAST - External coating of plaster or other coarse aggregate to make a building waterproof. The normal external finish of most medieval buildings originally, except those with ashlar-facing. HOODMOULD - Projecting moulding above an arch or lintel to throw off water. JAMB - The side of a doorway, window or other opening. KEEP - A citadel or ultimate strongpoint. The term was not used earlier than the 16th century, and such a building would normally be referred to as a "great tower" or "donjon". LIGHT - A compartment of a window. LOOP - A small opening to admit light or for the discharge of missiles. MACHICOLATION - A slot for the dropping or shooting of missiles at assailants. MERLON - The upstanding part of a crenellated parapet, the cut-away parts being crenels. In the later medieval period merlons in Ireland were commonly stepped in form, with a narrower topmost part. MOAT - a defensive ditch, dry or water filled either permanently or seasonally. MOTTE - A wholly or partly man-made castle mound. MULLION - A vertical member dividing the lights of a window. MURDER-HOLE - An internal machicolation, often in the vault of an entrance lobby, or at the foot of a flight of steps. OGIVAL-ARCH - Arch of oriental origin with both convex and concave curves, first used in Britain in the early 14th century. OILLET - Small round opening. PARAPET - A wall for protection at any sudden drop. PILASTER - A flat buttress. PORTCULLIS - Gate designed to rise and fall in vertical grooves, being hoisted up from above by a windlass. Occasionally all-metal, but more commonly of wood, but with an iron covering. POSTERN - A secondary gateway or doorway. A back entrance. SCALE-AND-PLATT STAIRCASE - Staircase with short straight flights and turns at landings. SHEELA-NA-GIG - Female figure usually with the genitalia exposed. SPANDREL - A surface between an arch and the rectangle containing it. STRONGHOUSE - A mansion capable of being defended against an attack. TOWER HOUSE - Self-contained house with the main rooms stacked vertically either for reasons of defence or as a status symbol. TRACERY - Intersecting ribwork in the upper part of a Gothic window. TRANSOM - A horizontal member dividing the lights of a window. WALL-WALK - A walkway protected by a parapet on top of a wall. YETT - Iron gate supported on hinges. In Ireland they usually opened outwards and were secured with a chain running through a hole on one side.

FURTHER READING

Castles in Ireland, Tom McNeill, 1997
The Architecture of Ireland, Maurice Craig, 1982
The Medieval Castles of Ireland, David Sweetman, 1999
Medieval Ireland, An Archaeology, Tadhg O'Keeffe, 2000
Irish Castles and Castellated Houses, Harold Leask, 1941
Guide to the National Monuments of Ireland, Peter Harbison, 1970
The Shell Guide to Ireland, Lord Killanin and Michael Duignan, 1969
Castles and Fortifications in Ireland 1485-1945, Paul Kerrigan, 1995

Loop at Ballagh

There are recent ancient monuments inventories published by the Office of Public Works
   available for the counties of Carlow, Laois, Louth, Meath, Offaly, Wexford and
   Westmeath. These contain more exhaustive bibliographies than can be given here.
See also the annual proceedings of the Royal Irish Academy, the Journal of the Royal
   Society of Antiquaries in Ireland, Kilkenny Archaeological Society, the Ulster Journal
   of Archaeology, Wexford Historical Society, and Medieval Archaeology.
Guide pamphlets exist for: Athlone, Dublin, Kilkea, Kilkenny, and Trim

BALLYLOO CASTLE S743698 D

Not much remains above the level of the vault, which has mostly fallen, over a loft over the cellar, and the NW wall containing the entrance is almost reduced to the ground. The tower may be of late 14th or early 15th century date and measures 12m by 8.2m over walls up to 1.7m thick. One embrasure and loop are fairly complete but the others are ragged holes. There are traces of a latrine chute in the east corner.

BALLYLOUGHAN CASTLE S746585 A

This early 14th century castle was later taken over by the Kavanagh MacMurroughs until it passed to the Bagenals in the 1650s. It was later sold to the Bruens. Little now remains of the 1m thick curtain wall around a courtyard 47m by 41m and the moat has been filled in, but there are ruins of a three storey gatehouse 10m by 9m with 5m diameter round towers 10m high on the southern corners, a staircase in the east wall and latrines for the upper rooms in the west wall. At the SW corner of the court is a two storey tower measuring 10m by 9m with one wall twice the thickness of the others to carry a straight stair to the upper room, which has a two light window facing south. Less survives of the NE tower measuring 7.8m by 6.4m which was added later and converted into a cottage in the 18th century, and only footings remain of a small turret at the NW corner.

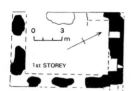

Ballyloo: plan

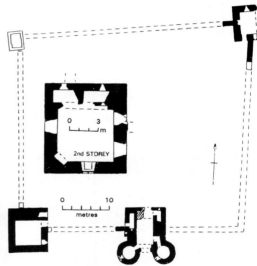

Plans of Ballyloughan Castle

Ballyloo Castle *Ballyloughan Castle*

Ballymoon Castle

BALLYMOON CASTLE   S740615   A

Nothing for certain is known of the history of this castle. Begun probably c1300 by either the Carews or the Bigod Earl of Norfolk, it was evidently left unfinished. A curtain wall 2.2m thick and 6m high surrounds an area 37m square containing footings for domestic ranges around all four sides of central court. Toothing stones on either side of the gateway suggest it was intended to add a gatehouse or barbican. A stair led to a room over the passage from which a portcullis was operated. There are no corner towers but the other sides are flanked by turrets containing pairs of latrines serving the upper rooms, plus a narrow turret with single latrines on two levels projecting NE from the east corner. The hall lay on the NW side where a large fireplace remains between traces of large windows high up, and the main private chambers on the NE. There are a number of embrasures with crossloops and lintelled rere-arches around the SE and NE sides of the building.

Ballymoon Castle

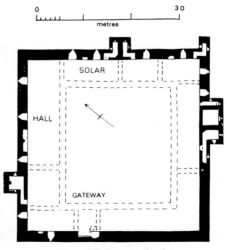

Plan of Ballymoon Castle

Carlow Castle

Plan of Carlow Castle

CARLOW CASTLE   S720766   A

Within the grounds of a factory stands the western half of a large keep remaining from a once extensive castle mostly demolished in the early 19th century to build a lunatic asylum. Hugh de Lacy is thought to have built a motte here c1180, and the keep was probably built by William Marshal in c1208-13. The castle was later held by the Bigod earls of Norfolk and their successors the Howards until it was confiscated in the 1530s. Some time during this period the town was probably walled but nothing is known of the layout of any defences. The castle was captured and briefly held by James FitzGerald in 1494 and again by Silken Thomas in 1535. It was granted to Edward Randolf in 1552, to Robert Hartpole in 1577, and was sold 1616 to Donough, Earl of Thomond. The castle was captured by the Confederate Catholics in the 1640s and was surrendered to General Ireton in 1650. It was eventually returned to the Earl of Thomond and was later held by the Hamiltons.

The three storey keep measured 21m by 14m over walls 2.7m thick above a battered plinth. The west wall contained staircases leading up and down from the hall on the second storey. A stub of the north wall contains the entrance doorway opening onto the hall. Two of the four corner towers 8m in diameter survive, the NW tower having a top stage of the 16th century, when mullioned windows were inserted to give more light to the state rooms.

CLOGRENNAN CASTLE   S697736

This castle by a crossing of the River Barrow was badly damaged during a siege by Sir George Carew in 1569. A sketch of 1680 shows the building as rebuilt or replaced by a five storey house with three gables on the side facing the approach and parapets on the end walls. It was converted into a gateway into the demesne of a new house in 1806 but was a ruin by 1870. Most of the building either fell or was demolished in 1931. The surviving footings may be no older than the 18th century.

CLONMORE CASTLE   S960761   C

This late 13th century castle has a court about 45m square enclosed on the north and west by a wall 1.6m thick, and by apartments on the east side, whilst the destroyed south wall must have contained the main gateway. There is a postern beside the NW tower, which measures 6.5m by 5.2m and has a stair leading direct from the court to a room over the vaulted cellar. A SW corner tower 10m by 8m is mostly ruined above the lowest level but there was at least one upper room with a latrine on the west. The hall block, now much ruined and obscured with ivy, is rather oddly located so that there is a re-entrant NE angle. Another such re-entrant angle is created by the placing of the solar block south of it further east, so that the two only touch at one corner. The hall lay over cellars or offices and seems to have had a latrine at the NW corner in conjunction with access to a passage along part of the north curtain wall. The private chamber had a latrine in the projecting SE corner, which also contained stairs down to the rooms below. Towards the end of the 13th century, or early in the 14th, another block was added further south, with a four storey tower beyond at the courtyard SE corner. This block in turn is set further east than the chamber block and contains vaulted cellars, a living room with a fireplace above, and a fine new great chamber on the same level as the old one. This room has a fireplace and a window with two trefoil-headed lights on the west and two more such windows on the east. A spiral stair in the adjacent tower gave access to a gallery at the south end.

HUNTINGTON   S913607

This still-occupied stronghouse with 1.8m thick walls, vaulted cellars, 17th century plaster ceilings and a semi-circular projection on the west side was built in 1625 by Laurence, Earl of Esmond. It was extended in the 1680s by Sir Laurence Esmonde, 2nd Baronet and further altered in 1720, and also in 1860 by Alexander Durdin.

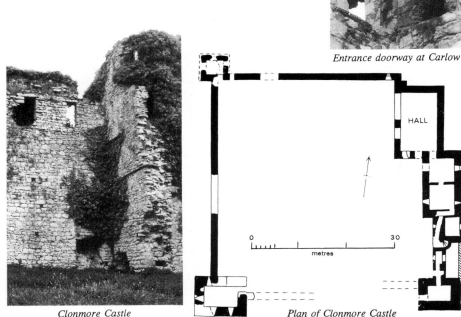

Entrance doorway at Carlow

Clonmore Castle

Plan of Clonmore Castle

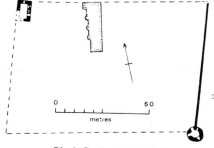

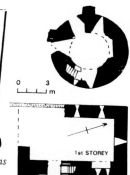

Clonmore Castle

Black Castle, Leighlinbridge: plans

LEIGHLINBRIDGE: BLACK CASTLE   S691654   B

On the east bank of the Bannow, guarding the bridge, is a tower known as the Black Castle to distinguish it from the vanished White Castle nearby supposedly built in 1408 by Gerald, Earl of Kildare. Probably of the 1540s in its present form, the Black Castle measures 11.6m by 8.2m and has an east wall 2m thick containing an entrance protected by a machicolation and a murder hole from a window seat above. A stair leads up to a loft under a vault and a single living room above. There are rooms in the haunches of the vault and on the north and south the wall-walk is enclosed as galleries, with a corbelled chamber over the NE corner spiral staircase. The tower lies in the NW corner of a bawn 100m by 80m now only represented by 1.8m thick fragments of the north and south walls and the overgrown circular SE corner flanker 8m in diameter equipped with stirrup-shaped gunloops. One jamb of the north-facing bawn gateway adjoins the main tower. A murage grant to raise funds for walling the town was made in 1310. A 10m long section of the wall remains standing 3.5m high together with one circular turret.

Two views of the Black Castle, Leighlinbridge

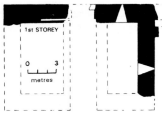

Rathnageeragh: plan

Rathnageeragh Castle

RATHNAGEERAGH CASTLE   S767566

Only the NW and NE walls remain of a 13th or 14th century building about 18m by 12m which contained rectangular vaulted chambers on either side of a gateway passage. The NE wall contains a latrine chute and has traces of a former adjoining curtain wall. A stair in the destroyed SW wall and surviving west corner led up to the second storey.

TINNAHINCH CASTLE   S708433   D

This building is thought to have been erected in the 1630s by James Butler. Of three storeys with corbels to carry the upper floors, it measures 13.4m by 9.4m and has a round bartizan on the north corner and a wing projecting west from the SW corner to contain a wooden staircase and a north facing entrance within one of the re-entrant angles with a machicolation at top storey level to protect it. The north wall contains a kitchen fireplace and oven at ground level and both end walls contain fireplaces on the two upper levels, so the top storey (at least) was probably subdivided. There was also an attic flanked by wall-walks on the east and west sides only.

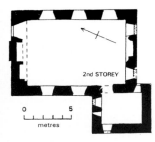

Tinnahinch Castle

Tinnahinch: plans

OTHER CASTLE REMAINS IN COUNTY CARLOW

ALTAMONT S864656 Lower part of house has thick walls, including one gunloop. The kitchen and service rooms are thought to have been at the south end.

BALLINREE S772555 Pile of rubble on site of gatehouse or hall house. Had three vaults at lowest level where walls were 1.8m thick.

BALLYNALOUR S752354 Just a 2m high fragment of the NW and NE walls with three steps of a staircase now remain of this tower house.

BALLYTARSNA S761672 Of a tower measuring 10.7m by 7.4m the north wall stands 3m high but only footings remain of the other sides.

CASTLETOWN S755717 North end of 18th century house incorporates base of tower with walls 1.5m thick with a stair, flagged floor and jamb of loop.

COPPENAGH S850761 Only the SE wall with openings at two levels below a vault now remains, along with large chunks of fallen masonry.

DUNLECKNEY S719629 Possible motte west of old graveyard. Nearby 19th century house incorporates parts of later stone castle revealed during recent repairs.

FRIARSTOWN S802764 SW corner fragment, footings of west wall, and rubble pile of tower of Knights Hospitallers. Cropmarks suggest a D-shaped moated court around it.

JOHNSTOWN S775765 House has cellars probably of older date which may represent castle shown on 1650 Down Survey or an outbuilding.

RATHVILLY S878818 Platform 50m by 40 with ditch on north. Castle here perhaps built by Hugh de Lacy in 1180s. Mentioned in grant to Earl of Norfolk in 1346. Damaged in the campaign of 1650 but remained occupied to at least 1730.

WILLIAMSTOWN S906790 10m length of wall base and pile of debris remain.

OTHER CASTLE SITES IN CARLOW

BALLYBAR S734712 Pile of debris still remained in 19th century of castle at Ballybar Upper. There was also once a castle at Ballybar Lower.

BALLYMOGUE S785640 Platform 50m across probably marks site of bawn.

BALLYNUNNERY S790696 Low fragment of tower and outbuilding with double-splayed window survived until c1930. Sketch of 1680 shows two gabled towers.

CLONMULLEN S897552 Nothing now remains of this building.

CLONOGAN S917623 Ruinous in 1540, having been forfeited by Earl of Kildare in 1534. Slight traces of earthworks marking a court 45m by 35m from which materials are said to have been taken c1820 to build Clonogan House.

DUNGANSTOWN S718794 No remains of castle depicted in 1650 on island in Barrow. Built by the St Ledgers, passed to the Butlers and then to the Bests (later known as Bestfield).

FARDURRAGHNAGRANBY'S S813750 Curved wall shown on old photo now gone.

GRAIGUE S766751 No remains of castle shown on 1839 map, which also shows the site of another castle in Bennekerry Townland close to the NW.

GRAIGUEALUG S767690 Castle site on 1839 map. Possible second site nearby.

GRAIGUENASPIDDOGE S772686 Nothing now remains of a tower measuring about 9m by 7.5m. with a low arched doorway.

HAROLDSTOWN S908784 Vanished castle stood close to graveyard.

KILNOCK S804677 Walled garden may represent bawn. Castle "out of repaire" in 1650.

KILLERRIG S814770 Plantation on site. Footings visible in field drain.

RATHMORE Described in 1598 as one of the eight principal castles of Carlow. Marked as "an old castle" on the 1650 Down Survey. No remains.

STRABOE S824796 Bawn outline suggested by cropmarks seen from the air.

TULLOW S851730 No remains of Hugh de Lacy's motte, or later stone castle shown in sketch c1680 as having a court with a house and a gatehouse with two round towers. Possible former town wall, since a murage grant was made in 1343.

22 other castles are shown on the Down survey of 1650 but their sites remain unknown.

Other sites: Ballinkillin S727556, Clowater S716549, Downings S845777, Moyle S768731.

MOTTES: Ballyknockan S689646, Castlegrace S844678, Castlemore S828738, Minvaud S968760, Rathvilly S890818, St Mullins S728380

CASTLES OF COUNTY DUBLIN

ASHTOWN   O113363   E

Beside the visitor centre in Phoenix Park is an early 17th century tower with a spiral stair in a gabled wing connecting three levels of a main block 8.6m by 6.6m. There are wall-walks with plain parapets on the south and north sides, but the end walls rise straight to gables, with a chimney stack on the east gable. In 1663 the Duke of Ormonde purchased the castle and its 200 acre estate from his friend and agent John Connell. The estate was made a deer-park with the castle as the keepers' lodge until in the 18th century it was incorporated into a new building called Ashtown Lodge. This became the official residence of the Under-Secretary for Ireland in 1782. In the 1920s it was used by the United States legation and then from 1929 until 1978 by the papal nuncio. The decayed house was then demolished to reveal the original tower, the windows of which have been reinstated by the Office of Works, and the entrance doorway moved back to its original position beside the stair wing. The original main house in the park was Kilmainham, originally a Knights Hospitaller priory, which stood where the Royal Hospital was established in the 1680s.

ATHGOE   N988269

Beside a house of 1750 is a round-cornered tower dated 1579, which could be when it was constructed by the Locke family. The tower measures 7.3m by 6.5m and has four storeys linked by a spiral stair in a semi-circular turret set close to the entrance doorway.

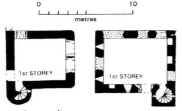

Athgoe: plan   *Ashtown: plan*

Breamore Castle

Athgoe Castle

Ashtown Castle

Bawn gateway at Carrickmines

BREAMORE O198646 D

The Barnewalls' house is now being renovated and many of the mullioned windows with hoodmoulds (some also have transoms) on the second and third storeys have been renewed. The second storey has an oriel at the south end with a five-light window with gunloops below. Other oriels are provided on the east side of a long gallery in a fourth storey within the roof. The gallery has a five-light window in a wing projecting from the east side. A later wing with stepped battlements at the north end of the west side contains a kitchen. In 1736 Captain MacCulloch defended this building against Captain Vernon, Sheriff of Dublin until he ran out of ammunition and the wall was breached.

CARRICKMINES O218240 D

Excavations prior to building a motorway through the site have revealed extensive foundations of buildings, and one fragment of the gateway stands 2.5m high on the west side. The castle existed by 1326, when Maurice Howel was desperately trying to hold on to his lands here in the face of attacks by the O'Byrnes. A siege by the latter in 1369 was raised by the arrival of the Justiciar, James Butler, Earl of Ormond, but there were two further sieges by the O'Byrnes in the 1370s. Henry Walshe is said to have rebuilt the castle c1450, financing the work by appropriating revenues of the port of Dalkey. Despite the presence of the Earl of Southampton's cavalry force in the castle, the O'Byrnes destroyed the adjacent village in a raid in June 1599. In 1642 the Walshes joined the rebellious Irish and Sir Simon Harcourt was mortally wounded in April whilst attacking the castle. After the wall was breach it was stormed and the garrison of 300 all killed.

CASTLEKNOCK O085365

Beside the college are formidable earthworks of a castle built c1180 by Hugh Tyrrel. The central mound has a wall up to 2m thick and 4m high externally around the north and western sides of a court 30m long by 20m wide with two outer ditches with counterscarp banks. At the NE end is the very patched western part of a polygonal tower keep 13m in diameter over walls 2.5m thick with slight remains of a spiral stair high up. Francis Place's drawing of 1689 shows extensive buildings adjoining the vanished eastern wall of the bailey and the keep as being of three storeys above a high plinth. The castle was captured by Edward Bruce in 1317. It was captured by General Monck in 1652 and the garrison then slaughtered.

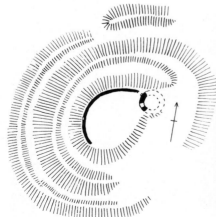

Plan of Castle Knock

Keep at Castle Knock

CORR   O268394

This tower measuring 6.4m by 5.8m over walls 1m thick has a damaged vault over the second of four storeys. The three upper levels each have a window in each of the four walls, including at least one with seats at each level. These rooms are connected by a spiral stair in a corner turret which has a blocked entrance doorway at the third storey level. There is a tiny room under the stair. The lowest level has its own entrance with a drawbar slot and has one double-splayed loop. The third storey has a latrine and a fireplace with a breast projecting upon corbelling.

DALKEY   O264269 & 263277   B

Of the seven castellated buildings known to have existed in and around the town, three still remain, all of three storeys. One, measuring 12.4m by 8.7m and now renovated to serve as the rates office, is thought to have originally served as a town hall or court house. It has stepped battlements, a chimney stack, and two turrets at diagonally opposite corners. On the other side of the road is Archbold's Castle, a ruin measuring 10.3m by 6m with a cellar and a sleeping loft below a vault and a living room above. An upper stair is contained in a turret carried out slightly upon corbelling. The entrance has a machicolation and leads to the foot of a straight stair rising up over a recess in an end wall. Bullock's Castle beside the harbour has a turret at one end of a long main block. At the other end is an added second turret over an arched gateway which gave access to the port, which was closed off by a wall leading 300m to the east to terminate at another tower.

Corr: plans & section

Town Hall, Dalkey

Archbold's Castle, Dalkey

Drimnagh Castle

Corr Castle

Drimnagh Castle

DRIMNAGH   O112319   D

In the grounds of a school is a court enclosed by a low embattled wall rising from a wet moat 4m wide. It is entered on the east side through a 16th century tower containing gateway passage and three upper levels of private rooms reached by a spiral stair in a turret projecting on the south side. North of it extends a 14th century hall block with carved Dutch gables surmounted by chimneys suggesting rebuilding in the late 17th century. The Barnewalls held this castle from the early 13th century until it reverted to the Crown in 1606. It was leased to Sir Adam Loftus and passed to Philip Ferneley in the 1650s, the hall then being altered. The Barnewalls of Braemore had a lease of Drimnagh from 1677 until 1718. It was then held by the Ennis family, who added the hall outer staircase. The Kavanaghs held the castle in the 19th century but it was the Hatch family who gave it to the Cistercians in 1954, although the monks only occupied the castle until 1958.

Archbold's, Dalkey

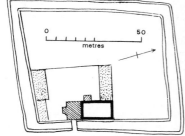

Drimnagh: plan

Bullock's Castle, Dalkey

Old postcard of Dublin Castle

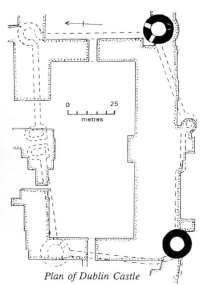

Plan of Dublin Castle

DUBLIN   O155338   B

There may have been a fortress here in the 1170s, and King John ordered the construction of a strong tower in 1204, but the main defences are thought to date from 1213-28 when Archbishop Henry de Londres was Justiciar of Ireland. In its long-lost medieval form the castle seems to have only endured one siege, when Silken Thomas made an unsuccessful attempt to take it in 1534, but lost most of his army taken prisoner by the townsfolk. A plot by Rory O'More and Conor Maguire to seize it in 1641 was betrayed, but another attempt to surprise it in 1646 came closer to success. Until 1922 the castle was the centre of English authority in Ireland and was the official residence of the Lord Deputy or Lord Lieutenant. Parliaments and law courts were often held within the castle and it served as an important political prison. Red Hugh O'Donnell managed to successfully escape from the castle in 1592, a year after he had been recaptured after a previous escape attempt.

Much of the castle was rebuilt after a fire in 1684, and several further campaigns in the 18th century resulted in the defences being swept away to make space for a series of palatial new ranges (details of which lie outside the scope of this book). From old records and excavations we know there was a rectangular bailey measuring 120m by 70m wide surrounded by a moat. There was a great hall in the western part with a prison north of it, and the Lord Deputy's residence lay on the south. There was a gatehouse with twin D-shaped towers about 8m wide on the north side and four large corner towers, some of them being up to 16m in diameter. The Record Tower (formerly the Gunners' Tower and later known as the Wardrobe Tower) at the SE corner still has two storeys of medieval work, whilst the thinly walled Birmingham Tower of 1775 stands upon the refaced massive base of the former Powder Tower at the SW corner. East of this tower lies St Patrick's Hall. The octagonal tower on the south side stands almost on the site of an intermediate D-shaped tower. In 1803 Robert Emmet led an attempt to occupy the castle, and it was the scene of another attempt to occupy it during the Easter Rising of 1916.

The castle lay on a rise above the Poddle in the SE corner of the medieval town, which had earth and timber defences in the 10th century, when it was under Viking control, and it was enclosed by a stone wall by c1100. The defended area was later enlarged by extending it northwards to the banks of the River Liffey. The earliest of the several murage grants for the maintenance of the walls dates from 1221. A few minor fragments survive of the walls at the western end. The archbishop's palace at St Sepulchre's also included a tower, and once bore the arms of Archbishop Inge, who improved the palace in 1521.

DUNDRUM   O171278   D

In the 1590s Sir Thomas FitzWilliam added a wing 7m by 5m to the north end of the NW wall of an older three storey main block 10.2m by 8.2m which contains stirrup-shaped gunloops and has now lost its NE end wall. A FitzWilliam possession from the 13th century, the castle was held by the Dobsons in 18th century, when the large upper windows were inserted. Excavations in 1987-90 revealed the base of a gatehouse of c1200 with a drawbridge across a moat filled in during the 14th century. See page 13.

DUNSOGHLY   O118432   E

The tower built c1450 by Sir Thomas Plunkett, Chief Justice of the King's Bench has four turrets of differing sizes and degrees of projection set at the corners of a lofty four storey main block 10.8m long by 8.4m wide. The entrance into the vaulted basement faces north towards a bawn 26m long by 15m wide enclosed by thin walls which have mostly been rebuilt except on the west side. The NE corner turret contains a wide spiral staircase. The second and third storeys have fireplaces in the north wall and enlarged windows facing east, west and south, whilst latrines are provided in the small SW corner turret, and private rooms (some with fireplaces) in the NW and SE corner turrets. A short length of thin walling containing a doorway connects the SW corner turret to the nave of a chapel probably dating from 1573, the year that appears upon it, along with the Instruments of the Passion and the initials of Sir John Plunkett and his third wife Genet Sarsfield. The chapel had a chancel which has been destroyed and the arch towards it blocked up. Surrounding the castle are earthwork defences of the 1640s.

Grange: plan

GRANGE   O040317

All three storeys of this tower 9.2m long by 7.7m wide have 18th century sash windows on the north side, and the only original openings are one loop on the stair turret projecting north at the NE corner and the doorway on the east wall, above which the upper storeys have fireplaces.

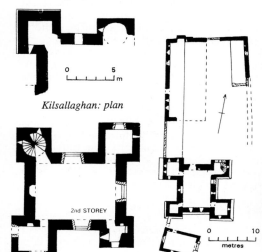

Kilsallaghan: plan

Plans of Dunsoghly Castle

Dunsoghly Castle

Kilgobbin Castle

Howth Castle

HOWTH CASTLE   O278390   C

The motte of Almeric St Laurence, granted Howth by Henry II, lay on the headland above the harbour, later occupied by a Martello Tower. One of his descendants has a splendid tomb of c1470 in the ruined church nearby. Of the castle erected in 1564 there remain the tower with stepped battlements in the SW corner and the gatehouse in the NW corner. The bawn walls connecting them have succumbed to rebuildings and additions of 1738 and the 19th and 20th centuries, and the ditch has been filled in. The custom of leaving the castle gates open during the main meal of the day is said to be in fulfilment of a ransom pledge made to the pirate Grace O'Malley, who took umbrage on being refused admittance and kidnapped the young St Laurence heir. After William, 4th Earl and 30th Baron of Howth died in 1909, the estate passed to his sister's son Julian Gainsford. He added the west tower designed by Sir Edwin Lutyens, and the chapel in the SE range. The gatehouse is a three storey structure with stepped battlements and a NE stair turret rising to a higher level. The 3.3m wide and 8m long entrance passage has a blocked stirrup-shaped loop on the south side and is flanked by a pair of unlit vaulted rooms on the north.

KILGOBBIN CASTLE   O193243   D

This tower measuring 10.7m by 7.4m had two storeys under the partly surviving vault and one lofty upper level with a fireplace on the west and a latrine in a turret at the SE corner. The SW corner is also raised up above the double-stepped battlements. The entrance with a drawbar slot lies on the west side. The stair must have been in the destroyed NE corner. The castle was held by the Walshes in 1476, when it was sacked by the O'Byrnes, and it later passed to the Coates, Hardings, Nutleys and Newguineys.

KILSALLAGHAN CASTLE   O117487   D

This tower seems to have been a smaller version of that at Dunsoghly. Parts of two walls remain of a main block probably about 9m by 7m with remains of a stair turret at one corner, a larger turret 4.5m square containing rooms at another corner, and traces of another turret at a third corner.

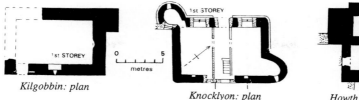

Kilgobbin: plan

Knocklyon: plan

Howth: gateway plan

KNOCKLYON   O115272

This building probably of c1600 was much altered by the Ledwich family in the 1780s and 90s and was further altered c1840, and remains occupied. It is a fairly thinly walled building measuring 10m by 7.2m. with circular turrets on the east and west corners.

LUCAN CASTLE   O036356

Agmondisham Vesey's mansion of 1772 lies beside the site of a castle probably built by Sir William Sarsfield, Mayor of Dublin after he acquired the estate upon the attainder of the 10th Earl of Kildare in 1534. During the 1650s and 60s it was held by the Cromwellian Sir Theophilus Jones but was restored to Patrick Sarsfield, who was created Viscount Tully and Earl of Lucan. A second castle site lies in Main Street at 032352.

MALAHIDE CASTLE   O220455   E

The former seat of Lord Talbot, now a portrait gallery, is a much altered late 15th century hall-block now of three storeys with 18th century interiors, and a four storey tower at its north end. The circular SE corner turret has authentic-looking mullioned windows on three upper levels over a basement, and a corbelled parapet. The western parts of the castle, with two more corner turrets of similar size, are 18th century. Except for a short period in the 1650s, when the castle was confiscated and given to Miles Corbet, the Talbots lived here from the 1180s until the last of them died in 1973. They were buried in the adjoining 15th century church and were taxed on 11 hearths here in 1664.

Malahide Castle

MONKSTOWN CASTLE   O233281   B

Two views of Monkstown Castle

The Cistercian monks of St Mary's Abbey at Budlin are said to have had a castle here in the 13th or 14th century but the present building could date from after the abbey was dissolved. It has a four storey tower 8.4m long by 5.8m wide which has later been extended on one side. A 20m length of modern walling connects it to a gatehouse with traces of an adjoining range, the upper level of which was reached by a stair reached directly from a bawn probably about 30m square, with the two surviving towers with stepped battlements occupying two of its corners. Monkstown passed to John Travers at the Reformation and was subsequently held by the Eustaces, Sir Henry Wallop, Henry Cheevers, the Cromwellian commander Ludlow, Archbishop Boyle, and Anthony Upton. A print of the 1790s by Berengar shows a second castle lying nearby.

NEWCASTLE CASTLES   N995285   C

The motte and bailey of an early royal castle lie near the church, the west tower of which contained habitable upper rooms for a priest. A nearby tower known as the Old Rectory measures 6.8m by 6.4m over walls 1m thick and has a SW stair turret and a tiny SE projection containing a latrine on the second storey, which has a fireplace and several windows. A second tower in a field nearby is similar in size and shape but without the latrine projection. Here the entrance lies beside the turret and is protected by a murder hole from the second storey, which was a vaulted loft. The upper levels are now missing.

Monkstown; plan

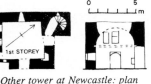

Other tower at Newcastle: plan

Old Rectory, Newcastle: plans

PORTRANE: STELLA'S TOWER   O251511   D

This tower measuring 7.4m by 5.8m has an entrance in a slight projection from the north end wall. Beside it is a spiral stair in a turret projecting eastward. There was a basement with double-splayed loops and a low loft above, then a vault supporting the floor of the main room, which has a fireplace on the west side. There is another room above it.

PUCK'S CASTLE   O243213   D

This building measures 10.4m by 7m. The 2.5m thick SW end wall contains the entrance and a straight stair rising up over a corner mural chamber. The lowest room has one double splayed loop, and this room and that above have later brick fireplaces against the NE end wall. The second storey has wide windows in each long wall and a latrine in a projection at the north corner, whilst the third storey has a latrine in the east corner.

Tower at Newcastle

Rush: plan

Puck's Castle: plans

Stella's Tower at Portrane

Puck's Castle

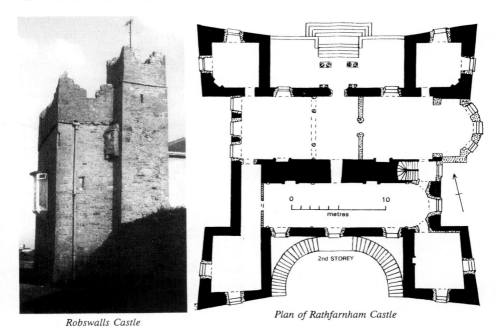

Robswalls Castle

Plan of Rathfarnham Castle

RATHFARNHAM CASTLE   O145289   E

Archbishop Loftus' four storey house of c1583 was surrendered to Parliamentary forces in 1647, but in 1649 was stormed by Royalists just prior to the battle of Rathmines. In 1664 the house was assessed for tax on the basis of having 18 hearths. The apartments were remodelled in the 18th century to designs by Sir William Chambers and James Stuart for the Loftus family, who had recovered the castle and become earls of Ely. In 1837 the Marquis of Ely sold the house to the Blackburns. The house was occupied by the Jesuits for most of the 20th century before restoration by the Office of Works began in 1987. The house measures about 22m by 16m and has rooms on either side of a thick east-west internal wall containing the fireplaces. The main rooms lie north of the crosswall and are now entirely 18th century, with an added elliptical bay at each level at the east end. The four corner towers are arrow-head shaped with acute outermost corners to allow flanking fire, although no gunloops appear to have survived the later remodelling.

ROBSWALLS CASTLE   O245454   C

By the shore not far from Malahide Castle is an inhabited embattled tower with a tiny latrine projection corbelled out high up between the main block and the stair turret on the south. There are two levels under a vault, a third storey with a modern bay window on the west side, and a fourth storey with an angle loop in the SW corner.

SHANKHILL CASTLE   O243213

This irregularly laid-out three storey building lying derelict beside an inhabited house probably dates from the late 16th or early 17th century. On the south side the upper two storeys project upon corbelling and there is a projecting wing at the east end.

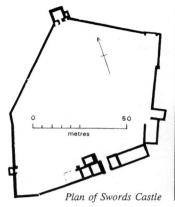

Plan of Swords Castle

Rathfarnham Castle

SWORDS CASTLE   O182460   B

The archbishops of Dublin had a house here by c1200 but the existing ruin seems to be 14th century work. At the northern angle of an irregularly pentagonal court 65m wide by 95m long is a tower about 9m square and 13m high with a stair turret at its SW corner and a latrine projection on the east. An upper fireplace on the west side has a projecting breast. The wall-walk on the west curtain adjoining still retains its double-stepped merlons. On the south side of the court is a gateway with a tower east of it, the top storey of which has a two-light window with a transom facing south. Beyond this tower is a range which contained a chapel with a fine east window on the upper level. The tower has a staircase turret at its NE corner. On the other side of the gateway another range with stepped battlements and a lofty polygonal stair turret overlooking the gateway extends westwards. A second block was later added to its northern side. There was another range further west, where a latrine turret projects from the curtain wall. Only the outermost two walls remain of the tower within the SW corner. The hall seems to have been on the SE side of the court, with a range of private apartments extending SW from it towards the chapel range, which it touches at one corner. See pages 10 & 43.

TALLAGHT   O094278   D

A four storey tower between the church and the domestic buildings of a Dominican priory formed part of a palace of the archbishops of Dublin later replaced by a house of c1730. The tower has a stair turret at the NE corner. The vaulted basement now forms a chapel with inserted quintuple east lancets. The vault over the topmost level is modern.

Swords Castle

Much-altered tower at Saggart

Tully's Castle, Clondalkin

Ballyowen Castle

OTHER CASTLES IN COUNTY DUBLIN

BALLYMOUNT O091304 Gatehouse with upper room beside motorway remains of Sir William Parsons' house built in 1646. His descendants became Earls of Rosse.

BALLYOWEN O052341 Three storey high 3m square corner turret of Robert Taylor's fortified house adjoins later building beside modern shopping precinct.

BALROTHERY O199610 Small ivy-clad four storey tower just south of churchyard with a west facing doorway now blocked up.

BELGARD O075294 NW corner turret of forms part of Georgian house now a company office. Possible birthplace of Richard Talbot, created Earl of Tyrconnel by James II.

CLONDALKIN O073312 This small 16th century tower adjoins a ruined 17th century block. It is also known as Tully's Castle from the family of that name.

DEANSRATH O052314 A low fragment with a staircase lies in a housing estate. An old print shows a tower house and gatehouse here, both of three storeys.

DONABATE O225500 Rectangular tower with higher stair turret lying in north transeptal position beside Church of Ireland church.

GLEAN O196256 Wall stands one storey high beside entrance gateway to later house.

LAMBAY O309508 One of the four corner turrets remains of Archbishop James Usher's fortified house. Similar in plan to Rathfarnham but much smaller.

LANESTOWN O210497 Three storey tower 8.4m by 7m with stair turret at SW corner in Newcastle demesne. Vaulted cellar. Occupied until mid 19th century, so altered.

LAUGHANSTOWN O231231 Much altered and cut-down tower forms core of farmhouse.

LUTTRELSTOWN O044371 Part of an old tower with 19th century mansion.

MILLTOWN O253228 Tall ivy-covered fragment amongst shrubs in garden of house.

ROCHES O134611 Slight remains upon cliff above glen. Probable de Geneville seat.

RONANSTOWN O065344 Only relic of thinly walled 17th century fortified house is a 4m square corner turret two storeys high lying within a modern housing estate.

RUSH O264560 Vaulted basement of tower 9.5m by 7m with room in wing facing east at NE corner, and entrance and stair in turret 3m square clasping west corner.

SAGGART O040272 Basement of tower with 18th century upper storey in stableyard.

SEATOWN O198472 Much altered tower in farmyard near shore.

STEPHENSTOWN O193622 1m high fragment and footings of tower 9m by 7m, probably the "burnt castle" held in 1650s by Elizabeth Finglas.

TERENURE O136296 Barnewall tower in college grounds. Altered by Deane family c1670-95 and rebuilt in 18th century. No medieval features remain.

TEMPLEOGUE O127283 Remains of Talbot family castle in early 19th house.

WESTOWN O128602 18th century house demolished in 1999 incorporated a Hussey tower captured by Cromwell in 1649 and garrison killed. Stair turret collapsed in 1966.

SITES OF CASTLES IN COUNTY DUBLIN

CHEEVERSTOWN O065285 Three storey tower 7m square with entrance in west wall of vaulted basement demolished c1980 and site now quarried away.

CLONTARF or CASTLE IVE O194364 1830s mansion on site of Vernon castle probably built after being acquired from Knights Hospitaller. Vernon seat until 20th century.

COLMANSTOWN N994261 A Locke seat. Small tower with vaulted basement and two upper storeys with fireplaces was demolished in 1960.

JOBSTOWN O069274 Earthworks were visible from the air. Housing estate now on site.

MERRION Only a wing remained of this FitzWilliam seat by the late 18th century.

ROEBUCK O186293 Later building used by University College on site of 5th Lord Trembleston's 16th century tower destroyed during the war of 1641.

TURVEY O212509 Barnewall tower incorporated in 17th century house with 18th century extensions. Demolished in 1987.

TYMON O108288 Entrance with machicolation over was flanked by NW stair-turret. Ruined in 1547. Passed to Cusacks, Sedgroves, and Loftuses. Sold to the Conollys.

OTHER CASTLE SITES: Adamstown O029326, Baggot O171378, Ballally O182269, Baldengar O241575, Ballycoris O221211, Bellinstown O186504, Booterstown O212298, Cappagh O127388, Cappoge O106397, Cardiff's Park O115378, Castle Kelly O107205, Censure O279363, Collinstown O218562, Corkagh O056302, Corballs O172431, Cornelscourt O224257, Donore O145376, Elmcastle O097293, Grace Park O167369, Hynestown O003306, Kilbride O038300, Kilmore O190383, Loughlinstown

Ballyowen: plan

O247234, Nagor O046311, Nelstown O067340, Palmerstown O161303, Raheen O095332, Shanagannan O254212, Simmonscourt O182318, Tolka O131377, Ulverton O263270 & 262278 (bawn), Ward Upper O101451, Westbourne O052315, Woodlands O045370, Woodville O049359

MOTTES: Brazel O152467, Dunsoghley O117431.

Swords Castle

CASTLES OF COUNTY KILDARE

ATHY   S683940   C

Athy was once a walled town and was burnt by the Irish in 1310, and by Edward Bruce in 1317. It was successfully held by the Earl of Ormond against the Confederate Catholics in 1642 but was captured by Eoghan O'Neill in 1645 and by Cromwellian troops in 1650. On the east bank of the Barrow by the bridge is White's Castle, a later enlargement (see the join) of a tower built by Sir John Talbot in the early 15th century. The openings of all three storeys and the battlements and corner turrets are now modern.

BALLYSHANNON   N787045

Only a motte and other earthworks survive but this was once a FitzGerald castle of some importance. It was too strong for Ormond to take in 1643 and remained in Confederate hands until September 1648, when it was surrendered to General Jones, who had failed to capture it back in February of that year. The Confederates managed to retake it by means of a ruse in 1649 but it was captured by Cromwellian commander Hewson after a short siege. The castle had a tower surrounded by bawn about 45m square with rectangular flankers at the SE and NW corners and a circular NE flanker. There was a wet moat up to 12m wide and beyond it lay a bastioned outer rampart, perhaps added in 1649.

BALLYTEIGE   N753243   C

Near the Royal Canal stands a derelict tower measuring 7.5m by 7.3m, in use until fairly recently despite the lack of daylight inside. The very few narrow loops include angle-loops in the southern corners just below the modern battlements. The vaulted basement has an entrance facing north and an adjacent stair.
The other floor levels have been changed.

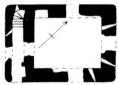

Blackwood: plan   *Ballyteige: plan*   *Backhall: plans*

White's Castle, Athy   *Barberstown Castle*

BARBERSTOWN   N298310   H

The Suttons were established here by 1473 as tenants of the Penkinsons. Their tower measures 8m by 7m over walls 1.4m thick and has a north facing entrance beside a NW corner stair turret projecting west (with an added battered base) and a latrine turret projecting south at the SW corner. The basement retains one double-splayed loop but the windows of the three upper storeys and the battlements are early 19th century. The castle was granted to John, Lord Kingston in 1666 but passed to the Youngs by 1703. It was later held by the Carncross family and then passed to the Bartons. It is now an hotel.

BLACKHALL   N792022

The west wall and parts of the adjoining walls of a tower 11.8m by 10.4m still stand four storeys high with a fine fireplace on the topmost level and traces of a vault over the lowest level. The spiral stair lies in the SW corner, whilst the south wall contained a tier of chambers over the entrance, which was surmounted by a sheela-na-gig.

BLACKWOOD   N795271

Beside a house lies the round-cornered lowest storey of a tower 11.8m by 8.4m with a 3m thick SW end wall containing the damaged entrance and steps to a spiral stair in the west corner. There was formerly a panel over the entrance dated 1584 with the arms and names of Piers and Eleanor FitzGerald. There are gunloops in the NE and SE walls.

BOLTON   S791902   D

Adjoining the domestic buildings of a convent is a square three storey medieval embattled tower with a staircase turret projecting from the west end of the south wall and a latrine turret projecting from the east end of the north wall. The third storey has a slightly projecting breast for a fireplace on the south side but the windows all look 19th century.

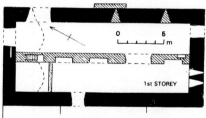

Plan of Castle Reban

Bolton Castle

Blackhall Castle

CALVERSTOWN   N805035

An older tower measuring 11m by 6.5m is incorporated into a ruined and very overgrown 17th century house of three storeys with attic rooms in the roof. There are chimney stacks on the NE and SW end walls (with projecting breasts) and in the middle of the NW side.

CARBURY   N687350   G

On the eastern side of Meiler FitzHenry's motte on Carbury Hill are remains of a wall around the east and south sides of a small bailey, perhaps the work of William Marshal, although the earliest specific mention of the castle is not until 1234. These walls later became part of a hall-block measuring about 18m by 12m the other walls of which are rather broken down, although there is an arcaded spine wall supporting two longitudinal vaults. This may have been the work of the de Birminghams. For much of the 14th century the castle was in royal hands and it was remodelled in 1447 by the then Lord Deputy, Sir John Talbot. It was held by O'Conor Faly in the 1460s, the Earl of Desmond being held prisoner within it, but in 1475 the castle was wrecked by the O'Donnells. It was restored but in 1546 was burnt by a combined party of O'Kellys, O'Maddens and O'Conor Falys.

In 1562 the castle was granted to the Cowley family, whose descendants later became the Wellesleys, one of which became the Duke of Wellington. The 13th century hall-block was extended to the north produce a house about 30m long with a stair wing in the middle of the west side. The northern part was later widened to produce a structure 16m wide extending across two parallel vaulted cellars with some sort of service tower (now mostly destroyed) at the NW corner. The east and north walls of this second extension stands complete to the parapet, with tall polygonal chimneys and three-light mullion-and-transom windows with hoodmoulds on the second and third storeys but the rest is too ruined and cluttered with debris and vegetation for the complete layout to be understood.

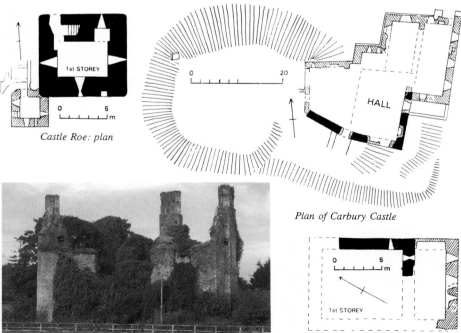

Castle Roe: plan

Plan of Carbury Castle

Calverstown Castle

Carrick: plan

Interior of Carbury Castle

Carrick Castle

Carbury Castle

CARRICK   N640369   C

Only the east corner and parts of the adjoining walls with one double-splayed loop facing SE remain of a building 10m wide and about 11m long. It has a doorway facing NE. More survives of a block 4.5m wide added against the SE end. It contained a kitchen with a fireplace at one end, a vaulted room above with a fireplace and angle-loop, and one upper storey. Here in 1305 Sir Pierce Birmingham and Jordan Cumin instigated a massacre of thirty-two O'Connor chiefs at a banquet, one them being Muirchertach, King of Offaly.

CASTLE MARTIN   N836102

The Blacker family's house of 1739 of incorporates the subdivided lowest storey of a Fitz-Eustace tower measuring 12.7m by 7.7m over walls 1.1m thick. It was captured in 1647 by Colonel Jones, and in 1648 by Colonel Hewson. Either it or an earlier tower was attacked in 1448 by Cathal O'Conor Faly. The church has dwelling tower and a fine tomb.

CASTLE REBAN   S648981   D

The fragmentary hall-house of the St Michael family has vaults on either side of a crosswall containing a stair. There are turrets at each end of the west wall and large mullioned windows high up. The castle was captured by Lysaght O'More in 1325 and was in Irish hands in 1527, but Walter St Michael was in possession in 1581. The castle was granted to Robert Carre in 1607. It was besieged by the Irish in 1642 but was relieved by Sir Charles Coote. Part of the north wall was dismantled in the 19th century. See p45.

CASTLE ROE   S736857   D

There is a latrine chute in the south wall of this round-cornered tower measuring 9.4m by 9m over walls 2m thick below a vault. The thicker north wall contains the entrance, from which a straight stair rises up over a recess to two low upper storeys. The turret adjoining the SW corner is the only relic of a later house added to the west. Kilkea church contains the tomb of William FitzGerald of Castle Roe, and his wives who died in 1623 and 1630.

DONADEA   N835351   C

This four storey tower bears the arms of the Aylmers, its owners until 1935, and may be as late as 1624, the year given on a date-stone over the pointed-arched entrance doorway, now blocked, in the 3.8m thick SE end wall. The tower measures 14m by 9.7m and has a pair of narrow vaulted cellars, each with a loop at the NW end, set on other side of a longitudinal crosswall. The building has been much altered and now projects out from the NW side of a ruined house of 1773 and 1827, but it retains a wide spiral stair in the south corner and an angle-loop in the north corner at third storey level.

GRANGE   N619365   E

In this tower measuring 8.5m by 6.6m the west end wall containing the entrance and a mural stair up to a spiral stair in the NW corner is only thick enough to accommodate a small latrine chamber at the third level, where the main room has a 17th century fireplace and a fine east window with a fine hoodmould over a pair of ogival-headed lights with carved spandrels. The ornamental parapets and chimneys are also 17th century additions. The castle belonged to the Tyrrell family and was occupied into the 19th century. The tower and its grounds, have recently been restored by the Office of Public Works.

Window at Grange

Grange Castle

Donadea Castle

Castle Roe

Kildare Castle

Inch Castle

Donadea: plan

Inch: plans

Grange: plans

INCH   S732947   D

Only the western half still stands of a tower 8.2m long by about 7.6m wide. The basement has a vault and an arched recess in the west wall, whilst there is another recess under the spiral stair in the NW corner, the destroyed entrance having faced north. The second storey has a latrine in the SW corner. The 6th Earl of Kildare may have built the tower c1420 on the site of a 13th century castle of the de Vesci family.

KILDARE   N730124   H

William Marshall's castle here later passed to the de Vescis and in 1316 was granted to John FitzGerald, 6th Baron Offaly, 1st Earl of Kildare. The existing tower is later and the upper parts (with angle loops) could post-date the destruction of the medieval castle by Elizabeth's officials in the 1580s. It adjoins the area of the castle bailey known as The Park which has 16th or 17th century artillery defences on the north side and one circular flanker since it formed the NE corner of the walled town. The town seems to have had three gates, one facing south, the White or East Gate just south of the castle, and the Clare or West gate, whilst the cathedral on the north side was also embattled.

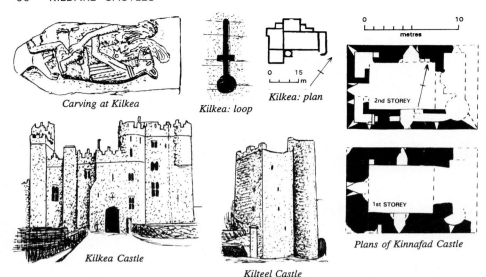

Carving at Kilkea

Kilkea: loop

Kilkea: plan

2nd STOREY

1st STOREY

Plans of Kinnafad Castle

Kilkea Castle

Kilteel Castle

KILKEA   S749884   H

Walter de Riddlesford's motte of 1181 by a stream passed in the 13th century to Maurice FitzGerald, 3rd Baron Offaly. His nephew and heir John was created Earl of Kildare and it was probably he who began the existing building SE of the motte. In 1414 the castle was besieged by the O'Mores until Thomas Cranley, Archbishop of Dublin, brought a force to relieve it. In the 1420s the then earl remodelled the castle and defeated another native Irish force which threatened it. In 1513 the 8th Earl died in the castle of wounds sustained whilst besieging the O'More castle of Leap in County Offaly. The estate was confiscated after the rebellion of Silken Thomas, heir of Garret, 9th Earl of Kildare and it was not until 1554 that Queen Mary restored the 11th Earl, Gerald, to his title and Irish estates. Kilkea was his principal seat and was improved, there formerly being a stone dated 1573 in one room. Suspected of treason by Elizabeth I's officials, he died in London in 1585.

Elizabeth Nugent, widow of the 14th Earl of Kildare, handed over the castle to the Jesuits in 1634 and in 1646 the papal nuncio Rinuccini stayed within it for the Confederation of Kilkenny. The castle changed hands several times in the late 1640s and was captured by Colonel Hewson in 1650. It was restored to the earls in the 1660s but was then leased to a series of tenants. In 1798 the castle was occupied by troops from Dublin after the tenant Thomas Reynolds betrayed the insurrection against the authorities. The earls of Kildare were raised to the Dukedom of Leinster in 1766 and in 1849 the then duke began the remodelling of the castle as his seat. Their fortunes broken by the events of 1919-23, the family finally sold the castle in the 1960s. It now serves as an hotel.

The castle is a large and complex building 30m long on the south side whose full development has yet to be unravelled. The five storey western part contained private apartments, whilst an east wing originally contained a hall over cellars, but a third storey was created within the old roof space in the rebuilding of 1849. All the battlements and most of the windows are 19th century but quite a number of old loops remain, including a NE corner loop in the end wall of the east wing. The south end of this wall forms a circular turret about 23m high. A lower wing extending towards the bawn gateway further east contains a crossloop with a bottom roundel likely to date from the 1520s or 30s, and set upon a corner here is the Evil Eye Stone depicting human figures with heads of a lion and a boar. On the north side is a projection containing a portcullis groove, whilst on the west, near the NE corner, is a square turret supporting a circular two storey bartizan.

KILTEEL   N983212   C

This tower with a circular stair turret formed part of a preceptory of the Knights Hospitallers, lying in ruins nearby. It has vaults over two of its five storeys and a gateway passage adjoins it. After suppression in 1541 the preceptory was granted to Sir John Alen. In the late 17th century it passed to Richard Talbot, Earl of Tyrconnell. It was sold to the Hollow Blade Sword Company in 1703, but they quickly disposed of it to William Fownes.

KINNAFAD   N615351   C

The thick east end wall containing the entrance, spiral stair and mural chambers of this 16th century Birmingham tower measuring 13.9m by 9.7m has collapsed. The second storey had angle-loops lighting the stair and western mural chambers, gunloops flanking the main room windows and a fireplace in the eastern mural chamber, whilst the third storey was vaulted. Both these levels have latrines in the SW corner.

LEIXLIP   O005357

Adam de Hereford built a motte at the junction of the Liffey and the Rye Water. Ralph Pepard surrendered the castle to the Crown in 1302. Henry VII granted the castle to Gerald, 8th Earl of Kildare. After the fall of the 9th earl in 1536 it was leased to the King and Vernon families, but in 1570 it was granted to Sir Nigel Whyte. The building is a two storey L-shaped structure of various dates with a circular three storey medieval tower with a battered base on the outermost corner. The Connellys made additions in the 1740s, having purchased it in 1728, and the Townsend family inserted new windows in 1767-72, and then provided new battlements in the early 19th century. Since 1958 the castle has been occupied by the Guinness brewing family.

Leixlip Castle

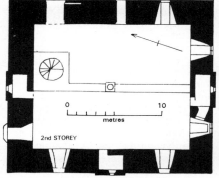

Maynooth: plan of keep

Kinnafad Castle

Keep at Maynooth

Oughterard: plans

Plan of Maynooth Castle

MAYNOOTH   N935376

Gerald Fitz-Maurice, 1st Baron Offaly, d1203 probably began the keep measuring 21.8m by 18.7m over walls 2.4m thick. The basement was probably always subdivided although the existing arched crosswall and vaults with low lofts squeezed underneath are 15th century, perhaps being the work carried out by the 6th Earl of Kildare in 1426. A block of masonry at one end contains a spiral stair up to the level above, where there was originally a hall and chamber side by side. This level has several window embrasures with seats and there are mural chambers in the centres of the north, west and south walls, which are here strengthened by broad pilaster buttresses. Another storey was later formed in the original roof space below the wall walk and a new roof then provided at a higher level.

Little remains of the walls of a court extending 40m NE from the keep to the River Lyreen, but there is a 15th century gatehouse measuring about 8.5m by 8m on the SE side, and a rectangular tower of that period in the east corner. The very mutilated tower containing a postern passage projecting diagonally at the north corner may be 13th century. Despite being strengthened with a new bastion during Silken Thomas's rebellion of 1535, the castle was breached by Sir William Skeffington's artillery after a five day siege which ended with the execution of most of the surviving members of the garrison, which had originally included 60 gunners. Maynooth was not restored to the 11th Earl until 1552 and the family subsequently lived at Kilkea. The castle was repaired in 1630, taken by the Catholics in 1641, and was dismantled by Eoghan Rua O'Neill in 1647.

MOONE   S790927

In the grounds of Moone Abbey is a tower measuring about 7m square above a broad battered base. The NE wall contains a tier of tiny chambers over the entrance, from which a straight stair rises to where a spiral stair begins in the east corner. It has a latrine beside it. There are vaults over the first and fourth storeys. The topmost levels later formed a dovecote but retain several original loops and one two-light window high up facing NW.

OUGHTERARD   N957258   D

This tiny round-cornered four storey tower measures just 7.1m by 5.5m over walls 1.1m thick. The lowest room has double-splayed loops, recesses, and an entrance in one of the long walls. There is neither a hatch in the second storey vault nor a lower staircase and the third storey was reached separately from the outside by means of its own entrance. At that level there is a latrine projection on one side.

RATHCOFFEY   N890320   D

The Wogans' chief seat here was attacked in 1454 by a junior branch of the same family. In 1642 the castle was surrendered to General Mant and Nicholas Wogan was declared an outlaw. In 1800 Archibald Hamilton Rowan replaced most of the castle by a new mansion, now ruined, but there survives an altered bawn gatehouse 10m by 7m with a passage flanked on one side by a guard room with a latrine and a spiral staircase.

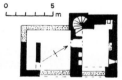

Moone: plan   *Rathcoffey: plan*

Rathcoffey Castle

Moone Castle

Oughterard Castle

REEVES   N958294   D

A tower 8m square with three unvaulted storeys connected by a staircase in a slightly taller semi-circular turret projecting from the south end of the east wall lies beside farm buildings. A doorway leads out over where there was a gateway of an adjoining bawn.

WOODSTOCK   S679945   B

The wing 4m wide projecting 5m at the south end containing gunloops on two upper levels may have been added in 1536 by Lord Deputy Grey. Although the main block 13m long by 9.8m wide contains several blocked 16th century upper windows of two and three lights with arched heads and hoodmoulds, the walls may represent a hall-house of c1250 built by Richard de St Michael. It has three storeys but there are four levels within the same height in the wing. Richard's daughter Rohesia brought the estate to Thomas FitzGerald, Baron Offaly, and their son John was created Earl of Kildare. The monkey on his arms recall when he was saved by the screams of the family pet when the castle caught fire. A small section of a bawn wall 1.7m thick adjoins the north wall.

OTHER CASTLES IN COUNTY KILDARE

ARDKILL N711352 Just the south end wall 1.2m thick remains of a tower 8.2m wide
    with a projecting turret still about 8m high at the west end.
ARDSCULL S729978 Huge ringwork 10m high and 50m across. Later stone buildings
    gone. Burnt in 1286. Edward Bruce won a battle nearby in 1315. Now public parkland
BARRETSTOWN N938125 19th century house now used as centre for children with
    special needs incorporates much altered medieval tower.

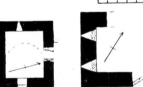
Blackrath

Blackhall

Moortown

Reeves Castle

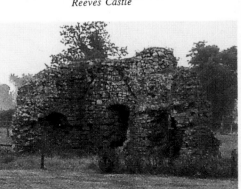
Walterstown Castle

Woodstock Castle

BLACKHALL N931161 Ivy-covered 6m high west wall 1.6m thick and 8.4m long of tower adjoins derelict farm buildings. Traces of blocked loops.

BLACKRATH N818999 Tower 7.2m by 6.4m by farmhouse. Vaulted basement and one higher fragment of SE corner with brick patching. Leased in 1536 by Eustaces.

CASTLE BROWNE N877298 Fitz-Eustace tower sold to Brownes in 1667 and altered in 1718 and 1788 may survive in Clongowes Wood College, a Jesuit school.

CASTLEDERMOT S782851 No obvious remains of Walter de Riddlesford's motte of 1181, but low fragments of town walls of 1295 remain between Barrack St & Main St.

CONFEY N011374 Lower part of three walls of bawn flanker or house corner turret.

CORBALLIS S820867 Buried footings and one defaced 1m thick and 2m high fragment.

HARRISTOWN N885112 Small 4m high fragment of Fitz-Eustace castle.

HAYNESTOWN N944196 Former bawn 50m by 25m with gateway with drawbar-slot. Probably built after c1550 when estate passed from the Travers family to the Aylmers.

JIGGINSTOWN N879188 Possible parts of a Fitz-Eustace castle remaining in outbuildings of the huge unfinished mansion begun in 1636 by Thomas Wentworth, Earl of Strafford.

KILBERRY S655989 Fragments of west gateway and other buildings of a Boswell castle.

LACKAGH N677127 Ivy-clad corner with walling 1.7m thick of tower of Sir Maurice Fitz-Gerald, d1575, whose effigy lies in Kildare Cathedral. A motte lies nearby to the west.

LYONS N975284 Site of fortified house by church containing monument of Richard Aylmer, d1548, who obtained the estate by marriage from the Tyrrels.

MOORTOWN N806064 8.6 long section of 1.4m thick west wall with double-splayed loop, traces of vaulting and part of second storey alone remains.

MYLERSTOWN N706372 Defaced fragments of south wall of tower about 13m long.

OFFALY N662179 Footings only of tower.

RAG N879189 Three storey tower with stair turret just west of Jigginstown House.

SEAGRAVES N964199 Modest gateway forms store adjoining house.

SHERLOCKSTOWN N904245 Remains of tower held by Sir Walter Dangan in 1592 within later mansion.

WALTERSTOWN N866233 Half of the tower stands two storeys high with several embrasures for loops.

CASTLE SITES IN COUNTY KILDARE

Athgarrett N953161, Ballygreany N682093, Ballyshannon N787045, Balrinnet N674389, Belan S772905, Belview S670962, Blackhall N885264, Boleybeg N900075, Brackagh N6440394, Brownstown N775092, Calf Field N694434, Carrickanearla N720173, Castlefarm N760028, Castlefarm N775008, Castlefish N844052, Castlemitchell S630949, Castlesize N887248, Cloney N642017, Clonkeen N666327, Coghlanstown N898103, Colbinstown N837985 & 833981, Confey N992379, Drinnanstown N708201, Duneany N693081, Dunfierth N781378, Flemingstown N897147, Gormanstown N855055, Graney N813841, Grangeclare N766238, Grangemellon S700894, Greenhills N836115, Hartwell N944214, Hobartstown S780887, Hortland N819366, Kildangan N673065, Kilgowan N828038, Killinagh N655385, Kilmeage N785241, Kilmeage N776226, Laraghbryan N923378, Moyvally N718429, Mullacash N888146, Mylerstown N876146, Newtown 968320, Nurney N707055, Oldtown N881155, Punchestown N919129, Rathasker N878170, Richardstown N888300, Rosberry N801168, Simmonstown N976319, Timahoe N774319, Timolin S801934, Usk N838205, Walshestown N814125 & 817127, Walterstown N705056, Wolfstown N966175

POSSIBLE SITES: Gragadder N895381, Mylerstown N705371, Rathsillagh N754009

MOTTES (* with baileys): Ballycore S814940, Bishopschair N812367, Castleruddery S919939, Castlewarden N968251, Clane N879279, Cloncurry N802414, Dowdenstown N919129, Kill N944227, Longtown N856259, Mainham N870300, Morristown N783148, Naas N893195, Oldconnell N811160*, Rathmore N960197, Sallymount N868095, Straffan 919292. RINGWORK: Rathangan N671194

CASTLES OF COUNTY KILKENNY

AGHAVILLER   S497351   A

In the mid 16th century the Comerfords converted the chancel of a church into a three storey tower house measuring 13.2m by 7.5m. There are doorways on the south and west but the main entrance was that in the 1.8m thick north wall containing a straight staircase. There is a chamber in the northern haunch of the vault over the second storey. The third storey has two-light windows and a fireplace. The graveyard also contains a round tower which may have been cut down to form a bawn corner flanker. See also page 15.

ANNAGHS   S704252   D

Like that at Danganbrack in Co Clare, this tower by River Nore measuring 11m by 9m has four gables with chimneystacks rising from the outer walls, so that the only sections of open wall-walk were at the corners. A straight stair in the north wall runs up from the entrance to a spiral staircase in the NE corner. The third and fourth storeys with gunloops are the work of Edmund Butler c1580, but the lower storeys below the vault may be older.

ANNAMULT   S541465   D

Also known as Friar's Castle, this tower measures 11.2m by 8.4m and is notable for having a service staircase in addition to the main stair, both of them having chambers underneath them, so that there is little solid walling, even at ground level. The entrance, now destroyed, lay at the foot of the main stair in the east wall. The second storey is vaulted. The third storey has a fireplace in the NW corner with two loops in its back wall.

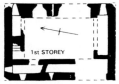

Annamult: plans

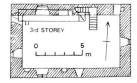

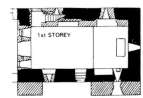

Aghaviller: plans

Aghaviller: chamber in vault haunch

Interior of Annamult Castle

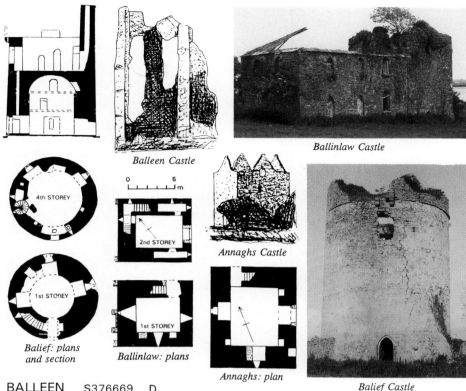

Balleen Castle

Ballinlaw Castle

Annaghs Castle

Balief: plans and section

Ballinlaw: plans

Annaghs: plan

Balief Castle

BALLEEN   S376669   D

Only the SW end remains of a 7m wide five storey stronghouse of the Mountgarret Butlers destroyed in 1650, although considerable sections also remain of the western parts of the bawn extending to the north. The house end wall makes a dramatic ruin with long vertical gaps caused by the fall of the parts between the heads and cills of the tiers of the windows. The fifth storey retains a jamb of a fireplace on the SE side.

BALIEF   S322635   D

The Shortalls' 16th century circular tower house has a diameter of 9m and rises 10m to the wall-walk, the parapet of which is very ruined, although a machicolation remains over the entrance. It contains a cellar with three loops, a main private room above, then a low dome-vault loft, and finally a larger main living room with a fireplace with a tall chimney, and three windows, the embrasure of one of them having a latrine and a murder-hole commanding the entrance.

BALLINLAW   S669170

Richard Butler forfeited this tower measuring 8m by 7.2m in 1653. A ruined house adjoins the NW side of the tower, the third storey of which has been rebuilt. A straight stair rises from the entrance, which faces NE towards a fragmentary bawn 22m by 19m. The second storey is vaulted and has tiny mural chambers in the south and east corners, the latter having a murder-hole over the entrance doorway.

Ballybur Castle

Ballycuddihy Castle

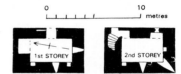

Plans of Ballycuddihy Castle

BALLYBUR   S476494   C

Thomas Comerford, d1588, may have built this tower measuring 11.4m by 9m over walls 2.1m thick. It was forfeited by John Comerford in 1653. The entrance protected by a machicolation on pyramidal corbels faces north and there are straight flights of steps in the west, north and south walls. The second and fourth storeys are vaulted and the third and fifth storeys have mullioned windows with hoodmoulds. The east wall has a fireplace breast. The parapet is mostly modern, but the circular SW corner bartizan is original.

BALLYCUDDIHY   S323668   C

There are roof marks of later ranges against the east and south walls of this small three storey tower 7.6m long by just 4.9m wide. The east wall contains an original lower entrance with a drawbar slot and an inserted upper entrance onto the base of the straight stair in the north end wall from the vaulted second storey to the main room above it. The second storey room has a fireplace in the east wall and a SW corner angle-loop.

BALLYDUFF   S612382

A block of uncertain date joins an 18th century west wing to the four storey tower which has a vault over the lowest of four storeys and chambers in the west wall. This part projects to the north as a wing or turret to contain the spiral staircase.

BALLYFOYLE S527635

This tower measuring 12.2m by 9.7m lying in a farmyard was probably built by the Purcells in the late 16th century but soon afterwards passed to the Cramers. Unlike most of the Kilkenny towers it has a fine spiral stair with a proper newel in the NE corner and the west of the north end wall contains two upper levels of rooms over an entrance passage and a guard room which has a vault, the only one in the building. The third storey room here had a NW angle loop, and there were others in the chambers in the southern corners at this level, where the main room has a fine fireplace and a blocked two light window in the south wall, plus two loops, whilst a latrine on the east is reached from the staircase. The east loop of the lowest level has a gunloop facing SE beside it.

BALLYNABOLEY S594504

David Hackett, Bishop of Ossory is thought to have built this tower c1460. It measures 10.4m by 9m and has straight stairs in the south, west and north walls, the entrance being in the west wall. The second storey is vaulted and the third storey has a fireplace in the south wall, whilst there are passages at the fourth and fifth levels.

BALLYKEEFE S414500 C

There is a squinch arch between the 20m long and 4m high bawn north wall and a circular NW flanker 5m in diameter.

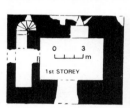

Ballyfoyle: plans

Ballyragget Castle

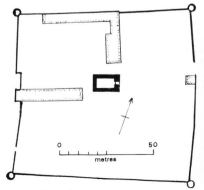

Plan of Ballyragget Castle

Ballykeefe Castle

Ballyragget Castle

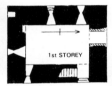

Ballyshawnmore Castle

Plans of Ballyshawnmore Castle

BALLYRAGGET   N449709   C

In the village is a roofed five storey 15th century tower said to have been built by Margaret, wife of Piers Rua Butler, Earl of Ossory and Ormond. It lies on the site of an older castle known as Tulla Barry. In the 16th century it served as the main seat of the Butler viscounts Mountgarret and was then given its spacious and well-preserved bawn with circular flankers. This branch of the Butlers resided at Ballyragget until 1788, when it passed to the Kavanaghs of Borris. The castle was captured by Essex during his campaign of 1599 and it served as a British military post during the insurrection of 1798. In the 1960s it served as a sawmill and timber store. The tower measures 13.2m by 9.4m and has an entrance in the east wall. The third storey is vaulted and has a fireplace dated 1591 with the initials E.M. The bawn has gunloops in the parapet and there are east and west gateways with further gunloops, the west gate also having a machicolation over it.

BALLYSHAWNMORE   S632539   C

This five storey tower Butler tower captured by the Cromwellian forces in 1650 measures 10.5m by 8.5m and has a basement with several double-splayed loops and an east facing entrance defended by a machicolation at the summit, where the adjacent north end wall is carried up one storey higher than the rest. A straight stair leads south off the entrance. The top level has a north window with a mullion and transom with all four lights trefoil-headed. The west wall has a finely moulded window with two step-headed lights.

BOOLYSHEA   S440570

An O'Shea tower measuring 7.8m by 6.4m, located far from any road, has gunloops on either side of the west and south windows at second storey level, and another off the SE corner latrine. The third storey may have only been an attic within the roof. The thick north wall which contained a stair leading of a west-facing entrance is reduced to its footings.

BROWNSFORD   S646345

This FitzGerald tower measuring 9m by 9.7m has four storeys and an attic. Straight stairs rise to the third storey, which has three loops, a fireplace and latrine, and then a spiral stair, now destroyed, led to the upper levels.

BONNETSTOWN   S468578

The west corner containing the staircase of this tower measuring 8.6m by 8m is missing, leaving just one jamb of the entrance, nor does anything remain above the vaulted basement.

Boolyshea Castle

Brownsford: plan

Clonamery: plan

Boolyshea: plans

Bonnetstown: plan

Bonnetstown Castle

BURNCHURCH   R952181   A (key needed)

Of a bawn about 30m long there survives only the 12m high and 5m diameter NW flanker containing three storeys of living rooms set over a basement and linked by stairs curving round in the wall-thickness. The late 15th century tower house of the Burnchurch FitzGeralds in the SW corner of the bawn is roofless but otherwise well preserved, having passed in the 18th century to the Flood family and remaining in occupation by them until 1817. It measures 10.2m by 9.5m and has five storeys, the topmost being set over a vault and having windows in all four walls and a fireplace with a tall circular chimney. A hatch in the floor of the latrine passage around the SW corner gives access to a room in the haunch of the vault. The end walls continue up one more stage to form fighting platforms, the south end reaching to a height of 18m. A zig-zag arrangement of passages gave access from the entrance in the north end wall to the basement. Off these passages lead straight stairs rising up in the north and east walls. The third storey room has a fireplace, access to a mural room in the north wall with a NW angle loop, a latrine in the SW corner, and a south window of three lights. The attic above is also reached from this room, the stair between them having a SE angle-loop.

Castle Columb

Flanker at Burnchurch

0   5
metres

Burnchurch Castle

Burnchurch: plans and section

CALLAN S414441 D

A large mound in the NW part of the town is all that remains of a castle founded in 1217 by William Marshal. Lord Callan's mansion of West Court to the NW dates from the 1790s but may replace or incorporate part of a tower of the Butler earls of Ormond. When a Cromwellian force attacked Callan in 1650 Sir Robert Talbot immediately surrendered the castle but the town on the south bank was held in defiance until Captain Mark McGeoghegan and his men were all killed. The town on this side of the river seems to have had three gates, a ditch and rampart, but there is no certain evidence of a stone wall.

CANTWELL S545593

The only remains of the bawn about 30m square are footings of its NW side and one jamb of its gateway with a drawbar slot adjoining the four storey tower measuring 10.5m by 8.8m in the western corner. Straight stairs lead up from the tower entrance in the SE wall to the west corner of the third storey, which lies over a vault. Above here most of the NW wall containing the continuation of the stairs above a latrine is missing. There are windows here in the NE, SW and SE walls, and the latter has murder holes commanding both the entrance and the doorway from the lower stair into the second storey room. The end walls continued up above the main wall-walk, the north corner being almost 18m high above ground. Originally a Cantwell seat, the tower later passed to the Sandfords, who had another house or tower at Sandford Court to the NE.

CASTLE COLUMB S543385

The NE wall of this chamfered-cornered tower measuring 9.6m by 8.7m contains the entrance and a stair which continues up in the NW wall. The second storey has a latrine in the SW wall. The third storey has a chamber in the east corner and a vault, above which nothing now survives.

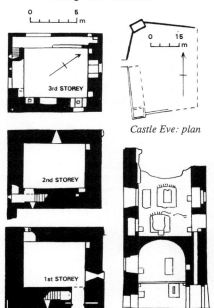

Castle Eve: plan

Cantwell: plans & section

Cantwell Castle

CASTLE EVE   S454433

A platform has a 1.6m thick north wall which may go back to the 14th century, when the D'Erley family had a castle here. A ditch remains on the west and projecting diagonally at the NW corner is a tower measuring about 7m by 5m containing a vaulted room with one cross-loop. A stone with the date 1580 and the arms of John Swetmans was transferred to Rothe House at Kilkenny in 1886. As a result of demolition in the 1990s only stumps remain of the end walls of a house along the west side, part of which was occupied until the 1950s. There was a second tower at the south end of the house.

CASTLE PIERCE   S245705

This four storey building has no vaults, nor is there a stone staircase. It was built by Peter Archdeacon and was forfeited in the 1650s but was burnt around that time.

CLARA   S574579   A (key at farm)

A 3m high wall pierced with musket loops was later added to the Shortalls to enclose a small bawn 13m long by 4m wide in front of the entrance of this fine 15th century tower, which is also protected by a machicolation with pyramidal corbels at wall-walk level and a murder hole from the floor of the lowest of a tier of three mural rooms above. The tower measures 10m by 8m and rises 19m to the top of the double-stepped merlons of the parapet. There are five storeys still complete with their original floors beams and an attic in the roof. The large fifth storey room has two-light windows, one of which was later closed up to allow the insertion of a fireplace. Beside it rises the flue of a fireplace on the third storey, at which level there are angle loops in the three corners away from the spiral stair. One of the loops opens out of one of the tier of mural chambers and the others open off passages either side of the embrasure of an inserted two-light window. One of these passages leads to the only latrine. One of the fifth storey windows has access by means of a hatch to a secret room alongside the haunches of the fourth storey room vault. The main stair ends here and a second stair rises over it to the wall-walk.

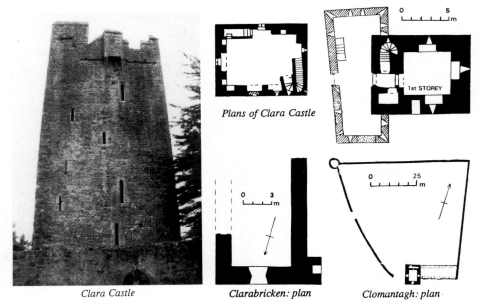

Plans of Clara Castle

1st STOREY

Clara Castle

Clarabricken: plan

Clomantagh: plan

Castle Eve

Clomantagh Castle

CLARABRICKEN   S579569

A motte lies NE of this castle, which originally belonged to the Archers but which in 1659 was occupied by Jacob Cornock. The west wall still partly stands 4m high with a latrine projection and there is also part of the north end of the building which was about 10m wide by 17m long, proportions suggesting a long, low stronghouse rather than a tall tower. Part of the SW corner nearest the farmhouse collapsed a few years ago.

CLOMANTAGH   S348638   D

Piers Rua Butler gave this estate to one of his sons, who became the 1st Viscount Mountgarret. After the forfeiture of Richard, 3rd Lord Mountgarret in the 1650s it was granted to the St Georges. There is a sheela-na-gig on the SW corner of the five storey tower, which is vaulted over the fourth storey and accompanied by a house and a bawn 60m by 52m with the SW corner cut off and the NW corner having a turret with a dome-vaulted roof and crossloops with triangular feet. Recently restored as a holiday home by the Irish Landmark Trust, the tower house measures 11m by 8m and is entered on the north side and the spiral stair lies in the NE corner. The lowest level has a crossloop commanding the entrance. The third storey has a fireplace on the south side.

loop at Castle Eve

Clomantagh

Bawn at Clara

Coolhill Castle

Corluddy Castle

COOLHILL   S726354   B

This circular tower house 10.3m in diameter over walls 3m thick in the vaulted basement was held by the Mountgarret Butlers in 1621. The three upper storeys each have latrines in a square projection opposite the entrance, which is covered by one of three machicolations at the top. The third storey has a fireplace. There appears to have been a small bawn extending east and north of the tower towards a cliff edge.

CORLUDDY   S542129

There are vaults over the second and fourth storeys of this five storey tower measuring 11m by 9.2m with the entrance and the lowest flight of straight stairs on the east side. The stairs continue along the south side to the third storey, which has a fireplace and a two-light window on the north side, a latrine on the south and a stair leading down to a chamber in the northern haunch of the lower vault. After the forfeiture of the Grants in the 1650s the castle went to the Jacksons and then passed to the Boyces.

Corluddy: plan

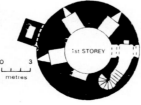

Coolhill: plan

Loops at Coolhill

Currahill Castle

Dysart Castle

CURRAHILL   S444352

The second and third storeys of this tower with ogival-headed loops are both vaulted and have latrines in the south corner. The second storey has a fireplace on the SW side and there is a chamber in the NE haunch of its vault. The fourth storey is very ruinous. Straight flights of steps lead up from the entrance in the NW wall to a spiral stair in the east corner. The tower measures 10.2m by 8.6 and has walls 2m thick in the lowest level, where there are three double-splayed loops in embrasures.

DUNKITT   S581157

Above the east side of the River Suir are two ivy-covered fragments of a castle of the Strang family buried deep in vegetation. One is a wing of a destroyed main block and the other, further south, is a polygonal turret 4m across set on a possibly older circular base.

DYSART   S596393

A tower 7.5m by 6.7m adjoins the west end of a ruined church beside the River Nore. The tower functioned independently of the church and had a cellar with recesses on each side and an entrance and spiral stair in a projecting turret at the SW corner which is now very badly cracked. Over the second storey vault were two upper storeys and an attic. Dysart belonged to Kells Priory until 1540 and then passed to the Berkeleys, who added another building, now very ruined, south of the tower.

Dysart: plan

Foulkscourt Castle

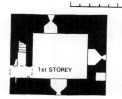

Currahill: plans

FOULKSCOURT   S283678

There is an oratory in the east wall of this Butler tower measuring 13.5m by 10.8m which passed to the Helys in 1698. The tower lay in the eastern part of a bawn 60m by 50m of which the south wall survives, complete with the gateway.

FOULKSRATH   S462667   H

On a low platform with traces of a moat is a large 16th century polygonal bawn with a wall up to 1.2m thick pierced with crossloops. There are three gateways, one of which may have formed part of an earlier building since it closed against the bawn. The five storey tower house measuring 13m by 8.8m with the end walls carried up one more stage to act as gables is thought to have been completed by the Purcells in 1510, they having recently succeeded the de la Frenes here. The spiral stair leads off a zig-zag entrance passage, an arrangement allowing the outer doorway to be commanded by a loop in the thin wall between the passage and the lowest room. The tower is now in use as a youth hostel and has seen some alteration over the years, but the topmost room retains its original two-light windows, and there are angle-loops at the third storey level.

FRENEYSTOWN   S602591   C

This four storey hill-top tower was built by Oliver Cantwell, Bishop of Ossory from 1487 to 1527. It has an entrance in the SW end wall and a turret on the north corner, whilst the fourth storey has a projecting chimney-breast on the SE side, above the roof of a two storey later range.

Plans of Foulksrath Castle

Foulksrath Castle

Foulksrath Castle

GARRYHIGGIN   S324592

This four storey tower measuring 6.5m by 6m and having a spiral stair in the NW corner has been rather altered. The entrance in the north wall has been blocked, the south wall has been rebuilt and the east wall modified as a result of a house having been added in the 18th or 19th century.

GLASHERE   S326709   C

There is a spiral stair in the NW corner of this Butler tower measuring 12.5m by 9.9m which was inhabited until 1840. The entrance has been blocked up but a ramp has been made up to an opening in the second storey. The third storey has a fireplace, a mullioned window on each side and angle-loops in the east and south corners. The fourth storey also has a fireplace and windows with pairs of ogival-headed lights with transoms. The fifth storey has 18th century brick windows and the parapet with round-topped merlons is of the same date.

GOWRAN   S636536

A house lies on or near the site of a castle which for a short while was the principal seat of the Butlers, who were buried in the collegiate church. After a destructive raid by the local Irish in 1414 a murage grant was made for a town wall, although nothing remains of it. There were two gates, and a western extension around the fair green with one further gate seems to have been added later. The town was also captured by Edward Bruce in 1317, and by the Cromwellians Sankey and Hewson in 1650, following which the officers were killed and the castle burnt.

Granagh Castle

Glashere Castle

Drum tower by the river at Granagh

Plan of Granagh Castle

Hall window at Granagh

GRANAGH   S573146   A

Beside the River Suir is a court 30m square surrounded by walls up to 2.4m thick with a
gateway with a drawbar slot on the east side. Little remains of a block containing an 8m
wide hall on the north side, although one surviving window has fine carvings of St Michael
and an angel with the Butler arms, but a solar tower in the NE corner still has four upper
storeys of private rooms over a pair of vaulted cellars. The rooms are linked by a stair in
the NW corner and have latrines in a turret raised above where the curtain wall adjoins the
SE corner. There are windows of two and three lights and the topmost room has a fine
oriel window facing south. The south curtain wall rises direct from the river and was
flanked by circular corner towers. That at the SE corner is mostly destroyed but the SW
tower has two levels of square rooms with access to latrines in the curtain. Below these
is a circular basement with crossloops with a bottom oillet probably intended for
handguns. A thinner wall, part of which has fallen into the river, linked this tower to a
third circular tower further west which may have formed part of a second court. Once
thought to have been built by the Le Poers in the 13th century, this massively walled
castle is now considered to have been built either by James, Earl of Ormond after he
obtained Granagh in 1375, or by his successor, the intention being to command the river
since the landward defences are comparatively weak. It was captured by the Cromwellian
commander Colonel Axtell in 1650.

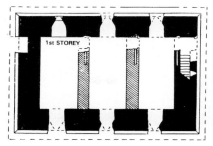
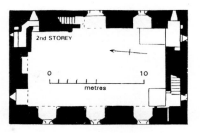

Plans of Grenan Castle

GRENAN   S593414   A

Set at the north end of a platform 55m by 35m and up to 3m high with traces of a thin outer wall probably of late date is a 13th century keep measuring 19m by 13m above a battered base. It seems to have had a solar or private room divided off at the north end of a square hall. The hall has a tiny oratory in the SE corner and two window embrasures on each side, off one of which is a stair to the wall-walk. The solar has two windows and a fireplace and latrine in the north end wall. The basement is now divided up into three chambers of equal size with vaults but the even spacing of the three loops on each side suggests there was previously a similar division with timber posts or partition walls. The middle and northern cellars are each entered in turn with doorways with drawbar slots through the crosswalls from the cellar nearest the entrance at the east end of the south wall. Where the straight stair from the entrance leads up into the hall SW corner there is a wide hatch in the vault, a security arrangement allowing a timber section of floor here to be removed should the entrance be in danger of being stormed. There are indications that a third storey, now destroyed, was later added to the building. This keep may go back to the time of Thomas Fitz-Anthony, who died in 1229.

Grenan Castle

Tower at Kells Priory

Tower at Kells Priory

KEHOE   S573543

The third storey room of this tower measuring 8.6m by 7.3m is irregularly shaped at the north end above where the staircase rises, and has been subdivided at a later date with an inserted fireplace. A second stair in the south wall leads up to the wall-walk. The lowest of the two rooms under the vault has a pair of double-splayed loops.

KELLS   S498432   A

The Augustinan priory has a outer precinct wall up to 4.4m high and 1m thick pierced with loops. It has a coved top without a wall-walk but along the circuit are four tower houses, mostly of five unvaulted storeys, which formed residences for lay officials. The south corner tower measuring 7.2m by 6.2m has a machicolation over its entrance and a fine two-light window on the third storey. The western corner tower measures 5.7m by 5.4m and the intermediate tower is 5m square. A sixth tower lies beside the gateway of the wall of the inner precinct which to the west of the tower has a wall-walk and a parapet with loops in the merlons. A seventh tower beside the church contained a vaulted sacristy. The north side of the priory is partly protected by a stream. The walls were not really intended to form a fortress able to withstand a siege, but they would have been effective against casual raiders or malefactors and there is a machicolation over the east gateway.

On the north bank of the river just west of the bridge are fragments of a wall 1m thick and up to 3m high around a bawn about 50m across, of uncertain date but probably on the site of the castle established here c1200 by Geoffrey FitzRobert.

Plans of Kilcurl Castle

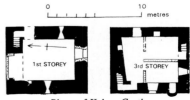

Plans of Kehoe Castle

Kehoe Castle

Kilbline Castle

KILBLINE S577474 D

On the second storey of this well-preserved tower is a chimneypiece dated 1580. Shortly after this date Kilbline passed from the Comerfords to the Shortalls, who adding during the 17th century the still inhabited two storey adjoining house. The castle later passed to Ralph Gore and was subsequently held by the Chandlers and the Ryans. Two storeys of the tower are used as storerooms. Two of the corners have round bartizans, one of which opens off a fighting platform raised up at one end of the tower.

KILCURL S529350

There are vaults over the first and third storeys of this tower measuring 9.8m by 8.5m. The east wall rises up one storey higher and has a machicolation over the rebuilt entrance, above which is a tier of chambers. The second storey has a fireplace on the north and the SW corner contains a second chamber tucked under where the straight flights of stairs continue up to the third storey.

0   5
└─┴─┴─┴─┴─┘m

Kells Priory

Kells Priory

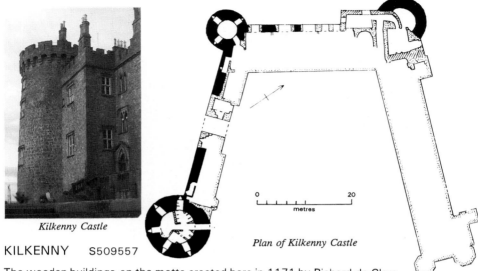

Kilkenny Castle

Plan of Kilkenny Castle

KILKENNY   S509557

The wooden buildings on the motte erected here in 1171 by Richard de Clare
were burnt by the MacGillapatricks the following year. The present castle has developed
from a quadrangular courtyard about 50m by 45m with walls 2m thick flanked by circular
corner towers which was built c1207-12 by William Marshal. Arrow-loops of that period
still remain in the lower parts of the five storey SE and SW towers which are about 13m
and 7.5m in diameter respectively, and in the curtain wall between them. The outer part
of the 11.5m diameter NW tower up as far as the third storey and the lowest parts of the
west curtain wall are also 13th century work.

The castle passed in 1245 to the de Clare Earls of Gloucester and lords of Glamorgan.
After Earl Gilbert was killed fighting the Scots at Bannockburn in 1314 Kilkenny passed
to the Despensers, and later went to the Staffords. In 1338 Olwen de la Freyne escaped
from imprisonment in the castle and returned with a force which broke into the building
to release his brother Fulk. James Butler, 3rd Earl of Ormond purchased the castle in 1391
and made it the chief seat of his earldom. From the later medieval period remain the vaults
over the lowest rooms of the towers. The town was besieged by James FitzMaurice in
1568. Cromwell in 1650 battered down the east side of the castle, which is now open but
which is thought to have originally had a gateway with twin round-fronted towers. The
west gateway dates from a remodelling in the 1660s by James, 12th Earl and 1st Duke
of Ormonde. The castle decayed after the attainder of the 2nd Duke for his support for the
1715 Jacobite rebellion but was renovated by Walter Butler of Garryrichen after he
inherited the title in 1766, the park and present approach being laid out and new stables
erected. In 1826 the north wing was rebuilt to house a picture gallery and the rest of the
castle remodelled to look medieval again. The castle was occupied by Republicans in May
1922 and besieged by Free Staters. Most of the furnishings were sold in 1935 and the
castle was left in a poor condition after military occupation during the 1940s, but it has
since been restored and refurnished as an ancient monument by the Irish Board of Works.

The castle lay at the SE corner of a walled town with five gateways on the west bank
of the Nore. There was an extra walled suburb named Irishtown which included the
cathedral precinct on its west side and had three gateways. Unimpressive sections of the
wall with one simple gateway arch remain near the Dominican Friary and other fragments
of the western walls and their D-shaped towers are hidden away within private yards
further south. At the NE corner of Bishop Este's palace of 1735-6 north of the cathedral
lies a tower built by Bishop Ledrede (1316-61). Cellars with vaults on piers adjoin it.

Kilrush: plans

Kilkenny Castle

KILRUSH S379644

This late 16th century Shortall tower measuring 9.4m by 7.6m was occupied by the St Georges from the 1650s until they transferred to a new house nearby in 1818. The studded door in the north-facing entrance is thought to be original. From it a straight stair leads up in the east wall, which has seen a number of modifications as a result of the addition of a now-vanished later range. The missing SE corner probably contained a spiral stair from the third to the fourth storey, which may have been subdivided. These upper levels above the vault have large windows and fireplaces in the west wall but no latrines.

LEGAN or BALLYDONNELL S568429 D

An ogham stone lies beside a bawn gatehouse retaining its north and east walls and part of the vault over the passageway. The main building collapsed c1880.

NEIGHAM S642509

Sir James Butler's tower of c1480 measures 12m by 10m and has three storeys under a vault and traces of a moat. His descendants were forfeited in the 1650s. Stairs lead off from the south-facing entrance, and the east wall contains a latrine. The SE corner is the only one without an angle-loop.

Gatehouse at Legan

Old door at Kilrush

NEWTOWN   S465438   C

The NE corner of this tower measuring 8.8m by 7.6m contains a spiral stair rising from the north-facing entrance up to the fourth storey. Another stair in the same corner then led up to the wall-walk. The end walls rose up one further level. The third storey has a fireplace and a hatch down into a chamber in the northern haunch of the vault below. The latrine chute was later adapted to serve as a flue for a fireplace in the lowest room. Footings of a bawn wall lie on the edge of a pit 10m south of the tower and to the west, between it and the adjacent lane, is a bowed stretch of bawn wall over 40m long and up to 3m high in parts, although it is completely covered in ivy.

PAULSTOWN   S662571

This still-inhabited tower with ogival-headed loops is thought to have been built c1440 by Sir Edmund Butler, son of Richard, 3rd Earl of Ormond. It passed to Francis Flood in the 18th century and in 1828 the Floods remodelled the tower and added a porch. They sold the tower to the Healys in 1892.

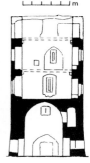

Kilfane: plan

Newtown: plans and section

Newtown Castle

Interior of Newtown Castle

THOMASTOWN   S585417 & 586418   C

Thomastown was a walled town with a gate facing the bridge over the River Nore on the SE and other gates facing north (Kilkenny Gate) and west. Murage tax was levied in 1374 and 1449 and the town was captured by Cromwell in 1650. Thomas FitzAnthony's motte lies in the middle and modest portions of the walls remain in fields on the west side. Near the bridge is a three storey tower called Sweetman's Castle, the second storey fireplace and upper windows being 16th century insertions. Further south, off Low Street, in a yard beside the river, is a second urban tower house called Brady's Castle. Also of three storeys, it had a well and remained in use as a store until fairly recently.

THREECASTLES   S458626   C

Set at the west end of the massively-walled nave of a church, but not communicating with it, is a tower measuring 8.8m by 8m containing two upper storeys over a vaulted basement. There were also once towers at the rectory just to the west and at the farm (beside a motte site) to the SE (457626 & 460625), hence the name Threecastles.

TIBBERAGHNY   S437215   D

This Mountgarret Butler four storey tower has been restored with new battlements and harling. It adjoins a later two storey house and lies beside a motte and bailey castle erected by Prince John in 1185.

Tower at Threecastles church

Tibberaghny Castle

Brady's Castle, Thomastown

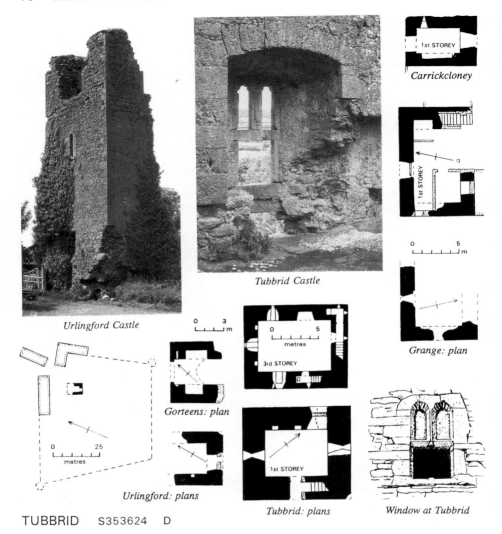

Carrickcloney

Tubbrid Castle

Urlingford Castle

Grange: plan

Gorteens: plan

Urlingford: plans

Tubbrid: plans

Window at Tubbrid

TUBBRID   S353624   D

This 15th century Grace family tower measuring 11.5m by 10.1m has four storeys connected by straight flights of steps, the lowest level having three double-splayed loops and the second level a vault. The third storey (also vaulted) has three windows with seat in the embrasures. This level and that above have in the NW wall latrine and fireplaces which may be a later insertions. One end of the tower continues up to contain a room level with the attic in the main roof and then provide a fighting platform on top.

URLINGFORD   S280638   D

The south end of a Mountgarret Butler tower 5.8m wide stands five storeys high with part of a vault and a fine window at the fourth level. Fragments of the SW and NE walls, and footings of the SE wall with a narrow ditch in front, remain of a bawn roughly 60m square.

OTHER CASTLE REMAINS IN COUNTY KILKENNY

BLACK CASTLE, Killaree S456606 Thick end wall of tower up to 4.5m high amongst row of derelict barns at abandoned farmyard.

CARRICKCLONEY S680220 Defaced tower measuring about 7.6m by 5.4m with second storey vaulted.

CASTLECOMER S538730 Motte in grounds of derelict house. Sir Christopher Wandsford's stronghouse of 1635 was captured by the Confederate Catholics in 1642.

CASTLE BANNY S556323 A 1.6m thick fragment of the west wall stands complete with the parapet and evidence of a vault over the second storey.

CLOGHASTY S730458 NE corner of O'Ryan tower 12m by 10m by the river stands four storeys high but rest is only 1m high. Lowest level has a fireplace in SE wall.

CLOGHSCREGG S633438 Just the corner of the tower remains.

CLONAMERY S658352 Overgrown four storey high fragment of FitzGerald tower on motte above River Nore. Abutted by crosswall. Evidence of vault on second storey and round bartizan at summit. See plan on page 61.

DRAKELAND S486554 The eastern part of a Grace family tower about 5.5m wide stands three storeys high. The western part collapsed in 1880 and other parts fell in 1903.

FRANKFORT S390341 Two walls of Butler house inhabited to c1800. Evidence of two periods of work.

GALMOY S721413 East wall with upper and lower fireplaces in breast and featureless south wall of two storey house about 9m square of Butler viscounts Galmoy.

GORTEENS S652138 NW-facing gatehouse 6.7m by 6.0m partly four storeys high with 2.7m wide passage flanked by recesses. Stair only between second and third storeys.

GRANGE S499181 East and south walls 1.6m thick with part of basement vault and one upper storey of tower 8m wide and about 10m long. Seat of Pierce Brennagh, d1575.

HIGHRATH S551542 Modernised tower shorn of top storey. Built by the Shortalls, held by the Jacksons in 1664, and occupied by the Ryans until recent times.

HOLDENSRATH S474563 Three storey tower 12m by 8m now missing SE corner with south facing entrance, but retaining part of stair in east end wall and most of vault.

KILFANE S598451 Four storey tower with fireplace on second storey over vaulted chapel adjoins church with thick walls formerly with wall-walks and parapets. See p21.

KILFERAGH S540526 House in wooded grounds incorporates castle of Forstal family.

KNOCKTOPHER S534370 Matthew FitzGriffin's castle passed to the Butlers in 1312. Stonework was wrecked by Cromwellian artillery in 1650 and only a motte remains.

LISMAINE S442660 Three storey high fragment of north wall and NW corner of stronghouse with gunloops on either side of a window.

RATHCULBIN S460433 Three storey high section of north wall of 17th century house with projecting chimneybreast. The eastern part collapsed in 1954.

TULLAROAN S382564 6m high motte. Grace chief castle to the north destroyed c1800.

CASTLE SITES IN COUNTY KILKENNY

CASTLE HALE S475356 Debris pile of former Walsh seat in Rossenarra demesne.

CASTLE KELLY S665552 Platform 65m across marks site of castle of Kelly family.

CLOGHPOOK S550651 Platform 40m across marks site of castle.

CLONE S475365 Piles of debris of tower and later structures nearby.

KILCRAGGAN S518179 Site of Walshe castle north of house of 1690s rebuilt in 1850s.

LISMATEIGE S513296 A motte remains but the stone castle has gone.

POTTLERATH S379519 Site of castle of Eamon MacRiserd Butler, grandson of the 3rd Earl of Ormond. Under his patronage here Sean Buidhe O'Clery wrote poetry preserved in the Bodleian library. The poems formed part of Eamon's ransom in 1462 after he was captured by the Earl of Desmond.

STROAN S595458 Traces of platform only.

TEMPLEORUM or OLDCOURT S478258 Platform 25m by 20m is site of Walsh castle.

Drakeland Castle

Gateway at Gorteen

Freneystown Castle

OTHER CASTLE SITES IN KILKENNY: Annamult S541465, Ardacoo S471622, Ardra S538730, Ballyhenebery S440255, Ballylarkin S386636, Ballynacooly S534250, Ballynooney S574264, Ballyspellan S316680, Barrabehy S511219, Baunanatyin S532378, Belline S449231, Blanchville S588523, Brittasdryland S392507, Cappagh Island S643397, Castleinch S476522, Castlemarket S456718, Castlemorris S489346, Castletown S266726, Clogaralt S725359, Clogharinka, Clogh S561782, Clonassy S556231, Coan West S594710, Corbetstown S513655, Courtstown S366558, Crowbally S560285, Dangan S571197, Dromdowney S660146, Duncarvan S615487, Dunamaggan S482390, Ennisnag S520441, Esker S450660, Farrantemple S710342, Fiddown S466199, Forestalstown S681244, Garrygaug S524263, Garryrickin S387376, Gaulstown S605178, Goulstown Lower S411590, Goslingstown S493525, Gragara S487661, Haggard S628231, Inchacarran S560242, Jamestown S472251, Kilcreen S490558, Kilkierain S649403, Killahy S353595, Killaroe S457606, Kilmacar S491688, Kilmurry S632141, Kilree 534400, Kiltown S525738, Knockmoylon S545284, Knocktopher S534371, 533373, 532373, Kyle Ballynan S370635, Lisdowney S408712, Lodge S394664, Lyrath S544555, Mansellscourt S566289, Meallaghmore S417321, Moonhall S595567, Mullinahone S648231, Oldcastle Lower S404330, Oldcourt S473230, Oldtown S394554, Pollagh S688509, Ratheealy S385605, Rathoscar S325688, Rochestown S539238, Rochestown S675190, Rossenarra S475348, Sart S404619, Seskin S416724, Shancashlaun S458357, Shanganny S484675, Sheepstown S 508372, Slievecarragh S668282, Troyswood S482599, Tullagher S645313, Tullowglass S473653, Upperwood S401639, Westcourt S409443, White Castle S623361, Whitescastle S533374, Whiteswall S285739.

MOTTES (in addition to others noted in gazetteer): Athclare S687446, Bootstown S408605, Castledough S471622, Grangefertagh* S301700, Kiltrassy S406320, Inistioge S634378, Listerlin S640291, Moat S411640, Owning S452282, Portnascully S516139, Powerstown S668510, Tullabarry* S445727, Tullahough S433302

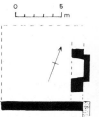

Galmoy's: plan

Bawn at Kells

CASTLES OF COUNTY LAOIS

BALLAGH   S224766   C

The fourth storey of this 16th century FitzPatrick tower measuring 11.2m by 9m has windows of two ogival-headed lights in the NE and SE walls, a chamber in a bartizan on the corner between them, and other chambers with machicolations projecting from the NW and SW walls, the latter being part of a tier of chambers over the entrance. The fifth storey has windows with pairs of segmental-headed lights facing NE and SE. The south corner contains a spiral stair reached from the entrance through a pair of lobbies, one covered by a crossloop from the cellar. The NW wall contains passages at the second and third storey levels and there are fireplaces in the third and fourth storey main rooms.

BALLAGHMORE   S197899   E

The NW corner of this recently renovated tower measuring 13.6m by 11.6m bears a sheela-na-gig in relief. Just 1m away from the walls lay a thin bawn wall of which there remain a slab-roofed circular flanker 3.5m in diameter at the SW corner. The tower entrance faces north and has a straight stair leading up through the north and east walls to a spiral stair in the NE corner connecting the fourth and fifth storeys. Another stair in the west wall then leads to the wall-walk. There are no vaults but the second storey has steps up from its floor to its entrance doorway and to the window embrasures suggesting that it was intended to have had a floor at a higher level over a vault which has been removed. Passages off the southern window embrasure at this level are lighted by crossloops and there is also a SE angle-loop. This level and the fourth storey have latrines in the SW corner. The existing battlements date from a 19th century restoration.

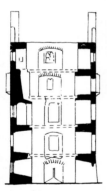
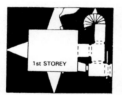
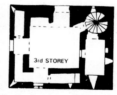

Ballagh: plans and section

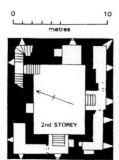

Ballaghmore: plan   *Ballagh Castle*   *Ballaghmore Castle*

Ballyadams Castle

Clonburren Castle (see also page 11)

BALLYADAMS CASTLE   S629908 D

Projecting from the northern half of the west side of a 17th century three storey house with a wing in the middle of the east side is an older six storey structure with two round turrets flanking an arched entrance set under a segmental arch with a murder hole. Below the top storey the turrets are connected by another arch with machicolations behind it. The NW turret contains a stairwell, and there were latrines in a NE projection behind it.

BALLYGEEHIN   S372834 C.

This castle of the Fitzpatrick lords of Upper Ossory was burnt in 1600 to prevent it being garrisoned by English troops. The thin ivyclad 11m long NE side of the building stands three storeys high and contains a wide blocked arch.

BALLYMADDOCK   S552990

The much altered northern half of a T-shaped 17th century building known as Cahernagapol's House remains inhabited whilst the south part lies in ruins. It has a fireplace in the SE corner, which adjoins part of the bawn wall. Another section of the bawn wall adjoins two gables of former outbuildings to the NW.

CASTLE FLEMING   S221796

Of a house 18.2m long by 9m wide there remain the 1m thick south wall with several large openings and the west wall with a slop-drain and a fireplace in a projecting breast. The jamb of an entrance of a projecting porch or a former bawn adjoins the south wall.

CASTLETOWN   S342920 C

A school lies on the site of the main tower of the castle of "Offerclane" shown in an old engraving with square corner turrets with double-stepped battlements. This building was probably of 15th century date as is the fragment of the NW corner tower 6.5m in diameter adjoining rebuilt walls, but there was an older castle here which Gilbert de Clare surrendered to the Crown in 1290. The castle was burnt in 1600 by Teige Fitzpatrick.

CLONBURREN   S249742   D

On a low rock is a tower rising 14m to a wall-walk, at which level there are corbels for former machicolated bartizans at the corners and in the middle of each side. The tower measures 12.6m by 9.5m over walls 2.3m thick. The NE wall is thicker and contains a tier of rooms over the entrance and a spiral stair in the east corner. Above the level of the former vault over the fourth storey the walls are just 1.3m thick with centrally-placed two-light windows. Some of the loops in the intermediate levels are oillets or cross-loops. The SW wall contains passages at the second and third storey levels.

CLONCOURSE   S218903

There is a machicolation high up over the doorway into a wing on the south side of this four storey house 13m long by 9m wide and there are corbels for a bartizan on the SW corner. There are chimney stacks on the east and west end gables but the north wall is destroyed. The house lies on the north side of a rectangular bawn about 56m wide with gunloops in the wall between it and the NW corner and a gateway on the south side.

CLONREHER   N446007   C

This building in a farmyard has a main body 13m long by 8.8m wide containing a hall over a vault over a cellar and loft. The hall is reached by straight stairs from the entrance (now blocked) on the east side. A badly cracked wing 4.2m projecting from the north end of this side contains rooms at all three main levels, plus two more levels under a topmost vault which are reached by a second stair in the main east wall. Another branch of the stair rises around the SE corner and up in the south wall to two upper rooms in a second wing projecting from the west end of that wall. A latrine in the main west wall adjoins the room in this wing at hall level, and there are two other vaulted rooms below which can only have been reached from the inside by hatches in the vaults. This former O'Dowling castle was granted to John Dunkirley in 1550 and was later held by the Hartpoles.

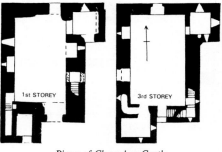

Plans of Clonreher Castle

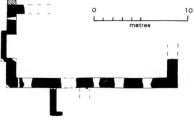

Plan of Castle Fleming

Clonreher Castle

COOLBANAGHER   N515033   C

NE of the church is a tower 10.8m long by 7.4m wide with a fine north-facing doorway and several ogival-headed loops, including one on the north side with sunk spandrels at fourth storey level. A stair in the SW corner linked the upper levels. There are no vaults. The badly cracked east wall contains upper fireplaces.

CULLAHILL   S356740   C

The wall of a 16th century inner bawn closely surrounds this lofty tower built c1425 by the MacGillapatricks which measures 15m by 12.6m. over walls up to 3.7m thick. Much of the north wall containing the entrance has fallen and this end of the bawn is mostly destroyed, perhaps the result of destruction c1650 by Cromwellian troops. There are tiny circular flankers with corbelled roofs at the southern corners of this bawn. To the north and east extends a seven-sided outer bawn with a fairly complete wall 1.1m thick with gunloops. The tower contained a cellar and an unlit loft under a vault. Level with the loft the SW corner contains a chamber and the upper levels have passages here to latrines in the west wall. The fireplaces in the east wall at the third and fourth storey levels are insertions, the upper one blocking a window. Behind the lower one rises a straight stair up from the entrance. The wall is thick enough to contain a second stair rising up beside it from a lobby near the SE corner. Originally there was a sheela-na-gig on this side. The fourth storey has a mullion-and-transom window facing south and the fifth storey has a SW angle-loop. There was also an attic in the roof, at which level the wall-walk tunnelled through the south wall, which rises one storey higher than the rest.

Coolbanagher Castle

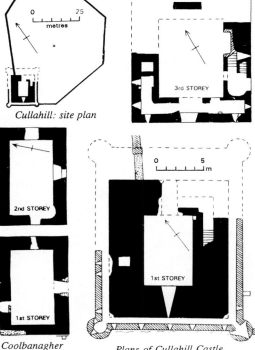

Cullahill: site plan

Coolbanagher

Plans of Cullahill Castle

Keep at Dunamase

Cullahill Castle

Cullahill Castle

DUNAMASE   S530982   A

A fort on the Rock of Dunamase was plundered by the Vikings in 944. It was given to Richard de Clare (Strongbow) by Dermot MacMurrough as part of the dowry of his daughter Aoife. William Marshal may have built the keep and the surrounding walls and the inner gatehouse and outer ward may be the work of his son-in-law William de Braose, whilst the Mortimers later carried out further improvements. The castle was later held by the O'Mores, from whom it was captured by Sir Charles Coote in 1641. It was captured in 1646 by Eoghan Rua O'Neill and occupied by Confederate Catholic forces until captured and destroyed by the Cromwellian commanders Hewson and Reynolds in 1650. It was partly restored by Sir John Parnell but soon allowed to decay.

The heart-shaped summit of the rock measuring about 100m across has fragments of a thin wall on the cliff edges on the north and SW sides, the latter having a postern approached by a ramp within a barbican. There are more substantial remains of a loopholed wall 1.9m thick on the weaker SE side with a central gatehouse with a passage with a portcullis groove flanked by small guard rooms, the outer parts of which are destroyed to the base. Excavations have revealed the lower parts of an older gatehouse measuring about 10m by 8m just NE of it, and there is a rectangular tower at the south corner where the wall of a triangular outer ward adjoins it. This outer ward has its own gatehouse with the outer corners rounded off. In the middle of the main enclosure are remains of a huge keep 34.4m long and 20m wide over walls 2.8m thick probably never much higher than their present height of about 7m. It is thought to have contained a hall with a chamber over an undercroft at the north end. In the 17th century the keep was remodelled as a stronghouse with a wing on the west side flanking an entrance and the hall was probably then divided into two storeys. Originally curtain walls extended north and south from the keep to close off an inner ward to the west of it. The lower parts of the destroyed SW end of the building have recently been exposed, showing a doorway on the SE side cutting through a very massive batter added against the vertical original wall.

Garranmaconly Castle

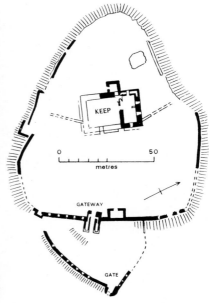

Plan of Dunamase Castle

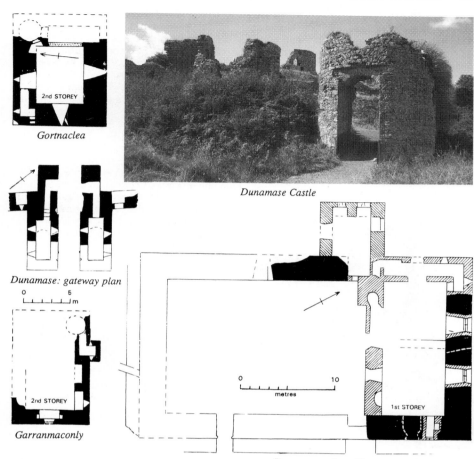

Gortnaclea

Dunamase Castle

Dunamase: gateway plan

0   5
m

Garranmaconly

0   10
metres

2nd STOREY

1st STOREY

Dunamase: plan of keep

GARRANMACONLY   S215841

This 16th century tower of the Fitzpatrick Lords of Upper Ossory was occupied by Peter Buckley in 1665 but later passed to the Vicars family. Set on a rock platform, it measures 12.4m by 8.3m and has a latrine projection on the north side near the well of the spiral stair in the NW corner. Further east the north wall has a high chimney stack serving fireplaces on the third and fourth storeys. There is a bartizan on the NE corner and a machicolation opening from the east end of the fourth storey room. The collapsed west wall contained the entrance.

GORTNACLEA CASTLE   S360862   C

This five storey tower house measuring 12.2 by 9.9m was held by Donal Fitzpatrick in 1566. Here the Black Earl of Ormond was held captive by Owney O'Moore in April 1600. The east end wall (now mostly destroyed) contained the entrance with unvaulted chambers above it and there was a spiral stair in the NE corner. Passages from the north windows on the second and third storeys lead to latrines in the NW corner. Some of the windows are of two lights and the lower part of a gable remains on the west wall.

GRANTSTOWN CASTLE   S332798   D

This five storey circular tower house 11.3m in diameter with gunloops was built by a lord of Upper Ossory in the 16th century. It was held by Gilbert Rawson in 1653, but had passed to Edmond Morris by 1691, and then in 1696 was granted by William III to Richard and Edward Fitzpatrick. The SE part of the tower containing chambers over the entrance has been destroyed but most of the adjoining spiral stair still survives. The third and fourth storeys are pentagonal and the fifth storey room set over a vault is almost square. At wall-walk level are remains of machicolations facing NE and south.

KILBREEDY CASTLE   S303799   D

This 16th or 17th century O'Phelan stronghouse measuring 17m by 10.3m contains one large upper room (probably once with a timber subdivision) with large windows. Under the vault below it is a chamber with loops set in deep embrasures like an arcade and a dark loft above it. Only the drawbar slot and murder hole from above remain of the entrance doorway at the east end of the south end wall.

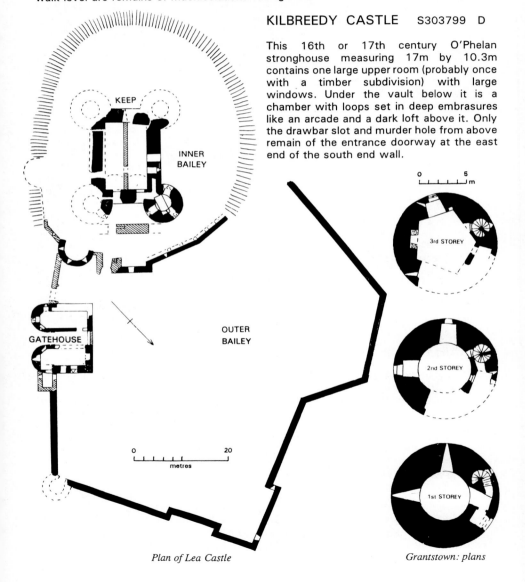

Plan of Lea Castle

Grantstown: plans

LEA CASTLE   N570120   A

William Marshal had a motte and bailey castle here in 1203 and is said to have built the keep, although an upper window in it with two trefoil-headed lights suggests a date of c1250-60, when Lea was held by Maurice FitzGerald, 2nd Baron Offaly. The castle was burnt by the O'Connors in 1285 and the new outer gatehouse added by Edward I in the 1290s to strengthen the outer ward failed to save the castle from being over-run and wrecked by the O'Mores in 1307 and 1346, or from capture by Edward Bruce in 1315. The adjacent town never recovered from these incursions. In 1422 the O'Dempseys captured the castle from the Earl of Kildare, only to lose it to the Earl of Ormond in 1452. Silken Thomas retreated to Lea during his rebellion of 1534. The O'Dempseys seized Lea for the Confederate Catholics in 1641 and it was blown up by the Cromwellians in 1650.

The four storey keep 21m long by 15m wide over walls up to 3m thick is very ruined and only one of the four corner towers 8.6m in diameter now survives. The entrance at second storey level lies in the east wall adjoining this tower. Some sort of barbican or porch was later added in front of it. The crosswall and vaults of the lowest level of the keep main body are probably later insertions. Around the keep was an oval court about 55m by 40m. The only remaining part of the curtain wall, on the north, was arcaded on the inner side to create enough thickness to carry a wall-walk. The wall was flanked by D-shaped bastions, one of which remains beside a square 15th century east-facing gatehouse. A short length of wall connects this bastion to the outer gatehouse, which has a long passage 3m wide flanked by elongated 6m wide round-fronted towers. This building was later adapted as an apartment block by blocking the passage at each end and adding a latrine turret beside the eastern tower. The outer court extending north and west behind it towards the River Barrow measures about 60m across. There seem to have been water-filled moats fed by the river as extensive outer earthworks still remain.

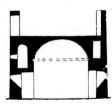

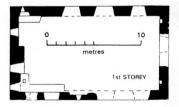

Lea Castle

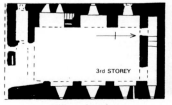

Kilbreedy: plans

Kilbreedy Castle

Shrule Castle

Timahoe Castle

MARYBOROUGH   S471985 B

The south, east and north walls up to 5m high remain of a bawn 130m by 100m erected by the crown c1548 and wrecked by Cromwell's forces in 1650. At the NE corner is a featureless bastion 11m in diameter. There was a range of buildings on the south side. The square SW corner tower has gone and little remains of the west wall containing the entrance. This side was the only one not enclosed by the now-destroyed town defences. The bawn walls originally had a wide earth rampart on the inner side.

MORETT   N541032   D

Of this large and massive FitzGerald tower measuring 16m by 11.3m built on a rock outcrop c1580 the SW corner and the east wall still stand complete, the latter having fireplaces on the lowest three of the four main storeys, plus another for an attic within the roof. An oven adjoins the lowest fireplace. Round bartizans remain on the SW and NE corners. There are no signs of vaults, latrines, staircases or an entrance.

RUSH HALL   S310899

A bawn 65m square with a wall 3.7m high has a southerly extension at the SW corner. This corner and those at the SE and NE have hexagonal flankers about 4.3m across but the flanker at the NW corner has been destroyed. The gunloops in the flankers are vertical slots with a central oillet. Projecting from the west side is a four storey house with parts of an annex alongside the north wall, in which are fireplaces. Most of the annex was removed in 1977 and little remains of the south wall of the main house.

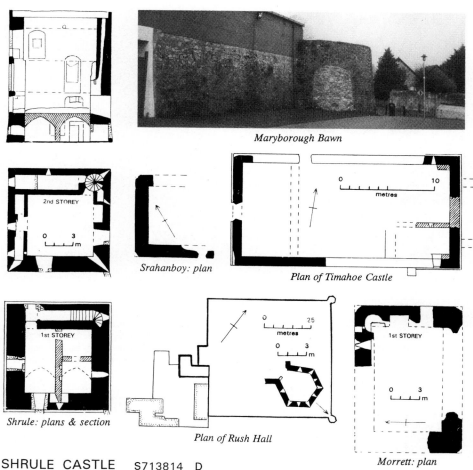

Maryborough Bawn

Srahanboy: plan

Plan of Timahoe Castle

Shrule: plans & section

Plan of Rush Hall

Morrett: plan

SHRULE CASTLE S713814 D

The lowest storey of Robert Hartpole's late 16th century tower was later subdivided by a crosswall to carry two vaults. High up on the south wall is a plaque with the date 1640 and the initials RHK. Only the south jamb of the east facing entrance remains. A passage leads from it to a spiral stair in the SE corner. The second storey has a fireplace on the south side and the third and fourth storeys have fireplaces on the north side. Latrines lie in the south wall beside the stair at the second storey, and also on the third storey, which has a passage to a NW angle loop. Some of the loops are ogival-headed with hoodmouldings and the fourth storey has a two-light window facing south.

TIMAHOE CASTLE S536902 A

After being granted Timahoe in 1609, Richard Cosby converted a 15th century church nave with the exceptional internal width of 10m into a castle by building a tower in the eastern part and using the rest as a bawn with a domestic building in the west end, thus leaving a square court in the middle. The chancel was levelled and the arch to it blocked up. A motte and bailey west of the village are mentioned by Gerald of Wales in 1182.

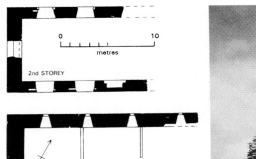

2nd STOREY

1st STOREY

Plans of Tullomoy Castle

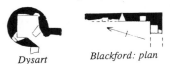

Dysart   *Blackford: plan*

Cody's Castle

TULLOMOY CASTLE   S603909   D

The east end of Billy George's early 17th century house 9.4m wide over walls 1.5m thick in the low basement has been destroyed but it was about 22m long. The upper windows were of three lights with hoodmoulds and there are fireplaces in the south and west walls on each of the second, third and fourth storeys. The lowest windows had iron stanchions.

OTHER CASTLES IN COUNTY LAOIS

AGHMACART S332743 NE corner stands two storeys high with remains of vault. Low bank and ditch enclose a bawn 27m by 22m.

AGHABOE S328895 Ditched motte has base of wall on summit 35m across. Traces of bailey to north.

BALLINAKILL S468805 Three storey north end wall with gunloops on two levels of Dunne family mansion of 1680 on site of Sir Thomas Ridgeway's castle of c1606-12 destroyed in the 1640s.

BALLYKEALY S383731 Featureless south and west corners two storeys high of tower 9.3m by 7m fortified by John McKeallagh Fitzpatrick in 1653.

BALLYKNOCKAN S490932 Lower parts of north and east walls of tower 8.6m by 8m held by Sir Thomas Colclough in 1598. Entrance and passage on north, latrine to SE.

BALLYMAHIMMY S262107 Wall fragment on SW side of ditched platform 20m by 16m.

BLACKFORD S614964 Three storey high fragment of east and south walls of tower shown on map of 1563. One loop facing east is only opening still complete.

CASTLEBRACK N405164 Pile of rubble SSE of church and fragment of south wall of bawn with ditch on east and south remains of castle built by Dunne family in 1427.

CODY'S S280797 8m long section of south wall 1.5m thick with upper loop, entrance drawbar slot and part of parapet for lost wall-walk. A possible early hall-house.

COOLNAMONY N339093 West wall of bawn with three gunloops and part of NW flanker near Glenlahan River. Probably built by Teige Oge O'Doyne c1551.

CULLENAGH S505909 North end of four storey stronghouse with fireplaces in projecting breast. Altered bawn wall with east half of circular SE flanker. Later SW flanker.

DYSART S517970 4m diameter NE corner bawn flanker remains of castle of O'Lalor family granted in 1577 to John Piggott. Captured by Confederate Catholics in 1646.

FERMOYLE S431784 East gable of three storey house with part of south wall with loops and windows. Part of bawn wall runs south from SW corner.

KILLEANY S378876 Featureless fragments remain of a tower marked on 1563 map.

MILLTOWN or BALLYVUILLING S624878 29m long length of 3m high bawn wall 0.9m thick. Tower house and later mansion now gone.

MONDREHID S252904 Featureless 14m long, 5m high length of walling with SW corner.

SCOTCHRATH S365858 Small house of uncertain date without defensive features but retaining a 40m length of a 3.5m high bawn wall.

SHAEN S504031 Walled garden on hill incorporates battered 3m high NW corner of tower said to have been destroyed in 1650.

SRAHANBOY S247966 4m high, 1.4m thick south and west walls of tower 9.2m wide. Held by the O'Connors in 1641. Occupied by the Calcutts until at least the 1780s.

TINTORE S356808 East wall of three storey Fitzpatrick tower now forms part of house. North wall modern. Fireplaces in NW corner but no other features.

Castlecuffe and Derrin are ruined 17th century houses without defensive features.

CASTLE SITES IN COUNTY LAOIS

BALLYFIN N381008 1820s house on site of late 16th century Crosbie castle granted to Piriam Pole in 1666 and replaced by a house built by his son William.

BALLYLEHANE S633860 Castle mentioned in 1346. Held by Hovendens in 16th century. Armoral panel of O'Connors of Offaly formerly on gate-pier of field but now lost.

BALLYMADDOCK S549989 Pile of rubble on site of castle demolished in 1940s or 50s.

BAUNAGHRA S227718 Site of former tower 9m by 6.3m over walls 1.2m thick.

BORRIS S252877 Vaulted lowest storey with entrance facing north and stair in east wall remained a century ago. Mentioned in 1581. House probably on site of outbuilding.

CLOPOCK S584907 Site of building with subdivided lowest storey in SE part of hillfort.

GRANGE S712832 Panel dated 1588 with initials of Robert Hartpole, Governor of Queen's County, lay over entrance of building possibly of later date demolished c1970.

MOAT S490813 Stone castle stood in SW part of bailey measuring 60m by 30m lying SW of 6m high motte with summit 12m across.

PORTARLINGTON N542126 17th century 20 acre town had River Barrow on east, west and north, and a canal on the south. Earthworks and corner bastions have gone.

RAHANAVANNAGH S482867 Site of O'Moore castle replaced by 18th century house.

RATHPIPER S296772 Castle named after Piper family survived until the 1830s.

REDCASTLE S372959 Site of tower built by the FitzPatricks in the 16th century.

STRADBALLY S573964 Site of Cosbie family stronghouse said to have replaced an O'Moore fortress known as the Castle of Palace.

WATERCASTLE S425805 Site of castle converted into a house in the 18th century.

OTHER CASTLE SITES: Abbeyleix S422831, Ballymanus S615991, Castletown S224892, Coolkerry S301777, Emo N537065, Farnans S626834, Glanmalira S574074, Gortnalee S250816, Grange Upper S542965, Grenan S438737, Harristown S258766, Killasmeestia S242833, Killeshin S674777, Prospect S539946, Roskeen N421176, Tankardstown S705873 (2nd possible site nearby), Timogue S554936

The location of castles mentioned or shown on old maps at Archerstown, Arless, Castledurrow, Castlefleming, Clonin, Grange More (a stronghouse), Kilmartyr, Kilminchy and Skirk are unknown.

MOTTES (* with baileys) See also entry for Moat. Ballinaclogh* S527895, Ballyroan* (Athronny) S466888, Castletown S645854, Donaghmore S269804, Dunbrin S688918, Grenan S440737, Haywood S468819, Kildellig S304841, Killabran (site only) S690856, Killeshin S674777, Kilmorony* S699891, Middlemount* S309791, Monelly S258979, Rathmananagh* N482012, Skirke* S229847, Srahanboy* S244967

CASTLES OF COUNTY LONGFORD

BALLINAMORE   N103678

Within a large walled enclosure without defensive features lies the loopholed east wall and other footings of the main block of a house about 12m wide built c1620 by Sir Richard Browne and Lady Mary Plunkett. Part also remains of the north wall of a SE wing 8.4m wide. Not enough evidence remains to show quite how the parts related to each other. There seems to have been a similar NE wing.

BAWN   N154697

A bawn east of the modern house is enclosed by a wall on the south side and a ditch on the other three sides. Within the SE corner lies the ivy-mantled NW corner turret 5.2m square and parts of the adjoining walls of a 16th or 17th century tower house. Old maps show this building much more complete with a circular turret on the SE corner.

BOHERQUILL or COOLAMBER   N345734   C

Set on a low platform are remains of a building 23.6m long by 11m wide over walls 1.1m thick. Only low fragments, some half buried in debris, remain of the two storey main part of the building but the north end (the only part not enclosed by the former bawn wall enclosing the platform) stands much higher. It contains a long narrow room with a fireplace and a NE angle-loop over a vaulted cellar and two low upper storeys reached by a spiral stair with another angle-loop in the NW corner. There is evidence of a second adjacent vault, but the rest of the building does not appear to have had vaulting. A gunloop opening off the NE angle-loop suggests a 16th century date for this O'Farrell seat.

Castlerea: plans

Bawn: plan

Gunloops at Boherquill

Ballinamore Castle

CASTLE FORBES   N096805

In 1628 Arthur Forbes was given this estate, complete with a tower house and a baronetcy of Nova Scotia. The vaulted basement of the old tower still remains. South of it Sir Arthur built a new L-shaped house with two storeys of living rooms over a basement. It had mullioned windows and high hipped gables and was complete by 1632, when he was killed in a duel in Hamburg. His widow Jane Lauder successfully defended the castle against the Confederate Catholics in 1641 and their son was made Earl of Granard in 1684. Arthur and Jane's arms lie upon the present building, most of which dates from after a fire in 1825, when the 6th Earl was saved from the flames by the efforts of his dog. There was a further remodelling after another fire in 1923.

CASTLEREA   N155677   D

The east wall of this 16th century O'Farrell tower measuring 10.6m by 9.2m contains chambers over a damaged entrance covered by a gunloop from an adjoining guard-room. The third storey is set over a vault and is well provided with gunloops, some flanking the main windows and one covering the stair from the room in the east wall. Both this level and that below have latrines in the NW corner. A chimney stack serves a fireplace in the east wall at fourth storey level.

CORROOL   N055560

2nd STOREY

Near the shore of Lough Ree is the lowest part of a building 10.2m wide over walls 1.7m thick above a battered base, probably a 13th century hall-house. Only traces remain of the west end, suggesting an external length of about 20m. The east wall has one broken loop and there are traces of two loops blocked by rubble on the north side.

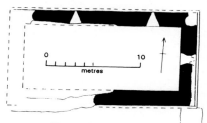

Plan of Corrool Castle

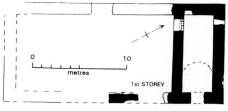

1st STOREY

Plans of Boherquill Castle

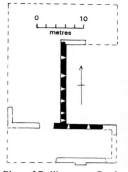

Plan of Ballinamore Castle

Corrool Castle

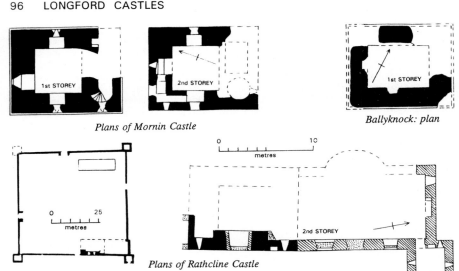

Plans of Mornin Castle

Ballyknock: plan

Plans of Rathcline Castle

ELFEET   N024593   C

A tower 6m square above a battered base lies at the east corner of a structure at least 16m long by 12m wide which could have been either a roofed building or an open court. The tower contained two upper storeys, one with a fireplace, over a vaulted cellar.

MORNIN   N173635   C

In 1612 James I confirmed Roger O'Farrell in possession of the "castle, town and lands of Mornyn", then the seat of the main branch of the family. The south end wall containing chamber over the entrance has fallen except for part of the SW corner containing a spiral staircase, but the other walls of a tower 11.6m by 9.6m stand high with evidence of a vault over the second storey and two upper levels. The north wall contains a latrine close to an ogival-headed loop, the embrasure of which was blocked to create a fireplace. Debris has buried the inner embrasure of a horizontal gunloop in the lowest level of this wall.

RATHCLINE CASTLE   N001669   C

Only the east wall about 12m long and 2.2m thick above a very substantial battered base remains of a large tower built by the Quinn family. The north and east walls also remain of a three storey 17th century wing 9m wide extending 14m to the north and occupying the NE corner of a bawn about 55m square. String courses mark the floor levels externally and there are fireplaces in the north end wall and large blocked windows of as many as five lights with two transoms. There are gunloops in a 5m square wing at the NE corner and also in a two storey flanker at the SE corner of the bawn. The NW flanker of the bawn is more ruinous and the SW flanker has gone. The bawn has unusually elaborate gateways facing south and west, and a third gateway on the east just south of the tower house. The bawn wall south of here is thicker than the rest and has loops and corbels for a floor, suggesting that it incorporates remains of a two storey late medieval building. The castle was damaged during an attack by Cromwellian forces but restored after being granted to Sir George Lane in the 1660s, to whom may perhaps be attributed parts of the gateways. It was wrecked again during the conflict of 1690-1 and a further restoration was planned but probably not executed. See page 16.

Mornin Castle

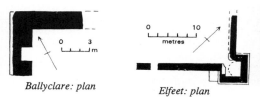

Ballyclare: plan

Elfeet: plan

Rathcline Castle

OTHER CASTLES IN COUNTY LONGFORD

BALLYKNOCK N113649 Defaced lower parts of tower 11m by 9m over walls 2.1m thick above battered base on summit of hillock with traces of surrounding bawn.

BALLYCLARE N093706 North corner and parts of adjacent walls of tower probably about 9.5m wide with walls from 2.0 to 2.4m thick.

BARRY N159609 Footings of tower and traces of bawn on ditched platform.

CASTLE COR N137570 Fragmentary walls of uncertain date upon a motte.

FORMOYLE N005637 Three storey high fragment of wall with part of gable of mid 17th century house of the Newcomen family.

GRANARD N330810 Huge mound of Richard Tuite's castle of 1199 which later passed to the de Gennevilles, and then to the Mortimers.

LISSARDOWLAN N186740 Motte & bailey destroyed by Aedh O'Conor in 1224 and later replaced by a stone castle of the O'Farrells, now gone.

LONGFORD N130756 Site of stronghouse built to replace O'Farrell castle c1627 by Francis Aungier, Lord Longford, whose descendants occupied it until late 18th century.

MOAT FARRELL N235755 & 239749 Motte and nearby house of two storeys and attic with apsed NE end.

PORTANURE N043565 Bawn with rebuilt north wall and missing south wall. Other walls and square SW flanker and circular SE flanker both with gunloops are about 4m high.

ROSDUFF N272936 Ivy-covered bawn wall 2m high on NE and south sides, the latter having a U-shaped flanker.

SITES OF OTHER CASTLES: Ardenragh N245625, Glen N257686, Moatavally N328734, Parkplace N187212, Screeboge N202643

MOTTES: Bohernacross N257687, Caherdague N326734, Garryandrew N271711, Kilglass N230647, Richmount N202643, Tachsheenod N186622

CASTLES OF COUNTY LOUTH

ARDEE N962907 C

A murage grant was made in 1376 for the maintenance of town defences. A fragment remains on the east side just south of the 3m high remains of the Cappock Gate, and there is a longer section of wall backed by a 17th century artillery rampart on the west side, where there is also a large pentagonal bastion and there were two more gates. Other gates faced south towards the river and to the north.

The much altered (and rebuilt at the NE corner) four storey tower known as the Court House (at 962907) measures 17m by 9.5m and has two turrets on the west side facing the street, and latrines in the slightly projecting SE corner. The NW turret contains a spiral stair and a north-facing entrance protected by a box machicolation at wall-walk level, where there is now a hipped roof. The other turret now contains a scale-and-platt staircase. The building has a vaulted basement and is now entered through a two storey extension added between the turrets. Further down the main street (at 962905) is Hatch's Castle, a round-cornered building 10m by 7.4m with three upper levels over a vaulted basement. A SE stair turret projects east, as does the NE corner to contain a latrine at third storey level. The original entrance beside the stair is now blocked, and all the other openings and the parapets rising to 15m above ground are 19th century.

A third tower measuring 9m by 8m lies just outside the walled area (at 962907). This is a rather lower building, 9m high to the wall-walk partly carried internally on corbelling and still retaining the stump of the corbelled parapet. Over a vaulted basement are two upper rooms with latrines in the NW corner, fireplaces (one removed) in the east wall, and various windows now altered or blocked up. The stairwell at the SE corner projects into the upper rooms and has the east-facing entrance at its foot.

Court House, Ardee

Hatch's Castle, Ardee

ATHCLARE   O56862 D

This four storey 16th century tower measuring 10m by 8m stands complete to the base of the parapet. The spiral staircase has a crossloop with oillets high up and lies in the SE corner and there are latrines in the NW corner. At least one of the two fine upper fireplaces has been removed to the adjacent house.

BALLUG   J202060

The west side of this tower measuring 9.4m by 9m has mostly collapsed. The entrance with a drawbar slot and murder hole remains on the south side beside an east facing turret containing the spiral stair reached though a doorway with another drawbar slot. A ruined house adjoins the north wall, and the east wall has modern openings at the lowest two levels and modern external steps outside.

BALREGAN   J025103

This building measuring 11.5m by 8.5m appears to have contained just one upper storey, possibly subdivided into a west living room and an east bedroom, set over a vaulted basement which has two blocked double-splayed loops and a possible fireplace in the north wall. A murder hole protects the entrance in the south wall, from which a stair leads up into a rectangular SW corner turret. Square turrets at the SE and NW corners contain small rooms, although the latter also has evidence of a possible spiral stair, but its base is now inaccessible. This part has a third storey room and stands over 11m high. The NE corner and east wall are missing.

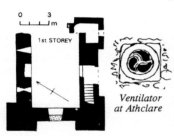

Balregan: plan

Ventilator at Athclare

Doorway at Athclare

Balregan Castle

CARLINGFORD   J188120   B

In c1185-1200 Henry de Lacy built a loopholed curtain wall 2.4m thick around an oval court 32m by 26m on a rock beside the sea. Only the lower part of one of the two rectangular towers 5m wide flanking the gateway passage on the west side now remains but a square tower to the SW with the upper corners chamfered off is better preserved. King John visited the castle in 1210 and had it repaired in 1211 and 1215. In the mid 13th century the eastern side of the court was filled with a plain but impressive hall-block 25m long by 15m wide over walls up to 2.8m thick. The lowest level is divided by a set of steps leading down to vaulted cellars of later date under the southern part and another cellar to the east. The upper parts of the south end were later built up as a chamber block but are now very ruined. Hugh O'Neill tried to take the castle by a surprise attack in 1596, and it was also attacked in 1642, 1649 and 1650.

Just west of the castle lay the north gate of the town. Neither this gate or the south gate remain, and there are only minor fragments of the western parts of the wall itself, but on the east (facing SE) is the Tholsel, a building 7.8m by 5m containing an upper room with a corner latrine, reached by external steps and set over a gateway passage flanked on the east side by a small room.

By the former quayside is Taaffe's Castle, a tower house of four storeys measuring 14m by 8.7m with a partly projecting thick end wall on the west containing small rooms and stairs, there being a stair in the NW corner up to the third storey and then another stair in the SW corner leads to the top. The upper levels have fireplaces in the north wall and latrines in the NE corner, but only on the third storey have the windows escaped being altered or blocked up. A slightly later two storey range 7.6m wide, also embattled, extends for 12m from the eastern part of the north wall. It has fireplaces at the north end.

The Mint, another urban tower house, lies in the main street supposedly on the site of the mint of 1467, although the present irregularly laid out building roughly 8.5m square over walls 1m thick without vaults is probably of c1600. It has a machicolation opening off the wall-walk over the entrance doorway but contains two-light windows with hoodmoulds facing towards the street at all three levels. The lowest windows have elaborately carved spandrels beside the ogival heads of the lights. The second storey has a latrine in one corner and seats in the window embrasures.

Carlingford Castle

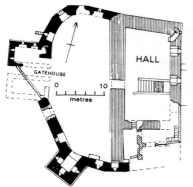

Plan of Carlingford Castle

Carlingford Castle

Tholsel: plan

Window at The Mint

Plan of Taaffe's Castle

Plan of The Mint

The Tholsel, Carlingford

The Mint at Carlingford

Taaffe's Castle, Carlingford

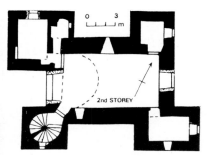

Plan of Castletown Castle

Clonmore: plan

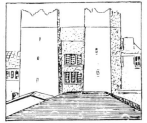

Castletown Castle

Barbican of St Laurence Gate, Drogheda

CARNTOWN   O092795

Adjoining a house is the Chivers' ruined tower measuring about 7m by 8.5m with a latrine turret at the NE corner and a stair turret at the SW corner. There are no vaults and the third storey has been cut down to take a gabled roof. The upper levels had fireplaces in the west wall. The second storey has a three-light east window and a two-light north window with round-arched lights. The third storey has a similar two-light east window.

CASTLETOWN   J032087   C

Now used as a convent school, this four storey tower was built c1472 by Richard Bellew possibly on the site of an earlier castle of the Verdons, part of which may have survived in the former bawn wall and outworks. The tower has a barrel vault over the second storey and has four rectangular corner turrets of different sizes and shapes. Three enclose angles whilst the NE turret only projects northwards. The entrance on the south side of the main block measuring 14m by 10.5m lies beside the spiral stair in the SW turret and is commanded by a murder hole. A row or corbels on the outside suggests that the parapet on this side was intended to be machicolated. The other three turrets contain small rooms, those on the NW having latrines beside them. At roof level the room in this turret has a fireplace and the turret top has a latrine for a sentry. The two uppermost main rooms have large fireplaces. Most of the windows have been modernised but the SE turret had until the 1940s one original window with a pair of cusped lights under a hoodmould which may have lighted a chapel here with a stair at the back to the chaplain's room above.

DARVER   O008987   C

Still inhabited, this rather altered four storey tower has a circular projection which contained latrines at the NE corner, and a north-facing stair turret at the NW corner, beside the west-facing entrance. The lowest storey is vaulted. The south windows, the battlements, the porch on the south side and the wing on the east are all modern.

DROGHEDA   O090748   C

South of the River Boyne is a motte rising 14m to a summit 23m across now enclosed by an early 19th century chemise breastwork around a Martello-type tower. Barracks lie within a bailey 65m by 46 to the west. Parts of the walls enclosing the barracks may be ancient on the south side since they formed part of the circuit of town walls of the part of the town south of the River Boyne. Fragments of the town wall around St Mary's churchyard in the SE corner show evidence of an outer wall 0.7m thick later increased to 1.6m thick by adding on buttresses with arcading to carry a wall-walk. On the west side the lower part of the Butter Gate, one of four gates. still remains, with a portcullis groove. North of the river lay a separate circuit of walls around a much larger area with up to a dozen towers and six gateways. Fragments remain in the SW corner and just south of the St Laurence Gate, an impressive structure 19m high standing isolated at a road junction. A barbican in front of a lost older gateway, it has a short passage with a portcullis groove flanked by two circular towers about 7m in diameter. The original late 13th century structure retaining several arrowloops in the towers was given a new upper storey in the 15th century. Vaults were used over the tower rooms in both periods. The southern tower contains stairs and a latrine. About 1.3km west of the southern walled town lay the Castle of Comfort (the Old Tholsel), a probable tower house depicted on a map of 1657.

DUNHAHON   J036020

A murder hole protects the north-facing doorway (with a drawbar slot) of this badly cracked late 15th century tower measuring 7.4m by 7m and rising through four storeys to a wall-walk 12m above ground. A square east-facing turret contains a spiral staircase beside the entrance and a north-facing turret at the NW corner contains latrines. The other corners have top turrets. The cellar has two double-splayed loops. The upper levels all have fireplaces in the east wall. Here in 1641 some 200 people were slaughtered during a surprise attack whilst they were attending mass. It belonged to Henry Townley in 1659.

Darver Castle

Dunmahon: plans & section

St Laurence Gate, Drogheda

Dunmahon Castle

GLASPISTOL   O158832 D

This 16th century tower measuring 9.8m by 8.6m has a vaulted cellar with three double-splayed loops piercing walls up to 2m thick. The north wall is still thicker and contains the entrance covered by a murder hole and flanked on one side by a guard-room and on the other by a wide spiral stair in an east facing turret 4m wide. The second storey has a fireplace on the north, windows with seats on the east and south, and a mural chamber and latrine in the west wall. This wall is reduced in thickness at the south end beyond the latrine of the third storey level, where an east facing window still remains complete with two arched heads. The very low fourth storey has one good window but was inaccessible from the staircase. Across its corners are squinch arches for top turrets now destroyed.

HEYNESTOWN   J043024 C

This small tower measuring 7.2m by 5.2m with four circular corner turrets has the arch of the basement vault continued through the outer walls making it look like a gatehouse with a blocked up passageway although there is no evidence that it served as anything other than a self-contained tower house. The basement is flanked on the south side by an unvaulted passage leading through from a doorway to a spiral stair with another doorway in the SE turret, which unlike the others only projects eastward. This turret and the two western ones are from 2.6m to 3m in diameter, but the NE tower measures just 2m across. This one contains a pit prison reached from a trapdoor above. The western turrets appear to have solid bases but contain rooms at the second and third levels, with latrines in the NW turret. The main second storey room has a fireplace in the north wall. On the east and west sides the turrets are linked by arches high up but there are no machicolations. The parapets do not survive.

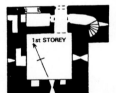  

Glaspistol: plans   *Mellifont: plan*   *Killincoole: plan*

Old print of Darver Castle   *Old print of Killincoole Castle*   *Milltown: plan*

Tower near Mellifont Abbey

Heynestown Castle

Plans of Roodstown Castle

Plans of Heynestown Castle

KILLINCOOLE   O001998

The second and third storeys of this four storey tower with a vaulted basement have fireplaces in the east wall. The tower measures 10m by 8m and has two D-shaped turrets, one containing the stair projecting north from the NE corner and the other projecting west at the SW corner to contain U-shaped rooms, those at the second and third storeys having latrines on their northern side. The entrance faces east beside the stair turret and has two murder holes over its passage. A squinch on the west side of the NE turret carries passages from the staircase to the main rooms.

MELLIFONT   O013781   A

This four storey tower is thought to have been built after the abbey was dissolved, perhaps by Sir Gerald Moore, who established his residence here in the 1560s. It is 7m wide and was probably 9.3m long, but the south end is now missing. The vaulted basement was later adapted as a gateway passage. Stairs in a SE turret projecting east led to three upper storeys with windows with seats facing north and latrines in a smaller NW turret projecting to the west. One window has a carved stone head beside it.

MILLTOWN   N951968   C

This 16th century tower measuring 7.5m by 6.6m has a round latrine turret clasping the SW corner. At the NE corner is an east-facing D-shaped turret now containing straight flights of stairs but probably originally fitted with a spiral stair, part of which still remains higher up. The other two corners have top turrets. The wall-walk is 13m above ground and the turrets rise up another 4m.

Roodstown Castle

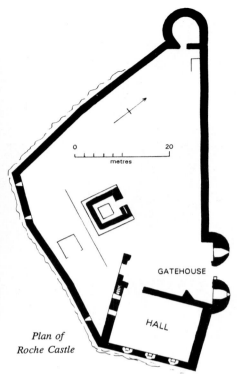

*Plan of
Roche Castle*

RICHARDSTOWN   O015905   D

On the south side of a mid 19th century house is a square tower with four round corner turrets rising one stage higher, both parts having 19th century battlements of rendered brick. The upper parts have generally been much rebuilt and all the windows in both the main tower and the corner turrets are 19th century.

ROCHE   H991118   A

Set on a rock is a kite-shaped court 60m long by 40m wide with a fairly complete and still embattled curtain wall 1.4m thick with holes for hoardings below the parapet. Towards the east end of the long NE front, facing the site of an outer ward beyond a rock-cut ditch, is a gateway set between two D-shaped towers, also with holes for hoarding beams below the parapet. There were apartments over the back of the gateway. Rising from a lower level beside the gateway on the south side is a block containing an upper floor hall 17.6m long by 12.8m wide reached from the court by steps through a later porch and having windows with seats in the embrasures in the south wall. The basement probably had subdividing arcades of timber to allow the flooring of such a wide span, and the hall itself may also have had timber arcades. Most of the castle is attributed to John de Verdon, who died in 1274, but the base of a building 9m square over walls 2m thick in the middle of the site could represent the castle recorded as erected by John's mother Rohesia before 1236, or may be the stump of a later tower house. West of it are loopholes in the curtain wall serving rooms at a lower level. Richard Bellew obtained a grant for the repair of the then ruined castle in 1464 and it may been in that period that the circular tower about 8m in diameter at the NE corner was abandoned and dismantled except for its low dome-vaulted basement, now hardly visible above the ground level outside.

Roche Castle

ROODSTOWN   N996925   B

This is a well preserved, although roofless, example of a small tower in the Pale with a vaulted cellar, a living room above with two-light windows with mullions and transoms, and two further storeys of private rooms. The NW and SE corners have projecting turrets containing the latrines and staircase respectively, with the entrance beside the foot of the stair, and the other corners have square top turrets.

SMARMORE   N945859

There are plain 18th century wings on the NE and SW sides of this tower, which was restored a few years ago. A series of remodellings have removed the basement vault, the stairwell in the turret at the west corner and the latrines in the turret at the east corner, whilst new windows and battlements have been provided. The entrance faced NW and lay beside the west turret.

SHORTSTONE   H989111

Footings of a wall up to 1.5m thick enclose a bawn 58m by 40m with traces of four circular corner flankers 8m in diameter and an entrance on the west side.

Richardstown Castle

Window at Roodstown

STEPHENSTOWN   J002023

There are three double-splayed loops in the vaulted cellar of this tower, which has an east-facing entrance beside a stair-turret at the NE corner. A turret at the SW corner contains latrines and there were two other turrets at the top. The second storey is now reached by an external staircase and has a fireplace in the east wall. The third storey room has remains of seats in the window embrasures.

TERMONFECKIN   O143803   B

Part of the small bawn to the west was later closed in to make a porch in front of two doorways on the NW side of this tower, which measures 6.8m by 5.8m. One leads to a stair to the second storey and then onto a spiral stair in the north corner. the other leads into a vaulted basement, beyond which is a second chamber added slightly later between two projections at either end of the SE wall. The second storey also has an extra room at this level, then the tower reverts to the dimensions already given. The upper storeys have fireplaces in the SE wall and rooms with latrines in the projection at the south corner.

The tower and bawn of the archbishops of Armagh at Termonfeckin has vanished. It lay at 139803 west of the bridge on the south side of the river. Old drawings suggest the main tower had two turrets and a later wing, and that the bawn had round corner turret.

THOMASTOWN or KNOCKABBEY   N932989

A much altered three storey tower with new battlements forms the NE corner of the mansion known as Knockabbey. The lowest storey retains its vault, one north loop and the blocked south-facing entrance set beside an east-facing square SE turret containing the staircase. The NW turret may have contained latrines.

Termonfeckin Castle   *Clonmore Castle*

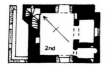

Termonfeckin: plans

Dungooly: old print

Milltown Castle

OTHER CASTLES IN COUNTY LOUTH

BALLYMASCANLAN J080191 Featureless defaced east and south walls up to 15m long, 2m thick and 2m high of medieval building of uncertain type.

BARMEATH O096876 House of 1820s incorporates part of old tower at NE corner.

CARSTOWN O110802 Two armoral plaques dated 1612 in core of house.

CLONMORE O113890 Three storey stair turret is only remaining part of tower house.

FAUGHART UPPER J057126 8m high mound with footings of 1.5m thick wall around court 13m across on summit. Damaged by quarrying on the south side.

GLIDEMOUTH or Dillonstown O097917 Part of a tower with a stairwell in the SE corner adjoins a house extending to the south.

LOUTH HALL N951968 The west end of the hall incorporates the lower part of a tower 14m by 13m with evidence of an entrance near the west end of the north wall.

MULATEE J214098 Sections of featureless walling only.

CASTLE SITES IN COUNTY LOUTH

CASTLETOWNCOONEY J176077 No remains of castle built c1543 by James Dowdall destroyed in 19th century.

DOWDSTOWN N978940 Lawrence Clinton's castle of c1570 demolished c1890-1900.

DUNDALK There were urban tower houses here at J047077, 048077, 048077, 048077, 048077, 056074, 047048, 048072 and nine other unknown locations. Lord Limerick had them all removed for redevelopment in the mid 18th century.

DUNGOOLY J002142 Site of O'Neill castle shown on sketch of 1758 with two corner turrets on the tower and with an arched entrance to a bawn.

EDMONDSTOWN N904961 Stones at farm dated 1574 with arms of de Verduns and Plunketts probably from a vanished tower on a nearby rock outcrop.

NISELRATH N946023 Site of castle described in 1599 as "a square castle and a great bawne with a good dytche rounde abowte it".

OTHER CASTLE SITES: Castle Bellingham O057950, Castle Moyle O0499001, Cookstown N932944, Dromiskin O054981, Haggardstown J062033, Paughanstown O003881, Stabannan O021920.

Taylor and Skinner's map of 1777 indicates former castles at Castle Curragh, Corbollis, Mullacurry, Mullanstown, Newrath, Salterstown and Tullydonnell.

MOTTES (* bailey also): Aclint* N894979, Artoney H955011, Ash Big H977054, Barronstown H978095, Castle Guard N971905, Castlering* H964040, Crowmartin* N880951, Derrycammagh N993947, Dromin O029894, Dun Dealgan* N029083, Dunleer O582877, Greenmount* O062932, Heynestown* J053021, Killanny* H893010, Louth Hall* N953979, Mayne O142849, Piperstown O077825, Priesttown* O061842, Stormanstown* N915937 There are 7 other possible motte sites.

Destroyed motte and bailey sites: Lurgankeel (excavated), Mountbagnall, Raskeagh

CASTLES OF COUNTY MEATH

ATHCARNE   O031647   C

At the east end of a ruined house of the 1830s lies a tower built in 1590 by William Bathe, a judge of the Court of Common pleas. A stone with his arms and those of his second wife Janet Dowdall has been transferred from the tower to the later house. Above a battered base surrounding the vaulted basement the tower measures 9m by 7.5m and has three upper storeys, most of the windows of which have been altered. A NW turret contains the entrance and spiral staircase, a slight projection at the NE corner contained latrines, and a wing at the SE corner measuring 6.2m by 5.6m above its own vaulted basement contained upper levels of private rooms. Parts of the parapets also still remain.

ATHLUMNEY   N876674   A

The 30m long mansion of c1600 with three levels of mullion-and-transom windows has a small wing projecting at one end where there was a kitchen with two fireplaces and an oven. Projecting from the diagonally opposite corner is the Dowdalls' 15th century tower with four corner turrets of different sizes and of different degrees of projection from a four storey main block measuring 10.6m by 7.2m. Two turrets contain small rooms, the third contains closets, probably latrines, and the fourth has a spiral stair with a doorway at the bottom with a drawbar slot. The cellar of the tower was reached separately through the base the corner turret now joining it to the later house. In 1649 the Maguires allegedly set the castle alight rather than let Cromwell occupy it.

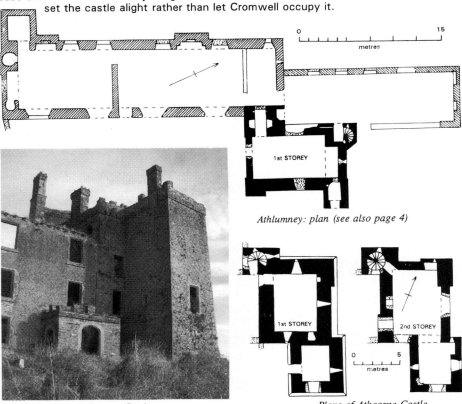

0 _____ 15
metres

1st STOREY

Athlumney: plan (see also page 4)

1st STOREY

2nd STOREY

0 _____ 5
metres

Athcarne Castle

Plans of Athcarne Castle

Athlumney Castle

BALLYGARTH   O145706

Originally a Barnewall seat, Ballygarth passed in the 1660s to the Peppers, who held it until 1979. The three storey tower lies on the west with an early 19th century porch tower between it and a range of 1791. The whole was given new battlements in 1861. The old tower has two square corner turrets both containing spiral stairs, one with 18th century shell patterns under the steps.

BECTIVE   N860600   A

The Cistercian abbey was provided with two towers during a 15th century remodelling which made it somewhat of a fortress. One of four storeys in the cloister SW corner has turrets on the southern corners. The other tower has two east facing turrets. After the abbey was dissolved in 1536 the buildings were leased to Thomas Agarde, but were sold to Andrew Wyse in 1552. It later passed to the Dillons and then the Boltons. See p20.

CARRICKDEXTER   N943730

Near the River Boyne far from any road is a four storey 15th century tower measuring 9m by 6.6m and an adjoining 17th century house with an oven and fireplace at ground level and two upper storeys with large windows. The tower belonged to the Dexters and has a vaulted basement and turrets 2.8m square boldly clasping two diagonally opposite corners to contain the staircase and latrines.

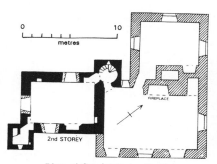

Plan of Carrickdexter Castle

Carrickdexter Castle

Clongill Castle

Flanker at Castle Jordan

CASTLE JORDAN   N590388   C

A length of a bawn wall runs SW from a flanker of spear-head shape with circular turrets on the corners nearest where the bawn walls adjoined it. The lowest of three unvaulted storeys has several gunloops. Further SW is part of the NE wall of a second tower with a very lofty north-facing stair turret now lacking any steps. To the west (at 588387) is a motte and bailey castle with signs of buried thick walls in the bailey.

CAUSESTOWN   N677624

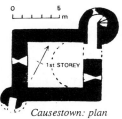

Of a tower 9.8m by 8m with a circular staircase turret at the NW corner and a smaller round latrine turret at the SE corner there remains the vaulted basement with two double-splayed loops and part of the south end of the second storey, whilst the latrine turret stands to the third storey level.

Causestown: plan

CLONGILL   N824760   C

A later two storey range 7.6m wide and now lacking its north wall extends for 17m from a tower house at the east end to a west wall with a projecting breast for a kitchen fireplace. The tower measures 9.8m by 7.6m and has two upper storeys over a vaulted basement. There are fireplace in the west wall, latrines in a square turret projecting northwards at the NE corner and slight remains of a circular stair turret at the SW corner.

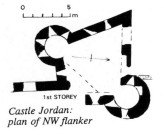

Castle Jordan:
plan of NW flanker

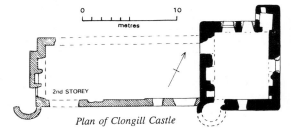

Plan of Clongill Castle

DARDISTOWN   N115696

This still-inhabited four storey tower has a vaulted basement and square turrets at all four corners. On the SW side is a range added c1550 which was heightened and extended in 1589 by Dame Janet Sarsfield, Lady Dunsany, as recorded on a plaque over the fine doorway. This range was remodelled in the mid 18th century by the Osbornes, owners since c1600, and then given a cross-range at the far end. John Walsh's original tower of 1465 has two original windows with cusped lights and hoodmoulds on the east side, one being tall enough for a transom.

DONORE   N703498   B

This tower measuring 8.2 by 6.6m tower has round corners, double-splayed basement loops, a round stair turret next to the entrance, and vaults over the first and third of four storeys. James, son of Niall McGeoghegan and over 40 members of his clan, including women and children, were executed after the castle was captured in 1650 by Commissary-General John Reynolds.

DUNBOYNE   O012421   A

In 1475 Edmond Butler was given a grant to build the tower now lying covered in ivy in the churchyard. It measures 8.1m by 6.6m and has a spiral stair in the SE corner and a blocked entrance facing south. The north wall has been destroyed above the vault over the lowest level. The second storey has a fireplace on the south side. See page 19.

Plan of Dunmoe Castle

Donore: plan

Donore Castle

Donore Castle

Castle Jordan

Plan of Fennor Castle

Dunmoe Castle

Plan of Killeen Castle

DUNMOE   N901702   A

Above a steep slope to the Boyne stands the D'Arcys 15th century hall-house measuring 18.5m by 9m. There were 4.6m diameter turrets containing square chambers at one end and 3.6m diameter turrets with solid bases at the other. One turret of each size and the landward facing wall between them has been destroyed. There is a keyhole-shaped gunloop opening off a stair in the SW turret. The main block contained a hall perhaps with a chamber divided off at the east end over vaulted loft over the basement. Cromwell is said to have bombarded the castle in 1649. The thinly walled two storey extension at one end and an old print are evidence that the building remained habitable until c1800.

DUNSANY   N915548

Hugh de Lacy is said to have founded a castle here in the 1190s but the oldest parts of the present building are probably the work of Christopher Plunkett, who was created Lord Dunsany in 1461. It seems to have formed two chamber towers at either end of a hall block now represented by a three storey range but possibly originally of wood, i.e a layout like that at Liscartan. A succession of rebuildings and extensions beginning with a campaign in the 1780s for Randall, 13th Lord Dunsany has removed all the medieval features. Further work was done for the 14th Lord after his second marriage in 1823,

FENNOR   965732   C

The wing with a battered base projecting north towards the River Boyne formed part of a medieval tower. The 16m long main block is 17th century although the difference in widths between the two ends again indicates the survival of medieval work in the stump remaining of the western part of the north wall. The east end contained a kitchen with a large fireplace an oven in a projecting breast. The upper storeys each have five regularly spaced windows facing south, clearly of late 17th or 18th century date.

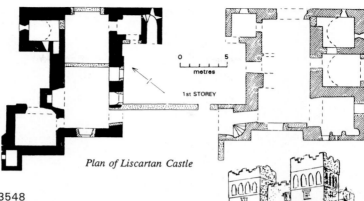

Plan of Liscartan Castle

KILLEEN N933548

There is said to have been a castle here in the 1180s, either the work of Hugh de Lacy or his tenants the Cusacks. The existing four storey tower with square corner turrets of differing sizes rising one storey higher was built some time after 1403 when the heiress Joan Cusack married Sir Christopher Plunkett, Sheriff of Meath and Deputy Lord Lieutenant of Ireland, their third son Thomas being the builder c1450 of the very similar castle of Dunsoghly in County Dublin. A wing was later added on the south side. Lucas, 10th Lord Killeen was created Earl of Fingall in 1628 by Charles I. The 18th century earls let the building to tenants but the 8th Earl had it repaired after reoccupying it in 1779, and major new works were carried out in the 1800s and 1840s resulting in the new battlements, windows and oriels on the old tower and extensions to the east, south and west which have caused the removal of the SW corner turret. The mansion survived the troubles of the 1920s, only to be burnt out by the IRA in 1981.

Dunsany Castle

Liscartan Castle

LISCARTAN N840695 D

This ivy-mantled castle is assumed to be the work of the Nangles, descendants of a Welsh knight named Jocelin de Angulo. The oldest part is a three storey block 14m by 7.8m probably of the early 16th century with rectangular turrets projecting from the NW, NE and SE corners, the wide staircase being in the last of these, which is the smallest. The NW turret measuring 6m by 5.2m and containing private chambers with latrines in a small NW corner turret of its own was perhaps a later addition, since its rooms are not vaulted like those in the NE turret. Both turrets have their own upper staircases. The main block contained a hall over a vaulted basement with a kitchen fireplace on the north side.

Just 13m further south lies another block 13m by 8m probably of the early 17th century. It was rather altered in the 18th century and now only stands two storeys high. It has turrets or wings at all four corners, those on the south side being the largest, whilst the NW turret contained a wide spiral staircase. In 1641 Liscarton belonged jointly to Sir Robert Talbot of Carrtown and Adam Minott of Bellewstown, and the second block must have been built to accommodate the second of these families. About a 100m to the SE lies a detached gatehouse with one upper room over a passage with a murder-hole. In the 1650s the manor passed to the Cadogans, who held it until the 19th century.

Monktown Castle

Newcastle Castle

MONKTOWN   N954636   C

Only the northern part of the four storey tower 7.8m wide now remains with an east facing turret at the NE corner which is roofed with a vault of overlapping slabs. The stair lay either in the thick west wall or in a turret at the SW corner with the entrance adjoining it. The basement has part of a vault and the next two levels have large north windows.

MOYMET   N778603   C

There are double-splayed loops in what was once a vaulted cellar in this tower with a NE corner turret. The three upper storeys all have fireplaces in what remains of the north wall, and there is a latrine on the second storey. About 15m to the west is a vaulted chamber of a 17th century range which originally had an oven and fireplace in the now destroyed west end wall. Some distance to the north is a gatehouse with stairs entered from outside leading to an upper room over a passageway flanked by a vaulted guard room.

Monktown: turret roof

MOYRATH   N725573

Lord Geoffrey de Montemarisio is said to have had a castle here c1220, but the existing three storey tower with round corners was probably built by the Nugents in the 15th or 16th centuries. In the 19th century it was occupied by the Pottertons as tenants of the Grattons. It has been much altered and has 19th century windows and battlements, whilst a 20th century house adjoins it.

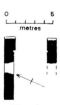

Moyglare

Newhaggard Castle

Moymet Castle

NEWCASTLE N773399

Within a farmyard lies a square tower with a vaulted basement, an upper floor containing the entrance, and a third storey on top, both upper levels having fireplaces and latrines. The unusual location of a round stair turret in the middle of the east side makes a late 16th or early 17th century date likely, although the windows were altered later. Fragments of a bawn wall adjoin the east and south walls.

NEWHAGGARD N782564

East of the 18th century house and mill lies a four storey tower measuring about 9m by 8m. On the north side, towards the river, the upper walls are projected out on a row of five four-centred arches carried on bold corbelling. The south side has a blocked arch high up and a portcullis groove, indicating that the building once served as a gatehouse of a bawn but that the vaulted passage later became a cellar with a low loft above it. The two upper storeys have latrines in a west-facing projection at the NW corner.

NEWSTONE N620704

Only the lofty barrel-vaulted basement remains of the main tower, but a west turret stands one stage higher with a latrine with loops piercing two of the corners. To the south are fragments of walls 1.3m thick with a fireplace and latrine chute of a later wing, probably early 17th century.

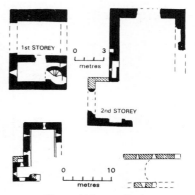

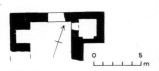
Monkstown: plan

Newhaggard: plan

Plans of Moymet Castle

ODDER   N912584

This three storey house was probably built by the Barnewells in the early 17th century. It has a corbelled chimney-breast on the east side and blocked original windows, whilst a large central stairhall was created during a remodelling of the 1880s.

RATHALDRON   N845693

The core of the embattled country house on the east bank of the Blackwater is a four storey tower built probably in the 15th century by the Cusacks, lords of Gerardstown. It has a staircase turret at the SE corner and the square NE turret probably contained latrines. A long wing added later was remodelled c1800 and further additions and alterations were made in the 1840s for the O'Reillys.

RATHKENNY   N893786

Only the east half, with a basement half full of debris from a vault, remains of the 7m wide tower of the Husseys, Barons Galtrim, one of whom married the Petit heiress in the 15th century. A later wing extending 13.4m to the south is 9.6m wide above the wide battered base of the east wall. The south end wall contains a huge kitchen fireplace, but little remains of the west wall. There was just one upper storey probably containing one room.

RATHMORE   N747668   D

Half the length of one wall of this four storey tower measuring 10.4m by 9.4m is thickened externally to contain the entrance and a spiral staircase. The cellars and the vaulted lofts above are divided by a crosswall. Above are two undivided rooms, the lower one having a latrine in the opposite wall. The tower may have been built by the de Verdons in the 14th century or by the Plunketts in the 15th century.

Riverstown Castle   *Doorway at Summerhill*

RIVERSTOWN   N874592

In a farmyard lies a tower with its entrance (protected by a murder-hole) facing a long later range with a vaulted basement to the west, both parts now being shrouded in ivy. Of five storeys with the second one vaulted, the tower is about 7m square and has two square turrets on the south side and a circular stair turret on the NE corner, in which is one stirrup-shaped loop high up. The main block upper levels have fireplaces on the west and large windows. Originally a Dillon seat, this is the alleged birthplace in 1717 of the antiquarian and classical scholar Robert Wood.

ROBERTSTOWN   N874592   B

Square bartizans at the SW and NE corners of this low three storey house has moulded corbelling of the type more common in Scotland. All the levels were subdivided, with vaults over the lowest. A wider eastern extension gives the building a length of 22.5m.

SLANE   N962751   A

A tower measuring 13.5m by 7m with NW and SW corner stair turrets forms the east end of the south range of the early 16th century college buildings north of the hill-top church.

SUMMERHILL   N844481   D

Named Lynch's Castle after the family of that name who built it in the late 16th century, this is a four storey tower measuring 10m by 8m with the second storey vaulted. The spiral stair in the NW corner has a newel and gunloops, and there is a tier of chambers over the west-facing entrance. The upper levels have fireplaces in the south wall and latrines on the north. There are fine upper windows with dished spandrels and hoodmoulds and an angle-loop high up in the SE corner. Another angle-loop facing SW was lost when this corner was broken out to give access to later range bearing a plaque with the O'Neill arms commemorating the priest Luke Wye with the date 1636. Containing mullioned windows, it was probably T-planned but nothing remains of the main block south of where a wing projected out west to contain a wooden scale-and-platt staircase. The old tower was re-occupied c1660 by Bishop Jones but the later wing was then left roofless.

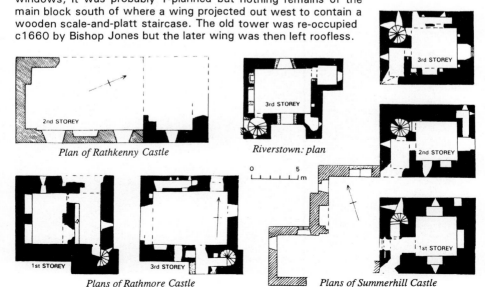

Plan of Rathkenny Castle

Riverstown: plan

Plans of Rathmore Castle

Plans of Summerhill Castle

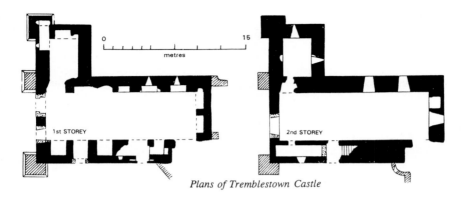

Plans of Tremblestown Castle

TREMBLESTOWN   N760575   C

This spectacular ruin above the Tremblestown river has a main block about 19m long by 8m wide containing a basement with many recesses and a loft (reached by a stair on the SE side) under a vault. Above were two upper storeys of large chambers with private rooms in a large NW corner tower rising one storey higher and bearing a shield with the Barnewall and Nugent arms. The south end of the main block has tall buttresses, at least two of which appear to be added. A SE tower was mostly destroyed to make room for a new wing c1800 but there are traces of a stair and a circular bartizan remains at the top. The castle was probably built by Sir Robert Barnewall after Edward IV created him Baron Tremblestown in 1461. The 8th lord was banished to Galway by Cromwell and the 13th Lord only recovered his title when he became a Protestant in 1795. The newer parts were added for the 14th Lord after his second marriage in 1797. It fell into ruin in the 1890s.

Tremblestown Castle

TRIM N802567 E

On the south bank of the Boyne lies the finest medieval castle in Ireland, the centre of the lordship of Meath granted by Henry II to Hugh de Lacy in 1172. Modern analysis of the unique cruciform shaped keep suggests that it was begun shortly after the original ringwork was destroyed in 1173 by Rory O'Connor. Measuring 19m square over walls 3.6m thick above a battered plinth added on later, it has wings 7m wide with walls 1.5m thick projecting 6m from the centre of each face, although the northern wing has been destroyed. Originally only one storey high, with a wall-walk high above the roof, it was heightened after Hugh's son Walter succeeded him in the 1190s and work upon it probably continued until c1215. It now has four storeys, all except the topmost subdivided by a crosswall, and there are square turrets on the corners of the main block. At second storey level the keep was entered by a doorway with a drawbar slot in the east wing north wall. Another doorway with a drawbar slot admitted to an entrance hall in the east part of the main block, from which there was access to rooms with fireplaces on two levels of the north and south wings and onto the main stair in the NE corner. A more private hall with a central fireplace lies in the western part. It has access to a spiral stair in the SW corner leading to a suite of two rooms on the third storey and then to a large single chamber on the fourth storey. At this level there was a timber gallery over the entrance. The keep was surrounded by the surviving ditch of the original ringwork and in the 13th century its entrance was strengthened by the erection of a small court in front of it with round towers 6m in diameter at the NW and SE corners. This court contained on its east side a waiting room 12m long for those seeking an audience with the lord.

NW tower, Trim

West gate, Trim

Gateway passage at Trim

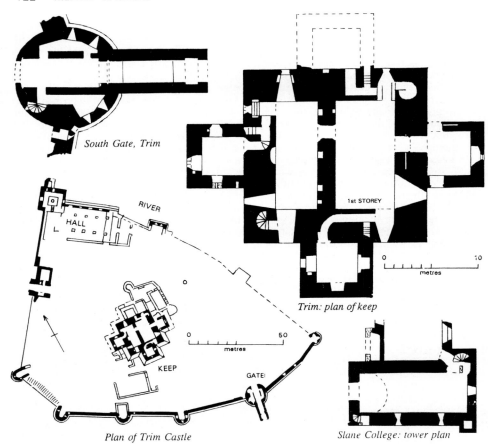

South Gate, Trim

1st STOREY

Trim: plan of keep

RIVER

HALL

KEEP

GATE

Plan of Trim Castle

Slane College: tower plan

The keep lies within a wedge-shaped bailey 150m by 100m which was enclosed by early 13th century walls 2m thick built against a rock platform with a wide rock-cut ditch in front. Footings remain of two rectangular towers about 9m by 7m facing the river, where the wall has vanished, whilst the more vulnerable south side, which remains more complete, has a series of four D-shaped towers up to 7m wide originally open-backed. A fifth tower at the east corner measures 5.6m in external diameter over walls 1.5m thick. This tower lies beyond the south gate, which is a circular tower 9.2m in diameter with narrow rooms flanking a passageway through its base. It has a rectangular barbican extending 9m in front to an outer archway surmounted by two chambers, the uppermost of which has corner loops, and beyond which was a drawbridge. The passage through the main tower itself was closed by a portcullis at either end. The flanking rooms have tall plunging arrowloops towards the field and one has access to a spiral staircase. There are further loops from the hexagonal room above, and this room and the ruined third storey had large windows with seats towards the court. On the NW side is an earlier gateway of the 1180s or 90s without portcullis grooves. It had a rectangular main body with a round outer arch and the upper corners chamfered off towards the field as in two of the towers at the de Lacy main seat at Ludlow in Shropshire. Another block adjoins on the NE to contain guard rooms.

South gateway at Trim

Keep at Trim

The 13m square tower at the NW corner contained private chambers opening off the dais end of an aisled great hall 18m wide and over 30m long of which only foundations now remain except for the fragmentary north side with traces of blocked two-light windows of later date. There were service rooms at the SE end, where there is a passage down to postern towards the river. Excavations have revealed the foundations of another domestic building south of the keep, and the flanking tower on the curtain wall nearby was later extended inwards towards this building to provide a tier of private chambers.

In the mid-13th century Trim passed to Geoffrey de Genneville, who married Walter de Lacy's great-grand-daughter Matilda. Their grand-daughter Joan brought Trim to Roger Mortimer, created Earl of March by Edward III in 1328. Richard II visited Trim in 1399 and left behind the future Henry V lodged in the south gatehouse with Humphrey of Gloucester. By this time the castle was little used, although the Mortimers' successor from 1427, Richard, Duke of York had it repaired when he was serving as Lord Lieutenant of Ireland. Silken Thomas captured the castle during his rebellion of 1534, and an artillery emplacement on the west side of the bailey may be a relic of Sir Charles Coote's siege and capture of Trim in 1647 or of another siege during Cromwell's campaigns in Ireland.

The castle formed the SE corner of a 13th century walled town extending across the river, the northern part eventually having two widely spaced lines of walls on the north and east sides. A long section of the outer east wall still remains, together with the Sheep Gate, which has a spiral staircase up to a room over a vaulted passage flanked by a guard-room on the south side. Nangle's Castle, an urban tower house, is no more than a shapeless wreck with a corrugated iron roof. It has a squinch arch between the main block and a destroyed corner turret and evidence of NE corner latrines. Nearby is a three storey tower and long building to the east which was probably the refectory of the Augustinian abbey, although long known as Talbot's Castle after an early 15th century Lord Lieutenant, Sir John Talbot, whose arms appear on the north wall of the tower. Still privately occupied, the building has 18th century windows and was remodelled c1909.

OTHER CASTLES IN COUNTY MEATH

ATHBOY N716640 Section of town wall with ditch and base of tower to SW of church. Murage for upkeep of the walls was granted in 1408, the 1420s and 1494.

ANNAGH N511738 Footings of building 20m by 7m with bawn 40m by 28m to west.

ARDAGH N831950 Just one wall 8m long and 1.2m thick remains.

ARODSTOWN N882500 Two levels of tower under vault, both with access to turret at south corner. Double-splayed loops facing NE.

BALLINLOUGH N541719 Basement of tower 10.7m by 7m with evidence of vault.

BALLYMACAD N508788 Quarried away except for featureless fragments of walls.

BALLYNADRIMNA N725590 Two storeys of round-cornered east wall with vault traces.

CASTLETOWN N773511 Two walls built against a rock outcrop. A rather doubtful site.

CASTLETOWN TARA N910611 Lowest storey only of building about 15m by 8m with mullioned windows and NW corner turret with two crossloops.

CLOGHREAGH N839922 East corner of tower or stronghouse stands 5m high.

DANGAN N820511 Thick walls with base batter survive in east wing of ruined 18th century mansion.

DERRYPATRICK N884512 Footings of tower 8.5m by 6m within bank and bitch of bawn.

DONACARNEY O136748 Fragment of north wall with part of fireplace and window above vault.

DOWTH O262738 Three storey tower with NE stair turret. Provided with new windows.

DRUMSAWRY N570784 Pile of stones with remains of north and south walls of tower 10m by 6m.

DURHAMSTOWN N808683 Stronghouse with upper storey and attic over four vaulted cellars. Stair turret at SE corner. Modified in 19th century when north wing added.

FRAINE N705616 Vaulted lowest storey of tower 7.4m by 6.3m with latrine chutes at SW corner. Footings of hall block 22m by 9.5m lie 5m to east.

GARADICE N860449 Thin east wall of three storey tower, and part of circular NE stair turret. Probably of late date. Evidence of later rebuilding with brickwork.

GRAVELSTOWN N784801 Featureless fragment of east wall of tower.

KELLS N741759 One three storey round tower to SE of site of the west-facing Cannon Gate is all that remains of the town walls.

KILBREW O012575 One end gable of ruined 18th century house includes older work.

KILBRIDE N772615 Stronghouse with three vaulted cellars and stair in NW corner turret to modified upper storey. Probably internal stair of wood to third storey.

KILMAINHAM N763753 Two corners three storeys high of tower 9m by 8.2m.

KILSKEER N662717 Just the NW corner three storeys high of tower 30m SW of church.

MACETOWN N998595 Part of corner turret amongst a pile of debris.

MILLTOWN N559751 Just a vaulted basement now with a trackway through it.

MOAT N544751 One wall with evidence of roofline lying on 15m diameter summit of 6m high motte.

MOYGADDY N945391 5m square three storey tower with second storey vaulted and spiral stair. No latrines or fireplaces. Probably a stonghouse or bawn corner flanker.

MOYGLARE N928399 North wall two storeys high with upper fireplace and SE corner of tower 6.6m by 5.6m.

MULHUSSEY N415436 Foundations only of tower 13m by 9.4m with base batter.

MULPHEDDAR N656449 Excavation evidence of palisade of c1275-1325 at ringwork.

NAVAN N870677 15m long section of thin wall with one bastion remain at NW corner of 15th and 16th century town defences.

NEWCASTLE N704882 Featureless west wall and circular NW flanker of bawn.

NEWTOWN N620704 Excavation revealed part of possible later tower close to the bailey measuring 35m by 30m of a motte rising up to 7m to a summit 15m across.

NEWTOWN TRIM N814568 Tower on west side of cloister of abbey retains stairs but has lost its basement vault. The third storey has a fireplace in the south wall.

ROSS N467831 The NW half of the four storey embattled building is original.

ST JOHNS N817568 Three storey tower 8m by 7.6m with fireplaces and machicolation on the west side, stair turret on NE and latrine turret on SW. Part of hospital priory.

SALESTOWN N973399 Vaulted basement only remains. Fireplace and other recesses.

SKREEN N953602 Thick lower walls and a mural staircase higher up remain of a tower incorporated in an 18th century house.

TIRCROGHAN N636432 Earthworks of bastioned fort with arrow-head shaped corner bastions. Captured by Hewson & Reynolds in 1650.

TUBBRID N497787 Footings of wall 7m long.

WALTERSTOWN N744837 Footings of building about 16m by 10m.

Moygaddy: plan

CASTLE SITES IN COUNTY MEATH

ARDNALLAN N624447 Last remaining corner of tower demolished 1985.

ASSEY N871611 Tower with round turrets at diagonally opposite corners destroyed in 1940s.

BALREASK N874592 Low banks define platform 22m by 14m beside road.

BRANNOCKSTOWN N758520 Rampart and ditch on hill-top now removed.

CARRANSTOWN N676557 Pile of stones only

CASTLETOWN N704630 Foundations of corner hardly visible under soil.

CROSSDRUM N532797 Footings of tower 6m square and building 10m long beside it within oval area 40m by 26m were removed in the 1970s.

GRANGEGEETH N960802 Square tower with four corner turrets shown on old map.

PLATIN O063720 House of c1700 now demolished probably lay on site of castle.

PROUDSFOOT O035750 Last remains of base of round corner turret now removed.

SCURLOCKSTOWN N834562 Site of square tower with two circular corner turrets.

SIDDAN N893851 Mound on site, but shown as ruin on map of 1783.

TRUBLEY N850590 Remains of square tower with circular corner turrets removed after collapse c1970.

VESINGSTOWN N983452 Fallen piece of masonry and other slight traces on site.

OTHER CASTLE SITES: Ardmaghbreague N762872, Drakerath N811808, Fyanstown N789756, Greencastle N559738, Killary N886818, Killengland O060523, Mornington O127745, Polecastle N897856, Staffordstown N943650, Strokestown N873844

Garadice

MOTTES IN COUNTY MEATH (* with baileys)

Agher N832455, Ardmulchan N908703, Athlumney N908703, Balgree B654783, Ballyhist* N644782, Ballymacad N507788, Castlecor* N524813, Castlerickard N717489, Castletown* N441823, Castletown Kilberry N876729, Clonard N657451, Clonbarton N884918, Clonymeath N859508, Coolronan* N679570, Cruicetown* N796846, Derver* N670780, Diamor* 609739, Drumbride N873940, Drumcondra* N887902 & 886894, Galtrim N861521, Gibstown* N819729, Ginnets N840530, Girley N708691, Glenboy* N532809, Kilbeg* N776817, Killadden* N863899, Lisdornin O126681, Loughbrackan N871882, Loughcrew N663763, Milltown N544751, Milltown N745721, Moat N760847, Moat* N511789, Moat* N707791, Moat* N784511, Moathill* N860676, Moat Town N751568, Moynalty N735825, Moyrath* N705586, Newtown* N620704, Nobber* 822867, Oldcastle N551792, Patrickstown N606775, Rathbeggan O000469, Rathfeigh O003613, Ratoath* O021519, Robertstown N784843, Skreen N960751, Slanecastle N960751. One motte has been destroyed.

Moyglare Castle

CASTLES OF COUNTY OFFALY

AGHNANANAGH   N280280

A collapsed vault fills the interior of the base of an O'Molloy tower 14.4m by 9.3m over walls 1.2m thick, but part of the south wall stands higher. A group of later outbuildings lies nearby. A datestone of 1641 now lies in the public house in the village of Blue Ball.

BALLINLOUGH   S014800

This late 16th century O'Carroll castle consists of a tower measuring 8.3m by 7.5m standing in a bawn about 27m across still enclosed on the SW and SE sides by a loopholed wall 1m thick rising 2.5m above the inner edge of a dry ditch. The tower has circular bartizans on the SW and NE corners containing tiny rooms at fourth storey level. Straight stairs rise up from the entrance in the east wall to a spiral stair in the NW corner. The second storeys has a latrines in the SW corner and the third storey has a fireplace on the east side. There are no vaults.

BALLYBRIT   S146955

An O'Carroll castle here was sacked in 1432 but the tower just 6.4m by 5.3m over walls 1.1m thick must be of later date, since the doorway facing SW has punch-dressed jambs and the three storeys are without vaults. There are later outbuildings adjoining the NE and SW sides and amongst them is part of a circular flanker 4.2m across of a former bawn.

BALLYBRITTAN   N568333

A two storey inhabited house, 18th century with older parts (including a carved head over the doorway), adjoins a ruined tower measuring 12.6m by 8.7m. A straight stair in the east end wall leads up from the entrance doorway. The single upper room over a vaulted basement has a fireplace, several windows and its own upper doorway. The tower retains a wall-walk without a parapet.

Ballinlough Castle

Plans of Ballycowan Castle

Ballycowan Castle

Ballinlough: bartizan

Ballybrittain: plans

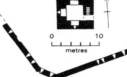

Ballinlough: plans

BALLYCOWAN N294252 C

Thomas Morres built the main block of this stronghouse 18m long by 10.8m wide over walls 1.6m thick above a battered base c1589. It was granted to Sir Jasper Herbert in 1623 and he added the wing near the south end of the east side which has an entrance doorway protected by a machicolation and surmounted by a panel dated 1626 with the Herbert arms. This wing contained a wide scale-and-platt staircase rising up to the second storey and then three upper levels of bedrooms, with the topmost in the roof. Each of these rooms has a two-light mullion-and-transom window facing east and a fireplace in the north wall, where there are three tall chimney stacks. The cross-walls dividing up the main block lowest level into a central lobby with three cellars and a NW kitchen with a fireplace may also date from the 1620s, since one wall partly blocks one of the loops. A service stair in the south end wall is now blocked and the whole of the SW corner is missing. Above the second storey main hall with a fireplace on the west side the main block contained two upper levels of rooms with mullioned windows, the upper level being within the roof. There were wall-walks and parapets on the east and west walls and there is a square bartizan upon the NE corner. Both main block and wing contain a number of gunloops. A bawn lay to the east and had the wall-walk continued along an outbuilding of some sort on the south side.

BALLYHEASHILL N573357

The south and west walls stand high of a tower without vaults probably dating from after 1550, when "an old ruynouse castell" is noted here. The only features are two loops in the south wall, various niches, and a straight staircase in the west wall.

BALLYKILMURRY N299272 & 298277

Originally an O'Molloy castle, it had passed to Sir Jasper Herbert of Ballycowen by 1641. A vault covered the second storey of a tower with a mural chamber at one end of the lowest storey. Other buildings adjoin the north and west sides, that to the west having a barrel-vault. The remains are choked with vegetation and debris. By the Silver River to the north (at 298277) is a 4m high fragment of a second tower with two drawbar slots.

BALLYKNOCKAN   S106951 D

A wall 0.7m thick surrounds a bawn 61m by 56m with 4.4m diameter circular flankers containing two levels of gunloops at the SW and NW corners. The castle belonged to the O'Carrolls but was granted to William Chandler in 1659 after they had been transported.

BALLYMOONEY   N128018

This house was built c1622 by Daniel O'Carroll, described as "Marshall for the rebels" in the war of 1641 and consequently transplanted to County Mayo in 1657. The remains comprise the 4.2m diameter SE and NE flankers of the bawn with gunloops at two levels and wall-walks at the top, and two wings and parts of the adjoining south facade of the 7.7m wide main house occupying most of the north side of the bawn. The west wing which contained a staircase is the smaller but higher of the two. It has the entrance covered by a machicolation off the wall-walk.

BALLYSHIEL   N081225

This T-plan 17th century house with projecting chimney stacks and part of a bawn wall with gunloops and traces of a flanker is named after the Sheeles family, although it may have been built after they were transported elsewhere in 1650s.

Birr Castle

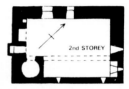

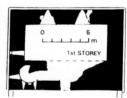

Castle Armstrong: plans

Castle Armstrong

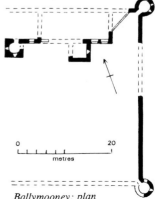

Ballymooney: plan

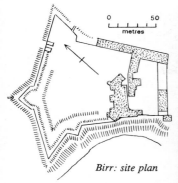

Birr: site plan

Ballymooney Castle

BIRR   N055050

In 1208 Murchad O'Brien besieged a castle here and burnt the settlement outside it. It was rebuilt by the English in 1214, but burnt the same year. Then known as the Black Castle, it was occupied by Tadhg O'Carroll in 1346 and by the 15th century it was one of the main strongholds of the O'Carrolls of Ely. The castle was damaged by the Earl of Ormond in 1432 and was besieged and captured by the Earl of Kildare in 1532 on behalf of Ferganainm O'Carroll during an internal family feud. Tadhg O'Carroll sold the castle to James Oge Butler in 1594, and in 1620 it was granted to Laurence Parsons. Nothing remains of the tower which probably stood on the original motte overlooking the Camcor River, nor of the bawn walls repaired in the 1620s, but a gatehouse 14m by 7.5m then added to the bawn forms the central hall of the present building of 1803, 1832 and 1846-8. It contains a late 17th century wooden staircase with turned balusters. The works of the 1620s also included the still surviving artillery ramparts around the bawn with one full bastion facing north and demi-bastions at the NE and NW corners, and the enclosing of a garden and orchard with a garden tower (perhaps a gazebo) and a service range and stables, most of them demolished in 1778 by Sir William Parsons. The castle was captured by the Confederate Catholics in 1642 and by General Ireton in 1650. James II confiscated the estate but the Parsons' regained possession after William III's victory at the Boyne and were able to hold out against an attack by Patrick Sarsfield, Earl of Lucan. The Parsons were later made earls of Rosse and still live in the castle.

CASTLEARMSTRONG   N178299   D

A stronghouse 11.8m by 8.7m over walls 1.6m thick above a battered base lies on a rocky ledge. The 3.1m thick SE wall contained mural chambers (now missing their inner walls) over the entrance and a spiral stair remains in the south corner. The second storey has a latrine projection and a fireplace in the SW wall, and the third storey has a fireplace at the NE end. The forecourt to the SE incorporates part of a later wing or outbuilding.

CASTLEROAN   S070828

A fetterlock-shaped bawn about 40m across with a 24m long straight west side has fragments and footings of a wall 1.2m thick above a battered base, beyond with is a ditch on the vulnerable south and west sides. There may have been a central tower house. The castle was held by Richard Butler in 1641 and was granted to Thomas Francks in 1666.

Clonmacnoise Castle

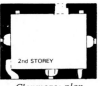

Clonmore: plan

Clonlyon: plan

0   20
⌞⌟⌟⌟⌟⌟⌟⌟⌟⌟⌟⌟ m

KEEP

Clonmacnoise: plan

Clonmore Castle

CLOGHAN   M972120

There is a square bartizan at wall-walk level on the NE corner of this tower measuring 13m by 10m, and another at fourth storey level on the SW corner, whilst a machicolation on the east side covered the former entrance there where a later building now adjoins. This wall contains mural chambers and a stair in the SE corner. The second storey has a latrine in the SW corner and the fourth storey has a fireplace on the west and a pair of windows of two lights with round heads. There is also a fireplace in the lowest storey, a feature suggesting that the tower was built after the destruction of an earlier castle here in 1595. The tower lies on the west side of a long narrow bawn with original flankers at three corners, but the square flanker at the SW corner and the adjoining outbuildings are 18th century work. The castle was held by Sir John MacCoghlan in 1620 but was held by the Moores in 1641 and they were confirmed in possession in 1666.

CLONLYON   N069261   D

The NW end wall of a 16th century tower 8.3m wide over walls 2.3m thick stands three storeys high with a latrine in the north corner at second storey level and a fireplace and passages to angle-loops at third storey level, which was covered with a lofty pointed vault. The entrance must have been in the collapsed SE wall and there are traces of a stair in the south corner. A wall 0.9m thick enclosed a bawn mostly filled by the tower in its west corner and a later outbuilding 5.5m wide internally occupying the whole of the NE side. This range was of two storeys and has a circular bartizan with gunloops on the north corner at the upper level. The southern corner of the bawn is missing. The castle is mentioned as a MacCoghlan possession in 1620 and 1641 but had passed to James Larkin by 1659 and in 1667 was granted to Robert Bowyer.

Cloghan Castle

Clonlyon Castle

CLONMACNOISE   N007305   C

The ringwork and bailey between the monastery and the River Shannon were built by King John c1212 and have a deep ditch and counterscarp bank on their vulnerable south end. They seem to have replaced an earlier fort burnt in 1135 and 1205 which guarded a nearby wooden bridge. It was probably during the early part of Henry III's reign that a hall keep measuring 19m by 11.2m over walls 2.2m thick above a battered base was constructed upon the ringwork. It had corner turrets 2.8m square rising from the battered base. Only the west corner containing a spiral staircase stands high, together with a leaning fragment of the south corner and footings of the rest. Walls up to 1.5m thick enclose a court 17m square to the NW of the keep. There is a round-arched entrance in the NW wall and a tower about 6m square with a second storey latrine in the west corner. There was also once a forebuilding in front of the keep to protect the upper storey entrance in its NW wall near the staircase. The court looks more like 16th century work than 13th and the keep looks like a victim of 17th century slighting but there is in fact neither historical or architectural evidence of the site being occupied after c1300.

CLONMORE   N587371

The ivy-clad two storey building measuring 10.2m by 8.2m with an entrance facing north and a latrine in the SW corner on the upper level may be one of the "two piles as bulwarks of defence, against any sudden attempt" erected by Richard Croft and Henry Dukes prior to their being granted lands here, although there were two "old ruynouse castles or piles" in this area in 1550, when Clonmore belonged to Sir Francis Rushe. Part of the parapet remains on the south side. There are no stairs or vaults.

CLONOGHIL   N073048

Defaced 2m high walls up to 2m thick remain of a tower 11.3m square lying in the NE quadrant of an earthwork enclosure perhaps of earlier date. It belonged to Owney MacWilliam O'Carroll until granted in the 1620s to Laurence Parsons. He leased it to the Bigo family, Huguenot refugees who established a glass factory here. The castle was captured and burnt by the Confederate Catholics during the war of 1641-2. See page 141.

Clonony: access to hidden chamber

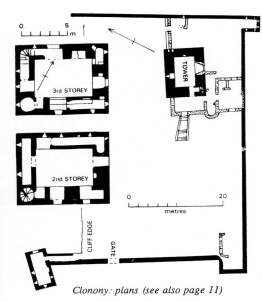

Clonony: plans (see also page 11)

CLONONY   N052206   E

This tower measuring 10.6m by 8.3m over walls up to 2m thick lies on a rock outcrop on the south bank of the River Brosna. It is mentioned in 1519 and was captured in 1553 during a war between the MacCoghlans, who had owned it, and the O'Molloys. In the early 17th century the tower was the residence of Matthew de Renzy, whose letters tell us much about the neighbouring castles and their owners. The rebuilt entrance in the SW wall has a murder hole and originally also had a machicolation off the wall-walk, and it adjoins a spiral staircase in the south corner. The second storey is vaulted and the room above has three mural chambers, one of them having steps down to a chamber in the south haunch of the vault. The openings have all been altered since the tower remained occupied into the 19th century. It stands in the west corner of a small court with various outbuildings filling the east corner of a main outer bawn with a SW entrance, and rectangular flankers at the west, south and east corners. There is no wall facing the river. A new owner of the castle is hoping to restore it as a private residence.

COOLE   N134227   C

A third storey fireplace has a Gaelic inscription which translates as John MacCoghlan began from here up 1575, which suggests that work on the tower had been interrupted by the rebellion of the sons of the Earl of Clanrickard in 1572 and was only resumed in 1575. The fourth storey is a vaulted loft, above which the building is fragmentary but has signs of a fireplace. The tower measures 10.4m by 8.7m over walls 2m thick and has an east facing rebuilt entrance with a murder-hole, with spiral stairs in the SE corner. The lowest level has three ogival-headed loops, and there are others higher up with decorated spandrels. Ornamental punch-dressing occurs on many of the openings. The second storey has a passage to a latrine in the SW corner with a small ornamental ventilator and at that level the NE corner had a two light window with the lost mullion forming the corner.

CROGHAN   N470329

Incorporated into farmyard buildings are fragments of the NW and SE corners of a three storey O'Conor stronghouse measuring 28.5m by 13.5m with brick patching on what remains of the wall-walk parapet. One fine upper fireplace and its chimney is the only feature of interest.

CULLENWAINE   S013824   D

A wall 0.9m thick with gunloops on either side of the projecting gateway on the north side encloses a bawn 48m square with footings of a circular flanker 6.6m in diameter at the SE corner and corbels for a bartizan at the NE corner. Only parts of the north and west walls remain of a building 15.2m long by 9.3m wide over walls 1.1m thick which formed the NW corner the bawn. It has one second storey mullion-and-transom window. On the south side of the bawn is a small late 17th century house with a projecting staircase wing in the middle of one side. The O'Carrolls seem to have had a castle here in 1532 but the present remains are probably rather later. John Carroll was replaced by John Desborough in the 1650s but was restored to Cullenwaine in 1660.

CURRALANTY   S047955

Ony O'Carroll held this stronghouse in the 1630s and may have been its builder. Two circular corner towers 4.8m in diameter well provided with gunloops on each of three levels and retaining timber door lintels lie at the north and west corners of a main block about 16m long of which only the patched and rebuilt NW wall now survives.

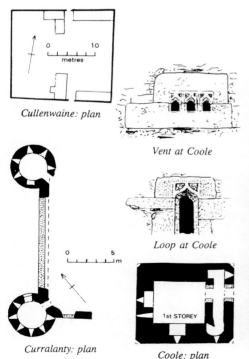

Cullenwaine: plan

Vent at Coole

Loop at Coole

Curralanty: plan

Coole: plan

Curralanty Castle

DAINGEAN or PHILIPSTOWN   N472273

In 1537 Lord Deputy Grey captured the new O'Connor castle of Daingean which was enclosed by wet moats and marshes. In 1546-8 the Crown had a new fort 75m square built around it and when the county of Offaly was created in 1556 the fort was renamed Philipstown after Queen Mary's spouse, Philip II of Spain. The fort was captured by James II's forces in the war of 1689-91 and was entirely rebuilt in the 18th century. Nothing remains of the walls built around the town to the north in the 1570s.

DOON or ESKER   N119317

This tower measuring 11.6m by 8.3m has an entrance lobby at the east end, from the south end of which a passage leads to a mural stair to the main second storey room. This room has a fireplace in the north wall, a latrine in the NW corner and access to a smaller east room from which in turn is reached a chamber in the SW corner with a murder-hole covering the passage to the staircase. A spiral stair near the SW corner led up to the third storey. A quoin at the SE corner has a sheela-na-gig. The letters of Matthew de Renzy tell us that this castle, then known as Esker, was rebuilt by the Nugents after an English-built structure had been destroyed by the MacCoghlans. It was held by Owen Mooney from the 1620s until he was transplanted to County Clare by the Cromwellians in the 1650s.

DUNGAR   S145912

There is a spiral stair in a semicircular turret on the south side of this circular tower house about 9m in diameter. The third and fourth storeys have slop-stones and mural chambers leading to latrines, the latter having a square main room. The wall-walk is also square, being corbelled out at the corners. The lowest room is still in use as a store. In 1640 the castle was occupied by Rory O'Carroll and his wife Finola O'Brien. About 180m to the east are footings of a second circular tower of uncertain date and purpose.

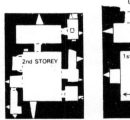

Plans of Doon Castle

Eglish Castle

Cullenwaine Castle

Blundell Castle at Edenderry

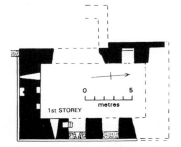

Blundell Castle at Edenderry: plan

Dungar Castle

EDENDERRY or BLUNDELL   N632325   A

On a hill above Edenderry is a ruined tower named Blundell Castle after the family that owned it from the 1650s until the 18th century. In 1556, then known as the castle of Edenderry, it was held by Sir Nicholas Herbert, but it was granted to the Cooleys in 1562 and was still held by them in 1622. The now fragmentary building measured about 16m by 10m over walls 2.2m thick still rising three storeys high on the east and south. There are double latrine chutes at the south end and a blocked narrow straight service staircase in the east wall. The fireplaces here and the large windows and the almost vanished wing (probably for a staircase) on the west side are 17th century additions and alterations.

EGLISH   N099098

The north and west walls of a tower 10.4 by 9.9m over walls 1.9m thick stand two storeys high, the north wall forming part of a derelict late 18th century house and containing a mural stair up to the second storey, where there is a passage in the west wall and a NW corner chamber with an angle-loop. A bawn enclosed the south and east sides with later outbuildings adjoining it. The castle existed by 1532 when it was captured by Ferganaim O'Carroll during his quarrel with the sons of John O'Carroll. The Earl of Kildare supported Ferganaim, and a later earl held the castle in 1612. It was held against an attack by a Jacobite force led by Lieutenant-Colonel Connor in 1689.

EMMEL   R985846

This five storey tower has a circular stair turret at the NE corner and an east-facing entrance towards where there is now a three storey late 17th century house five bays long. A corbelled projection on the north side contains the third and fourth storey latrines and there are square bartizans on the SE and NW corners, plus a machicolation over the entrance. The parapet has been partly rebuilt in brick and there are several 19th century houldmoulded windows. The lowest room contains an inserted fireplace and has a gunloop off one of the window embrasures. After "Long Anthony" O'Carroll was transported to Galway in 1657 the castle was granted to Captain John Rosse, but it was sold back to Anthony in 1676 and remained with his descendants for about another hundred years.

GARRY   N021137   D

The 9.9m long and 2.2m thick north wall still stands four storeys high of a tower thought to have been built in 1450 by Felim Maoil MacCoghlan. At the NE corner is a corbel for a former bartizan adjoining a sheela-na-gig and there are chutes for latrines. In the 17th century a range 18.7m long by 10.7m wide over walls 1.3m thick was built to the south of the tower. The west wall formed part of a bawn about 53m by 50m with a circular SW flanker 4.5m in diameter reached from the stronghouse itself. Another flanker at the NW corner lies just west of the older tower house, 12m east of the other side of which is the projecting north-facing gateway with a machicolation over the archway. The later range has a fireplace in the south end wall and a mural stair leading up to the wall-walk on the west. There is a still occupied farmhouse of c1800 on the east side of the bawn.

Plans of Kilcoursey Castle

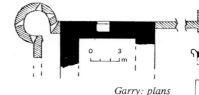

Garry: plans

Emmel Castle

Garry Castle

GEASHILL   N455208

Set on what looks like a 4m high motte measuring 20m by 25m on top is a three storey high fragment of a tower about 8m by 7.5m with a later doorway inserted in it. There was a vaulted basement. A fireplace to the SW served an outbuilding and there seems to have been a small bawn with an east flanker. In 1203 Meiler FitzHenry, Justiciar of Ireland was ordered to hand over the castle of Geashill to William Marshall, Earl of Pembroke. There is a mention of a new castle being built here in 1307 by Lord Offaly and in 1538 it was seized by Lord Leonard Grey and the O'Molloys. It was handed over to Lettice, Baroness Offaly in 1625 and was attacked by a Confederate Catholic force in 1641.

KILCOLGAN   N146246

Until the 1950s the bawn entrance facing north was surmounted by a stone dated 1649. It was built by Terence MacCoghlan, whose family was transported to Galway in the 1650s but Francis MacCoghlan regained Kilcolgan in 1663. The two storey L-plan house with diagonally placed chimney stacks and a crenellated parapet was mostly demolished in 1954 to provide material for the foundations of the power station at Lumcloon, but a wall 1m thick still surrounds a bawn 75m by 70m. The three storey circular flankers 6.4m in diameter each have a prow or angle strengthening the part furthest from the bawn enclosure, thickening the wall to allow upper fireplaces. The bawn wall has gunloops at a higher level suggesting an internal wooden firing gallery.

KILCOURSEY   N267323

Hubert Fox of Lehinch may have built this tower measuring 8.2m by 7.2m after being granted Kilcoursey in 1600. The north wall contains the entrance and a stair up to the third storey set over a basement with gunloops and a low vaulted loft. This upper room has several gunloops, including one piercing the SW corner. Another stair into the north wall led up to the fourth storey. The tower overlooks a drop to the south and lay in the SE corner of a bawn, part of the south wall of which remains.

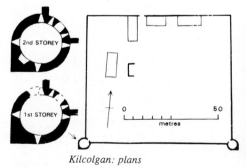

Kilcolgan: plans

Kilcolgan Castle

Kilcoursey Castle

KILLOOLY   N221173

Beside the hall are remains of a stronghouse with two levels of fireplaces in a projecting breast and the south wall of a bawn with a circular NW corner flanker with gunloops. The house may have been built c1622 by Peter Salconstall.

KILLYON   N125053

Originally perhaps the site of a nunnery, Killyon was held by the Herberts in 1634 and has footings of a bawn of that period 52m square with a standing portion of the wall with gunloops on the south, a 3m high fragment of a circular flanker at the NW corner and footings of another at the SE corner. Inside are footings of a house measuring 33m by 12m and a 19th century account describes a gatehouse projecting within the bawn. Killyon later passed to the MacCoghlans and was then sold to John Asgill of Ross Castle.

LEAP   S129974

The Ely O'Carrolls built this tower as a defence against the Butlers of Ormond and it became their principal seat. Gerald, Earl of Kildare failed to capture the castle in 1513 but a second attack in 1516 by his son was more successful. In 1558 the castle was burnt in an unsuccessful attempt to prevent English forces under the Earl of Sussex from occupying it, but it was soon recaptured by William Odhar O'Carroll, rebuilt, and a wing added on the north side. Tests on timbers from the added wing confirmed a date in the 1570s. By 1659 the castle had passed to the Derby family, who subsequently remodelled and extended it, remaining in occupation until it was burnt in 1922. The tower measures 13m by 10m over walls 2m thick and the fourth storey room retains an original two-light window on the west side and a bartizan on the NW corner. A machicolation off the wall-walk defends the entrance with a surviving hanging-eye in the south wall. The second storey has a late 16th century fireplace with a joggled lintel and smaller more modern fireplace inserted into it. The third storey is a low vaulted loft.

Leap Castle   *Rathmore Castle*

Rathmore: plans

Newtown: plan

Newtown Castle

MOYALLY   N214377

There is a U-shaped bastion at the NE corner of a bawn 47m long by 33m wide, the south wall of which, closest to the existing house, has vanished. There is a circular NW flanker and a square projection on the east side. There was a ruinous O'Melaghlin castle here in 1603 but the bawn may be the work of Richard Burke, Earl of Clanrickard, who was granted the estate here. It was sold to Colonel Richard Grave but he was dispossessed during the war of 1641, regained it in 1660, only to be dispossessed again in 1672.

NEWTOWN   S173993

A fragmentary wall 0.6m thick encloses a bawn 23.6m by 21.6m around a two storey house with fireplaces at either end probably built by Sir William Sinclair after he was granted Newtown in 1621. It passed to William Parsons in 1637 and was later held by John Carroll. Both house and bawn are mostly destroyed in the NW side, where there are traces of a moat and bridge. The bawn has north and south corner flankers 4.2m in diameter with two levels of gunloops.

RATHMORE   S074978

This four storey circular tower 10m in diameter had a thatched roof in 1642 when it was burnt by the Confederate Catholics. It was then held by Teige Carroll, whose son Donough was transplanted to County Clare in 1657 but recovered Rathmore in 1661. The entrance and staircase lay in the destroyed eastern part which faced towards a bawn. The second storey has a passage to a latrine on the SW. Ivy obscures the uppermost features.

Toberdaly Castle

Srah Castle

SRAH   N328251

Built in 1588 by the Elizabethan officer John Briscoe from Cumbria, this tower measuring 8.9m by 7.2m is notable for its numerous gunloops, the bartizans containing rooms opening off the fourth storey, and the third storey level two-light angle loop with the mullion forming the SW corner which opens off one of a tier of rooms over the west-facing entrance. There is also a single loop piercing the NE corner. The building is much defaced inside, the inner parts of the western rooms and NW corner stairwell having gone, but there is a fireplace on the north side at second storey level and the exterior is complete to the parapet with a machicolation over the entrance. There are windows with pairs of ogival-headed lights. Ruins of a 17th century house with a fireplace adjoin the NW corner.

TOBERDALY   N521320   D

Probably dating after 1550, when a survey mentions only "an old ruynouse base courte" is a tower measuring 9.4m by 7.8m containing three low storeys under a vault and having a circular bartizan on the SW corner and a square one on the NE corner. In 1654 it was occupied by Margaret and Mary Warren. The entrance doorway was moved further up the east wall in the 19th century when an octagonal gazebo was built on top of the tower.

Togher: plan

Plans of Toberdaly Castle

House at Leitra

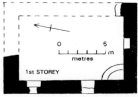

Cloughmoyle: plan

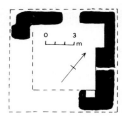

Clonoghil: plan

Togher Castle

TOGHER   N119314

Castle Roan: plan

Srah: plans

Most of the south wall of this tower measuring 12.6m by 11.3m over walls 2.3m thick has been destroyed, so that only traces remain of a stair in the SW corner and just one east gunloop of the guardroom flanking the entrance. There was a second straight service stair in the east wall. There are two pointed vaulted cellars divided by a thin wall which appears to be an insertion. The second storey is very ruined but two latrines remain in the NE corner.

WHIGSBOROUGH   N098133

Only a fragment remains of a circular tower 6.5m in diameter over walls 1.2m thick on a rock outcrop, and there are only traces of a possible bawn. This O'Molloy castle, also known as Dowris or Inchloughcurry, passed to the Earl of Kildare. It was leased to Bernard Fitzpatrick in 1575, to Shane Oge O'Molloy in 1607, and Neill Moore in 1609, but it was acquired in the 1630s by Sir Laurence Parsons.

OTHER CASTLES IN COUNTY OFFALY

AGHADOUGLAS S102931 Footings of tower 12m by 9.5m and traces of bawn on knoll.
ANNAGHMORE N170073 Heavily overgrown last traces of thinly walled building about 16m long with corner turrets at the northern corners. Belonged to the O'Molloys.
BEHERNAGH S010879 Fragment of circular bawn flanker is only relic of a castle held by Charles O'Carroll in the 1630s. Marked on a map of 1654 as a "stumpe of a castle".
BRACKLIN N387306 Low featureless fragments of east and south walls.
CASTLETOWN N216285 One 4m high fragment and footings of a tower held by Owen Molloy in 1641 and granted to John Hurd in 1666.
CLASHAGAD S085848 Footings of building 17m by 13m over walls 1.5m thick with traces of NW corner tower 7m by 5m and traces of bawn ditch to east and west.
CLOGHMOYLE S046924 Defaced and overgrown west and south walls of stronghouse 14.2m by 10m held in 1640 by Daniel MacGilfoyle. No remains of reported flankers.

CLONYHURK N485130 Two storeys remain of 8m wide tower over walls 1.5m thick now lacking its east end. Latrine chute in north wall at second storey.

FAHEERAN N235389 Footings of building 14m by 9.5m over walls 1m thick within circular enclosure with ditch up to 2m deep.

GARRYMONA or CASHLAN BLOCK N513197 Low fragments of three walls of structure 11m wide.

HOLLOW HOUSE N354286 Farmhouse of c1800 with remains of the bawn of Tinnycross with one flanker. It was held by the de Renzys in the late 17th century.

KILCLONFERT N426309 Footings of tower 10m by 9m with NE and SW corner turrets and traces of bawn 80m by 53m to south. Built by the Fludds on site of "old ruynouse castell" noted in 1550.

LEITRA N2006267 Two storey stronghouse 6.5m by 6.2m. with walls 0.9m thick with two gunloops and upper fireplace. Traces of a bawn to the east.

LEMANAGHAN N170270 Just the SW corner with walls 1m thick still stands 2.5m high of a MacCoghlan castle which by 1641 had passed to the Duke of Buckingham.

LISCLOONEY N034208 L-plan house may incorporate parts of castle built by Melaghlin O'Dalaghan in 1550s to replace an earlier building, parts of which remained in 1620.

KNOCK S127979 Footings of building 13m by 10m, walls 1.1m thick, on low mound within ringfort.

PALLAS N264196 Corner fragment 1.5m thick and footings of tower 10m square within platform 70m across with ditch. Granted to Francis Blundell in 1613, but held by the O'Molloys in the 1630s.

RATHLIHEN N236165 Remains of O'Molloy tower 17m by 10m over walls 1.5m thick with crosswall and bawn wall fragment.

SHANCOURT or MEENEGLISH N330318 Possible de Lacy castle. Footings of building 22m by 14m over walls 1.5m thick and NW corner turret with latrine chutes lying within moated platform.

Clonyhurk: plan

CASTLE SITES IN COUNTY OFFALY

ANNAGHMORE S307148 Evidence of bawn and flankers visible from air.

BALLINDARRA N049036 Ackland, subsequently Parsons family, house and bawn attacked in 1642 and 1691. Last remains collapsed in 1848. No remains now visible.

BALLINDOWN N069078 Site of castle seized by Earl of Kildare and O'Carrolls in 1532.

BALLYBOY N203139 Site of O'Molloy stronghold occupied in 1690 by Earl of Drogheda's regiment.

BALLYBURLY N552352 Ruined house on site of castle of Wakerley family destroyed in 1590s.

BALLYCUMBER N211307 Stone from top of window reset at back of house of 1736 has inscription "Dermot Coghlan made this castell in anno dni 1627".

BALLYKEAN N493194 Site of an O'Dempsey house and bawn with flankers.

BALLYMACADAM N222083 Loose stones on site of main seat of Carrolls of Leitir Lugna.

BALLYNASRAH M994114 Site of castle held c1620 by Sir John MacCoghlan.

BANAGHER N009154 Pynnar's sketch of 1624 shows a building in a bawn with crenellated walls with a round tower with crossloops towards the river and a twin-turreted gatehouse on the other side.

BELLMOUNT N068220 Site of castle of Lisdarry held by the Coghlans in the 1650s-60s.

BROUGHAL N163150 O'Molloy castle described as strong and well kept in 1537   and destroyed by Lord Deputy Grey in 1538. Tower remained until destruction in 1930s.

BUSHERSTOWN S043825 18th century house on site of O'Carroll castle.

CANGORT S032033 House on site of Atkinson seat destoyed by Cromwellian troops.

CASTLE BARNAGH N481282 Earthworks or buried footings of house and bawn.

CASTLE BERNARD S203056 Vanished castle which stood upon the earthworks of the motte and bailey castle of Kinnitty erected in 1214.

CLOGHAN N076194 Post office on site of Coghlan 17th century stronghouse probably built on site of earlier castle. Mentioned in 1641 and 1663. On map of 1657.

CLONEARL N471300 Earthworks and traces of stonework on site of castle built c1550 and occupied by the Leicester family in the 17th century.

CLONLISK N050886 Site of seat of Fearganainm O'Carroll mentioned in 1541.

DERRYDOLNEY N208159 Later house has reset stone with year 1684 and names of Philip and Mary Molloy. Evidence for building in adjacent field by the late 16th century.

DURROW N318307 A stone castle of c1214 may have stood on Hugh de Lacy's motte of 1186. Herberts made agreement for the construction of two castles here in 1567-9.

ERRY N258320 Site of bawn 40m by 35m. Passed to Sir Edmund FitzGerald after Edward MacGeoghegan was killed in rebellion but described as ruined in 1621.

FADDANMORE N070232 No remains of MacCoghlan castle mentioned in 1520 when passed to Richard Boyle, Earl of Cork after the wars of the 1640s.

FRANCKFORT N061852 18th or 19th century building on site of the O'Carroll castle of Dunkerrin which went to the Francks family in the 1650s.

GARBALLY N230181 Site of 16th century tower held by James Griffin in 1641.

GLENACURRAGH S120992 No remains of house show as a gabled ruin on map of 1657.

KILCUMMIN N046233 House on site of castle described in 1620 as having been built by the English and ruined by Art MacCorman MacCoghlan.

KILMAINE N124050 Ditch around of rubble of castle mentioned in 1677.

KILNAGARNAGH N139295 House on site of tower held in 1641 by John MacFir MacCoghlan.

KINCORA N128240 Slight traces of footings west of house mark site of tower built by Sir Richard Tuite, to which James Og MacCoghlan had added a bawn.

LEHINCH N282328 House on site of castle held by Hubert Fox in late 16th century.

MILLTOWN N032121 House on site of Goghlan castle granted to Joshua Hensy in 1666.

MOUNTHEATON S097903 Mount St Joseph Abbey lies on the site of a castle.

MOYSTOWN N029203 Site of MacCoghlan castle destroyed in 1548. An embattled three storey building with a bawn is indicated in papers of the 1620s.

RAHAN Symon Clifford's castle of 1227 probably lay near the monastic site.

RAHEEN N468184 A few stones mark the site of the castle.

RASHINA N130301 House on site of castle.

RATHDRUM N414284 Mound rising 3m to summit 30m across. Site of stone castle.

RATHROBIN N261163 Hoodmould of window in outbuilding of ruined house is relic of tower held by Dermot Doogan until he was transported to Galway in the 1550s.

ROSCORE N260229 Part of west end of stronghouse with gunloops and SW corner tower still remained in the 1640s. Held by Laurence Hammond in 1641.

SHINRONE S048924 Site of bawn built c1620 by Donough MacGilfoyle.

SIERKERNAN Casemate 4m in diameter with upper level of gunloops built against lost SE corner of very ruined priory church. Older round tower formed flanker at NW corner.

STREAMSTOWN N030162 Mound on site. Ogee-headed windows reused in nearby buildings.

TULLA N187001 House beside site of castle.

TULLAMORE N337253 Site of castle held in 1583 by Theobald O'Molloy. Sold to the Moores c1610.

OTHER CASTLE SITES: Aharney N284279, Ballinrath N588288, Ballyleakin N588298, Bellair N178320, Clonbeg S086991, Clonymoan S037844, Cully S237208, Gorteen N232355, Loretto N077031, Newtown N398208, Pigeonstown N221052, Raheenakeeran N523196, Tober N226364

MOTTES: Ballyboy* N203139, Ballymooney N421233, Castletown N203055, Down* N458170, Drumcooly* N626306, Durrow (8m high) N318307, Garr* N534378, Glendine S010781, Knockbarron N181062, Lynally* 297238, Rathlihen N235165.

RINGWORKS: Ballynacarrig N219132, Dungar N157921, and Sierkieron N139022.

CASTLES OF COUNTY WESTMEATH

ARDNURCHER   N278388

In 1192 Hugh de Lacy created a motte and small bailey here by digging ditches across an esker. It was burnt by Felim O'Connor in 1234. There were formerly traces of a round tower and a curtain wall upon the mound summit.

ATHLONE   N039415 E

The medieval walled town lay on the east bank of the Shannon, although the slight remains of the town defences there were part of a 16th and 17th century refortification with two demi-bastions where the wall met the river bank and four arrowhead shaped bastions on the landward side, the most southernly of which guarded the Dublin Gate. Nothing remains of a second walled enclosure of that date with several bastions on the west bank. The castle lies on this side near the bridgehead and lies on or near the chief seat of the 10th and 11th century kings of Hy Many. A new bridge and a fort to guard it were built in the 1120s by Turlough Mor O'Conor, King of Connacht and High King of Ireland. Both were destroyed and rebuilt several times during the contests of the next thirty years. During the initial Anglo-Norman invasion Geoffrey de Contentin built a motte and bailey castle. The bailey was looted and burnt by Cathal Crovderg O'Conor in 1199. The decagonal central keep 12.5m across over walls 3m thick is a 19th century rebuilding above the battered base of a 13th century keep which had been mostly destroyed by 1793. The medieval keep was itself a rebuilding or replacement of 1215 of a strong tower erected in 1210 by John de Gray, the English Justicier, which collapsed in 1211, killing Richard Tuite and eight others. Perhaps the motte proved unable to provide a secure foundation for the weight of such a structure. The Crown had the castle repaired in 1251 and further work was done in 1273-9, to which period can be assigned the curtain walls and the three-quarter round towers flanking them, although in their present form much of the walls and buildings are 19th century work. The original bailey entrance was in the east wall, towards the river, and the present approach ramp on the north is modern. The wallheads of the keep and curtain walls were lowered and remodelled to take heavy cannon after the sieges of 1690-1, and the castle remained in military use until the 1920s.

In 1641 the town and castle of Athlone were successfully held for 22 weeks against the Confederate Catholics of Connacht, but in February 1642 the English garrison and colonists were forced to withdraw and Athlone was taken over by Viscount Dillon of Costelloe. In 1650 the Cromwellian commander Sir Charles Coote captured Athlone after two attempts. In July 1690 Colonel Richard Grace successfully held the town against a Williamite force of 10,000 men, but in June 1691 General Ginkell captured it after a fierce bombardment of the castle, bridge and the western walled town.

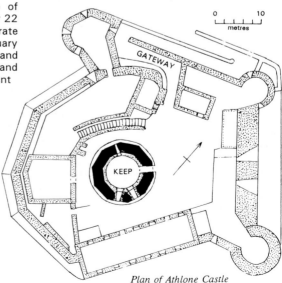

Plan of Athlone Castle

Athlone Castle

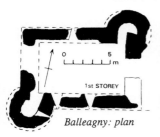

Balleagny: plan

Keep at Athlone

Balrath Castle

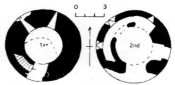

Ballymore: plans

BALLEAGNY   N346540

Only the very defaced lowest storey remains of a tower 12.7m long by 9m wide over walls 1.8m thick with traces of three loops. There are circular turrets 5m in diameter at the SW and NE corners, the latter containing the lowest part of a spiral staircase.

BALLINLOUGH   N637655

At the SW corner of this 18th century house is evidence of a narrower older building with an original chimneystack and blocked window. The heraldic stone dated 1617 on the attic may refer to its construction. The O'Reillys here managed to remain in possession despite the 17th century wars and changed their name to Nugent in 1812.

BALLYMORE   N222490   D

All that remains of the principal de Lacy seat in Westmeath, which later passed to the de Verdons, is a circular tower 8m in diameter with a stair rising from a south facing doorway into a vaulted basement to a single upper room. There are traces of outbuildings and earthworks but no indications of a bawn wall adjoining the tower, which appears to be late medieval. An account of 1682 describes Ballymore as being the chief English fortress in County Longford during the war of 1641.

BALRATH   N348393   D

The first recorded use of siege-guns in Ireland is when Lord Deputy Kildare besieged and captured this castle in 1488. It was granted to William Taaffe in 1603. Just the NW corner remains of the original tower but the north and west walls remain of an extension about 4m wide. A farmyard now occupies and obscures a D-shaped bawn platform to the east.

BILLESTOWN   N588617   D

A fragmentary three storey tower measuring 9.7m by 7.4m over walls 1.5m thick stands amongst earthworks. The vaulted basement has two loops and an entrance doorway with a narrow stair in the broken corner adjoining it. Only half of the more thinly walled upper rooms now remain. None of the levels was vaulted.

BOLEYVILLISH   N303499   D

Three walls up to 1.4m thick stand two and a half storeys high of a late 16th century tower 9.1m wide by probably about 11.7m long. The basement has a wide doorway with a drawbar slot and four narrow loops, two of them set either side of a fireplace.

CARLANSTOWN   N445767

A bawn measuring 60m by 45m serves as a farmyard with a modern house in the SE corner. There is a slight rounded projection at the SW corner, whilst the northern corners have tall circular flankers about 4.5m in diameter with horizontal-slit type gunloops.

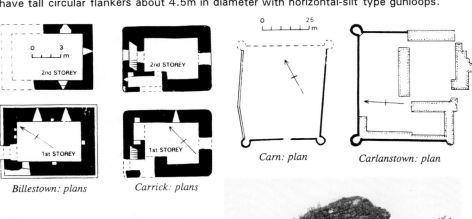

Carn: plan

Carlanstown: plan

Billestown: plans

Carrick: plans

Carlanstown Castle

Boleyvillish Castle

Carrick Castle

Castle Lost

CARN   N134416

The 38m long SW side of a bawn built by the Magawley family has a loopholed wall 2.5m high with a circular flanker 4.2m in diameter at each end also with gunloops. Also surviving are the featureless 50m long SE wall, and a retaining wall on the NW side which faced a slope and had a slight angle near the middle of its length. See page 159.

CARRICK   N366635   D

This round-cornered tower measuring 9.6m by 7.4m has a stair rising in the NW wall from a broken entrance facing SW. There are two storeys under a vault and one more above. The windows are 18th century enlargements, as are the gables rising from the outer walls.

CASTLELOST   N451414   D

The western half of Hugh Tyrrel's motte of c1186 has been destroyed to make an adjacent road. About 60m to the SE lies the vaulted basement of a building 15m long by 8.8m wide over walls 2m thick which may be a 13th century hall-house. It has a doorway at the west end and traces of a stair in the very ruinous east wall, whilst there are three loops facing south. The Tyrrels were still living here in Elizabeth I's reign, when Sir John Tyrrel, d1607, built the nearby church, the effigy within it probably being of him.

CLARE   N236472

A very ruined Dalton tower measuring 12.4m by 8m over walls 1.8m thick partly projects out from the east side of a hill-top bawn 40m by 50m marked by a stony bank. The only feature is a very broken basement loop at the west end.

Clare: plan

Castle Lost: plan

Boleyvillish: plan

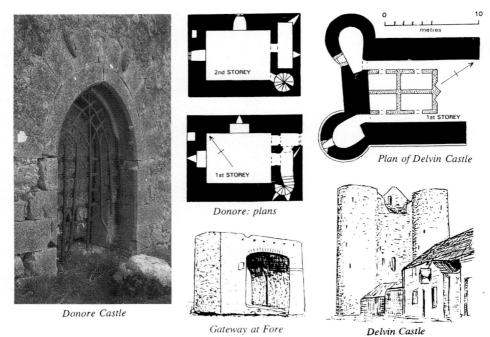

Donore Castle

Donore: plans

Plan of Delvin Castle

Gateway at Fore

Delvin Castle

DELVIN   N601628   C

The scrub-covered motte at the south end of the village represents the castle built in 1181 by Hugh de Lacy for his brother-in-law Sir Gilbert Nangle, to whom he granted the barony. From Sir Gilbert are descended the Nugents, who held land in the barony down to modern times. They now reside at Ballinlough Castle but also had a house (now ruined) at Clonyn just NW of Delvin which is dated 1639. Beside a shop near the motte is a castle with a layout more typical of the 13th century although it has no specific early features and is now regarded as a 15th century building. It has a main block 11.7m wide over walls 2.5m thick and is now 15m long, the eastern part having been destroyed after the Nugents defied Cromwell. The western end has two circular corner towers about 5.5m in external diameter which contain various rooms on five levels, the lowest being vaulted and the uppermost at the level of the main block wall-walk. In the main block a hall lay over cellars, with a private chamber on top, and there was an attic within the roof.

DONORE   N295386

This five storey tower measuring 12.3m by 9.5m with very fine quality stonework has on the SW side a Latin inscription of 1809 recording its construction in 1598 by Brian McGeoghegan and his wife Catherine O'Connor. The entrance on the SE side has geometrical patterning on the jambs, carved heads of a king and bishop, and retains an iron yett with a tracery pattern at the top. The third storey has a fireplace on the SW side and a latrine in the NW wall. The upper windows are lancets set in the centre of each side and having delicately carved spandrels. A gunloop opens off the staircase in the south corner. The east corner has angle loops on the second and fifth storeys. Despite having no road or track out to it, the castle remained occupied until the middle of the 20th century but is now ruined. After it was captured in 1650 by the Cromwellian John Reynolds, James McGeoghegan and his garrison of forty or fifty men were all executed.

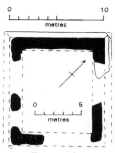

Emper: plan

Fore Abbey

EMPER   N274619

The Dalton's tower is now very fragmentary and defaced, although the north corner still stands 10m high, showing that the third storey was thinly walled. It measured about 12m by 10m above a broad battered base and there are indications that the basement had a longitudinal crosswall to carry vaults. Footings of a later wing extend to the SE.

FORE   N516704 & 511708, etc

Two archways remain of the east and west gates of the town defences. The west gate has a murder hole and the east gate has the base of a spiral stair to the lost upper room. There is no certain evidence that the defences were more substantial than a palisaded bank and ditch, although a murage grant of Edward III's reign provided for building a wall of stone. A tower house named Christian's castle lay 100m east beyond the east gateway, and a further 200m NE of there lie the motte and bailey earthworks of Hugh de Lacy's castle on the slope of Ben of Fore, occupied by King John in August 1210. The Benedictine abbey is a compact group of four ranges set around a small cloister. As remodelled in the 15th century it was made defensible, despite lying at the foot of a rocky crag upon which lies a dovecote. There are crossloops in the NE stair turret of the tower at the west end of the church, and there is a bellcote upon the tower over the sacristy between the choir of the church and the east range. A latrine turret adjoins this tower and there is another latrine turret projecting from the west range.

Fore: gates

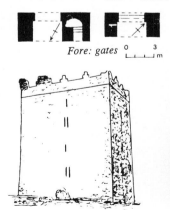

Donore Castle

Emper Castle

HEATHSTOWN   N532487

Defaced walls remain 7m high of a tower measuring 10.7m by 8.1m over walls 1.4m thick, now lacking its SE corner. There is evidence of two parallel longitudinal vaults.

HILLTOWN   N494754

In the yard of the 18th century house remain the lowest storey and a higher fragment of the SE corner of a round-cornered tower measuring 13.3m by 11.7m. There is a doorway and blocked stair in the south wall, a fireplace in the north wall and a double-splayed loop in the west wall, from the northern part of which projects a square turret.

KILBRIDE   N441439

Very ruined, and partly obscured by vegetation and a collapsing galvanised roof, this is an impressive remnant of a large and massively walled building of uncertain date about 29m long by 13m wide with a straight staircase in the south wall, which is over 3m thick. Another stair descends in the projecting SW corner to a postern in the west end wall, whilst there were latrines in the SE corner and mural chambers in a NE corner turret.

KILLAGH   N577575   D

Square turrets project from the north and south ends of the west wall of a ruined and overgrown tower 8.8m long by about 6.5m wide with a vaulted basement and two upper storeys. The blocked entrance doorway towards the north end of the east side now faces towards an 18th century house. The spiral stair beside the entrance is incomplete.

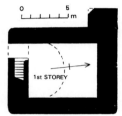

Hilltown; plan

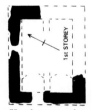

Heathstown: plan

Kiltober Castle

Killeenbrack Castle

Kilbride Castle

KILLEENBRACK   N236471

Gunloops open off the window embrasures of the lowest level of this four storey tower measuring 10.8m by 8m. The third storey has a fireplace in the north wall and there were mullioned windows in all the upper levels. The east wall has a gable over the outer wallface and contained mural chambers (now very ruined) over the entrance passage and the spiral stair occupied the SE corner. Only the southern corners and the lower parts of the west wall remain of a later two storey south wing 13.2m long by 8.8m wide. The south wall formed part of a surrounding bawn 52m by 42m, the SW corner of which still survives with a circular flanker and the 3m high adjoining walls.

KILTOBER   N394327

A very ruined and overgrown tower by a farm has a crosswall supporting two vaults and a latrine chute on the SE side. The semi-circular stair turret standing two storeys high is probably a later addition, as is the closely surrounding bawn wall, now just footings.

LARAGH   N263415   C

A D-shaped bawn platform 28m across extends 20m to the south of the two storey high 12m long south wall 1.8m thick of a McGeoghegan tower beside a public road. See p152.

LOUGH SEWDY   N221499

The island of Eilean Mor is mentioned as a crannog in 11th and 12th century annals. Hugh de Lacy's motte of 1184 on a former peninsular on the south side of the lough probably was a refortification of an O'Melaghlin fort on the site. Edward Bruce spent Christmas there in 1315, and the position was garrisoned by the English in 1641 and by the Jacobites in 1690. Near here in 1648 Eoghan Rua O'Neill and the Ulster Catholics, marching to relieve Athy, defeated a force under the Earl of Ormond.

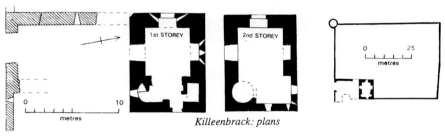

Killeenbrack: plans

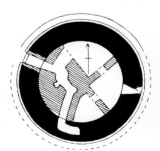

Plan of Low's Castle

Low's Castle

Laragh Castle

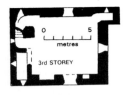

Martinstown: plans

Newcastle: plans

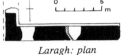

Laragh: plan

Moate Castle

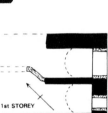

Newcastle: plan

LOW'S CASTLE   N382370   D

This castle is named after the Low family, who were granted the Maddens' estate here in the 1650s. Set on a mound, it consists of a circular building 13.2m in diameter over walling 2.2m thick above broad battered base. It could be a 13th century keep (originally with only an upper entrance) cut down in the 16th or 17th century to its present height of 7m and provided with a new pointed-arched entrance at ground level and a set of internal crosswalls creating three cellars, two of them vaulted, and one using an original outer loop. There is also a tortuous passage rising up from the entrance to the platform over the vaults. It clearly did not provide any living accommodation in its later phase, but there are traces of buildings to the NW and a thinly walled bawn extended to the SW.

MARTINSTOWN   N606604   D

A turret 2m wide containing latrines on the second and third storeys and facing towards a huge natural boulder projects 1.2m from the north end of the east end wall of a badly cracked tower 10.4m by 8.4m above a battered base. From the south facing entrance a straight stair in the west wall leads past a doorway into the vaulted second storey and onto the third storey, which has a fireplace on the south, a mural chamber in the SW corner, three windows, and another stair in the west wall to the top storey.

Newcastle

Newcastle

Martinstown Castle

MOATE   N188384   D

Moate is named after Richard Tuite's motte of the 1190s on the south side of the main road. To the NW, on the north side of the road, lies a much altered tower occupied by the O'Melaghlins until they were forfeited for rebellion in 1596. It was purchased and repaired in the 1650s by Captain John Clibborn, and in the 1730s James Clibborn added another range to the west over the entrance of which is reset sheela-na-gig. An outbuilding has a cusped lancet with dished spandrels taken from a nearby church.

NEWCASTLE   N416751   D

This tower measuring 8.6 by 7.6m may have been built under the terms of the 1429 act of Parliament allowing a £10 grant for the construction of such buildings. From the east facing entrance a straight stair in the south wall leads up past a doorway to the vaulted second storey with angle loops in the northern corners and on to the third storey, from which another stair leads to the fourth storey and wall-walk. The SE corner contains a mural chamber at third storey level. There are no fireplaces or latrines.

NEWCASTLE   N422395

The SE end of this seat of the O'Melaghlins granted to James Stopford in 1640 appears to have been a 13th century hall-house 15.2m long by 10.2m wide over a battered base which contained just one main room over a pair of vaults supported upon a longitudinal crosswall which was probably a later insertion. The whole of the northern corner and adjoining walls and that end of the vaults are missing. Just part of the SW wall and a projecting wing or turret remain of a later extension to the NW.

PORTLICK   N063504

After the attainder of Garret Dillon in 1696 this tower was granted to Thomas Knightly, but it later reverted to the Crown and was sold to Robert Smyth. His descendants added a two storey wing in the 18th century and then a new castellated front block was erected in 1860 for Robert Ralph Smyth. Of that period are the small mullioned windows in the old tower. It retains, however a machicolation over the entrance and four turrets at the top.

RATHWIRE   N566513

There are buried footings of stone buildings destroyed in 1450 by the MacGeoghegans within the bailey of Hugh de Lacy's motte and bailey castle. Negotiations held here between King John and Cathal Crovderg O'Conor came to nother since Cathal had failed to bring his son Aedh to John as a hostage. The manor was granted to John D'Arcy of Platten in 1336 but was probably occupied by tenants.

RATTIN   N552441   C

As originally built probably in the 15th century this tower measured 9.9m square over walls 1.6m thick except on the NE side where a thickness of 2.2m was required to accommodate a stair rising up from an entrance doorway facing SE. There were five storeys, the third level being a low loft under an unusually wide vault, now gone. In a 16th century remodelling the tower was given a new battered base and extended at the SE to provide a tier of mural chambers there and a new entrance, thus increasing its basal dimensions to 13.8m by 11m. In the 17th century the castle was held by Nicholas D'Arcy of Platten but it may originally have been built by a tenant of the D'Arcy family.

SCURLOCKSTOWN   N569667   C

Part remains of the east wall of a de Lacy tower with a 9m high circular SE stair turret. There are traces of a second turret at the NE corner.

0   5
metres

Syonan: plan

Rattin Castle

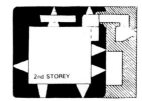

2nd STOREY

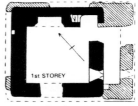

1st STOREY

Rattin: plans

Simonstown Castle

Syonan Castle

SIMONSTOWN   N453446

A battered base has been added to the SW wall of a building originally measuring 14m by 7.6m. A stair in the NW end wall leads from the vaulted basement to just one upper storey, possibly subdivided into two rooms and having a latrine in the west corner.

SYONAN   N280401   C

Two ogival-headed lancets now reset in the tower at Tyrrelspass were recently taken from this four storey McGeoghegan tower measuring 9.5m by 7m which existed by 1566. The east wall contains the lobby of the original blocked entrance and a spiral stair in the SE corner. The second storey has a vault and a fireplace in the south wall. The third storey also has a fireplace on the south side, and a latrine in the NW corner.

TAGHMON   N485616   B   (Church)

Part of a possible bawn wall remains to the south of a corner turret 5.8m long by 3.9m wide of a building of unknown date or character. The turret has a straight stair leading up from one end of a tiny vaulted cellar to two upper storeys. To the SE, beyond the public road, lies the well-preserved 15th century fortified church of St Munna measuring 19.8m by 8.2m above a battered base and having a four storey tower at the west end of a single chamber with a vault and its own battlements. The tower contains two vaults and has double-splayed basement loops and the church just narrow cusped lancets. It stair lies in the NE corner, close to the only doorway into the church.

0   10
metres

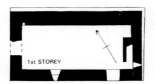

Taghmon   *Scurlockstown: plan*   Simonstov *Plans of Simonstown Castle*

1st STOREY

2nd STOREY

Tullynally Castle

TULLYNALLY   N442704

An early 17th century house here was granted to Captain Henry Pakenham in 1655. The family became Barons Longford in 1756 and were later given an earldom, the house remaining their seat until 1961. It was remodelled in the 1780s and then in 1801-6 the 2nd Earl had it castellated with Gothick details. Further work on the building it was done in 1839 and consequently little or nothing now remains of the original building.

TYRRELSPASS   N412375   H

Dendrochronological tests upon an oak floor beam over the lowest level of this tower built by the Tyrrel family suggested a construction date of 1410. During the 1980s it was restored from a derelict state by Laurence Ginnell, and on the south side are ogival-headed lancets then brought from the castle of Syonan, whilst three two-light windows came from the ruined church at Kilbeggan. The SE end contains a tier of small rooms over the entrance and the spiral stair. There are five storeys, with a pointed vault over the second level, and there are double-stepped battlements and two circular bartizans. A modern wing is hidden away at the back. Adjoining the tower on the SE is a circular flanker of the former bawn. Near here in 1597 Richard Tyrrel and Piers Lacy ambushed and destroyed an English force under Christopher Barnewall.

Tyrrelspass Castle

Doorway at Tyrellspass

OTHER CASTLES IN COUNTY WESTMEATH

ADAMSTOWN N325452 Footings in NE part of enclosure with stoney bank and ditch.
ARDNAGRAGH N134464 20m long east wall and other footings of Dillon castle.
BALTRASNA N475506 Three storey tower 9.8m by 7.8m partly rebuilt in brick in 18th
century adjoins two storey SE range of that period. No stairs or vaults.
BALLYLOUGHLOE N152419 De Lacy motte destroyed by the O'Melaghlins in 1208.
BALLYNACLIFFY N083527 Footings on knoll beside earthwork complex.
BALLYNAKILL N084496 Two walls of tower basement. Traces of barrel-vault and loops.
BALROWAN N546515 Small 2m fragment of tower near modern house.
BIGWOOD N454775 Only fallen fragments remain amongst vegetation.
BOARDSTOWN N451515 One defaced and overgrown wall of tower 5m high behind
stableyard. Evidence of a vault and blocked doorway.
BRACKNAHEVLA N266451 2m high fragment at SW end of oval enclosure.
BROCKAGH N440576 3m SW wall & footings of round-cornered tower of uncertain date.
BROTTENSTOWN N353524 Lower parts of building 18m by 8m with wing on SE side.
BUNOWN N083476 Two storey building with blocked pointed-headed doorway on south.
CARN N291464 Corners of tower 9m by 7m stand up to 6m high.
CASTLETOWN GEOGHEGAN N342438 Fragments of thin bawn wall by derelict cottage.
CLONCULLEN N538527 Pile of debris marks the site of a tower.
CLONLONAN N159368 Ivy-covered 7m high west wall of O'Malaghlin tower by farm.
COOLALOUGH N295377 NW corner stands 7m high, but the rest is only 0.5m high.
CORCLOON N491441 Except for the collapsed NE wall, this tower
stands 4m high and has a doorway facing SW.
CORREAGH N296359 Minor fragments and a pile of debris remain.

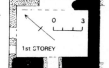

Baltrasna: plan

Scurlockstown Castle   *Baltrasna Castle*

CREEVE N132435 Footings of Magawley tower 8.5m by 6m in northern part of circular platform 34m across.

CREGGAN N076397 Footings and pile of rubble of O'Brien tower.

CROUGHMALL N317491 Pile of debris and one fallen fragment of tower.

DERVOTSOWN N657654 SE corner turret stands three storeys high. Other fragments also remain.

DUNDONNELL N347504 Enclosure with footings of building.

DUNEEL N243506 Fragments of tower up to 2m high beside farm.

DUNEGAN N167410 6m high west wall and part of north wall of Magawley tower 10m by 9m. Latrine chute at SW corner. Occupied by Homans from 1650. Burnt in 1826.

EDMONDSTOWN N555542 Tower 7.2m by 6.4 partly 3m high but lacking north wall.

FARNAGH N157382 9m long and 5m high fragment of tower.

GARRYCASTLE N070406 4m high fragment of SW wall with part of large fireplace and footings of O'Brien tower 15m long by 9m wide.

KILBIXIE N315629 Traces of shell wall and square base on Geoffrey de Costentin's motte of 1192. Nearby tower with subdivided vaulted basement possible leper-house.

KILFAUGHNY N095505 One wall 11m long and 6m high remains.

KILKENNY WEST N122489 Four storey high SW corner fragment of a Dillon tower.

KILLARE N280484 Motte only remains of Hugh de Lacy's castle of 1184 burnt in 1187.

KILTOOM N442685 Platform 70m by 40m with east end damaged by road.

KNOCKDRIN N455585 6m high tower 7.5m by 5.5m with good quoins by buildings north of house. Patching and openings in brick. Base of second building at 465583.

LYNN N423496 Garden ornament behind house possibly built of old materials.

LOCKARDSTOWN N283503 Fragment 1.5m high and footings of other walls of tower.

MILLCASTLE N470730 Two storey high fragment of NW wall with mural stair. Footings of second tower to the SE.

MONTRATH N412331 The ivy-covered SW and NE corners of a tower stand 9m high.

MORTIMER'S COURT N435668 Rampart and ditch protect NE side of enclosure on east shore of Lough Derravaragh. Minor ruins in west corner.

MULCHANSTOWN N570601 3m high, 5m long fragment of south wall, west wall stub.

MULLINGAR N438529 Courthouse on site of castle of Petits, tenants of Hugh de Lacy. Description of the town in 1682 suggests existence of several urban tower houses.

NUGENT'S N393474 2m high fragment of east wall and two other fragments on motte by Lough Owel.

OLDTOWN N340489 Low and defaced base of tower filled with rubble.

PORTERSTOWN N553505 Footings of one wall by farm.

RATHDRISOGE N335457 5m high fragments of SW and SE walls of building once 40m long on SW side of D- shaped enclosure.

ROBINSTOWN N406445 5m high 12m long wall of tower said to be unfinished.

ROGERSTOWN N330472 7m high fragments of north and south walls and cross-wall of stronghouse 18m long by 9m wide. Traces of vault over second storey of eastern part.

SIMONSTOWN N329552 Short low fragment of walling 1.6m thick.

STREMMINGSTOWN N305462 3m high and 2.4m thick fragment of tower with latrine chute plus fallen fragments and buried footings.

TOGHER N252812 South wall and traces of other sides of tower 7.5m by 6.6m.

TUITESOWN N365517 Base of tower with evidence of staircase to SE of footings of range with dividing walls. Base of third building to NW.

TULLYSTOWN N453806 South and west walls remain in 19th century building behind restored house.

TYRRELSTOWN N444463 6m high fragment of south wall and SW turret incorporated in modern house.

WATERSTOWN N100456 Ivy-covered base of tower on island 42m long by 35m wide.

WILLIAMSTOWN N425702 5m high northern half of round-cornered tower 8.4m long in farmyard.

The north and west bastions survive of a 17th century fort at Finnea N400813.

Carn Castle

CASTLE SITES IN WESTMEATH

Archerstown N596675, Balleagny N346539, Ballinacarrow N306513, Ballinaspick N249447, Ballinderry N209398, Ballintue N303591, Ballybroder N357318, Ballycahillaroe N141374, Ballyclogher N265457, Ballycorkey N311638, BallymacHugh N374362, Ballynacor N592599, Ballynafearagh N345520, Ballynagall N440589, Ballynahow N097335 Ballynahown N097335, Ballynalack N349647, Baltrasna N175382, Barbavilla N521652 Barradrum N337703, Baskin High N186482, Baskin Low N180488, Bracklin N603582, Bunanagh N294436, Carrick N414462, Castletown N445784, Catherinestown N463480, Clonarney N612658, Cloonbonny No74834, Colava N394671, Conlanstown N295603, Cooksborough N504544, Coola N338357, Coollamber N352735, Coosan N045440, Coyne N322479, Creeve N289441, Crosserdree N539593, Cullenhugh N351630, Culvin N340684, Cumminstown N356367, Cushinstown N573499, Dardistown N570582 & 568575, Davidstown N310553, Drumcree N543659, Dunnamona N148496, Dysart N383463, Farrow N363615, Farthingstown N294530, Fennor N542603, Finnea N403815, Garrynafela N056443, Gaybrook N461458 & 465464, Gigginstown N529615, Glascarn N334527, Glomerstown N336466, Griffithstown N565464, Hightown N543476, Hiskinstown N571593, Hogan N112516, Hopestown N393518, Irishtown N420546, Johnstown N542674, Kilgawny N273541, Killadoughan N573645 & 575644, Killbillaghan N105352, Killinure N066472, Killynan N518573, Kinnegad N600453, Kilpatrick N520636, Kinturk N462697, Knockmany N535510, Knockycosker N368398, Lackan N380653, Ladestown N401490 & (bawn) N401483, Laragh N319579 & 322568, Laughanstown N429595, Lismagree N271417, Lisnabin N553530, Littletown N096517, Loughan N310518, Lissanode N174453, Lynn N423496, Magheramore N145386, Milltown N304546, Milltown N501438, Mosstown N262458, Moyvore N243539, Moyvoughly N197439, Newdown N511519, Newtown N634679, Paddinstown N277573, Pakenhamhall N444705 & 445705, Piercefield N368598, Piercetown N216564, Raharney N600531, Rathaspick N301653, Rathcaled N265577, Rathganny N396637, Rathskeagh N254489, Rathtrim N319535, Rowlandstown N274557, Shinglis N214513, Simonstown N327549, Streamstown N276428, Tevrin N533579, Tromra N453720, Tubotstown N421728, Tullaghin N412558, Wardenstown N597514, Williamstown N242571, Williamstown N562593.

MOTTES AND RINGWORKS

Ballybrickoge N237429, Ballyglass N318535, Ballyharney N359658, Ballymorin N282520, Ballynacarrow N310502, Balreagh N514600, Banagher N537502, Boherquill N660724, Bredah N315404, Camagh N395759, Carnakilla N060490, Castlelost N450413, Castletown N442794, Castletown Geoghegan N342438, Coolnagun N360724, Coolvuck N111441, Dromore N315416, Drumraney N170488, Dunnamona N144500, Gallstown N481431, Glebe* N489612, Gneevebeg N314404, Griffinstown N567477, Kenny N359527, Kerinstown* N332514, Kilbride N515442, Killagh N579575, Killare N280248, Killucan N566514, Kilpatrick N515642, Knockdommy N158399, Labaun 152418, Mount Temple N150421, Multifarnham N404640, Porterstown N537502, Portlick N060490, Rathconnell N468550, Rathcreevagh N450741, Rathin N318535, Rathskeagh N249495, Rathwire N566513, Russagh N327683, Tinnode N336703, Tonashammer N502766, Tuitestown N359926, Williamstown N561599.

CASTLES OF COUNTY WEXFORD

ADAMSTOWN   S869284

A ruined tower house 9.3m by 9m lies in the north corner of a scarped enclosure 40m square which lies within another scarped platform 70m by 60m which was once a walled bawn. Built into the nearby farmhouse is a plaque from the bawn gateway proclaiming that the castle was built by Nicholas Devereaux in 1556. The tower north corner is missing but the other corners have gunloops off the vaulted cellar. A stair covered by a murder hole leads up from a destroyed entrance facing NE. A spiral stair in the east corner connected three upper levels, the lower two of which have fireplaces and windows with gunloops, one third storey window being of two lights. See page 162.

ARTRAMON   T036262   D

This tower house of the Roche family later passed to the Mastersons. It measures 8.5m by 8m and has a cellar and loft under a vault and two upper levels, the uppermost now having a later brick vault. One corbel remains of a parapet-level machicolation over the entrance in the south wall, the west jamb of which is missing. Straight stairs in the south and east walls connect all the levels. Only the third storey has a fireplace. There are latrines in the NW corner. Some of the upper windows (which are small where they survive) have embrasure seats.

1st STOREY   2nd STOREY   3rd STOREY   3rd STOREY   1st STOREY

0   5 metres

Ballyconnor: plans   *Baldwinstown: plans*

Artramon Castle   *Baldwinstown Castle*

BALDWINSTOWN   S971104

This badly cracked tower is thought to have been held by the Keatings until they were dispossessed in 1654. It measures 9.5m by 8m and had a cellar with double-splayed loops and a loft under a vault, three upper storeys, and an attic within the roof. The west wall contains the entrance (with a portcullis groove) and a lower stair. The loft has a chamber over the entrance. The next two levels are linked by a stair in the north wall and have latrines in the SE corner and fireplaces in the south wall. Spiral stairs in the NE corner then lead to the top room and a wall-walk with stepped battlements. Of a bawn extending towards a stream to the west there remains only a short 5m high wall from the tower south wall to a 7m high SE corner turret 3.5m in diameter, solid except at wall-walk level.

BALLYCOGLY   T038112

The tower of the Wadding family here is first mentioned in 1585. It measures 10.9m by 7.9m and had a cellar with one double-splayed loop and a loft under a vault and three upper storeys reached by stairs rising in the east and north walls from a destroyed entrance at the east end of the south wall. There are hidden chambers in the north wall level with the vault. The room over the vault has a north window with an ogival head, and the room above has a north window of two lights with seats. These levels both had fireplaces in the east wall, but the only latrine is in the west wall of the loft. The top room only has one slit window. There is a turret over the spiral stair to the wall-walk in the NW corner. East and west gables remain within the wall-walk.

BALLYCONOR   T118106

On the north side of a bawn 34m by 24m is a building which may have been a church of St Nicholas, and on the east side is a tower house 7m square partly standing up to 8m high with a house of similar width extending 17m north of it. The house east wall is missing but the west wall retains a doorway, gunloop, and a window with four ogee-headed lights, and the north wall has a blocked fireplace. From details on a lost datestone it appears that the house and bawn were added to an older tower in 1570 by Dionisius Stafford and his wife Katherine Synnott. The tower has a north facing doorway with a portcullis groove and has a number of blocked gunloops and several recesses in the vaulted cellar. The loft under the vault has a chamber over the entrance and firing loops facing east. There are more gunloops from the room over the vault reached by a spiral stair in the NE corner. The upper storeys of the tower were removed in the 19th century.

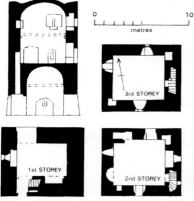

Artramon: plans & section

Ballyconor Castle

Ballyfarnoge Castle

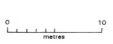

0 _____ 10
metres

Ballyhack Castle

Adamstown: plan   *Ballyfarnoge: plans*

BALLYFARNOGE   S709186

This tower was confiscated from Edmund Prendergast in 1654. It measures 7.4m square and had a cellar and loft under a vault and two upper storeys. From a doorway in the west wall stairs lead up in the north wall to a lintel-roofed passage in the east wall from which there was access to the top storey (now covered by a later brick vault) and (via a hatchway in the passage roof) to the wall-walk. The room over the original vault has a tiny fireplace on the south, a latrine in the SE corner, a chamber in the NW corner, a recess covering the entrance, and a passage through the north wall, probably to give access to the wall-walk of a later house, the roof-mark of which can be seen.

BALLYHACK   S706109   E

The tower here belonged to the Knights Hospitallers of Kilcloggan and on their suppression in 1541 passed to the Etchingham family. It measures 10.7m by 9.8m and has a cellar and loft under a vault and three upper storeys. The rectangular doorway on the SW is protected by a machicolation opening off the top room. The loft has a chamber in the NE wall with access via a hatch into another chamber below. The same wall contains chambers and latrines at the next two levels and a chapel with a piscina, aumbry and shelf-altar at the fourth storey level, which is reached by a spiral stair in the east corner. The fourth and fifth levels have windows with single and paired lights with ogival heads. The parapet is missing but corbels remain of a former bartizan on the southern corner.

Ballyhealy Castle

Ballykeerogemore: plan

Ballykeerogemore Castle

BALLYHEALY T004056 C

The Cheevers family held Ballyhealy from the 13th century until at least the mid 17th century. Their tower measures 10.3m by 7.8m and has been remodelled as a modern dwelling and the parapet (but possibly not the corner lookouts) has been rebuilt. Two of the six embrasures in the cellar are for double-splayed loops. A stair rises in the west wall from the round-headed south-facing entrance past a doorway to the loft and up to the room over the vault, which has a fireplace and slop-stone on the north, a latrine at the NE, windows of two cusped ogival-headed lights facing east and north, and a modern window facing south. A second stair in the west wall rises to another similar room above, and on to a fifth storey with simple slit-windows facing north, east and south.

BALLYKEEROGEMORE S725174 D

Doorway at Artramon

A two storey house probably of 17th century date lying on the west side of an earlier bawn 28m by 22m formed the main seat of the descendants of Robert FitzStephen's follower Roger de Sutton. Only the west and south walls, with projecting chimney breasts, remains of the 7m wide house. At the NW corner is a flanker about 6m by 5m with musket loops on each of three storeys, the upper two levels having been reached from the wall-walk. Of the bawn itself most of the east wall still stands 4m high, but the 6.3m diameter SE flanker collapsed in the 1970s. The 2m thick lower walls were able to contain stairs curving within the thickness up to a second storey and then another stair rose to serve two further upper storeys.

Bargy Castle

Ballyteige Castle

BALLYTEIGE   S967044   C

The original seat of the Whittys here was burnt by Art Mac Murrough Kavanagh in 1408 and the existing tower and bawn may be about a century later. The bawn measures 30m by 22m internally and has an entrance with a machicolation in the south wall, which stands complete with a wall-walk 8m above the court. The wall only stands 4m high on the west and north sides but retains circular turrets about 5m in diameter on the NW and NE corners. The 9m high NW turret has four storeys with separate entrances to the two lowest levels. The 7m high NE turret is 7m high and has three storeys, the lowest of which contains a well. The tower house measuring 10.5m by 7.8m in the SE corner of the bawn has a north-facing entrance protected by a machicolation which leads through a lobby into a cellar with five embrasures. The loft under the vault has an inserted west window with a square hoodmould. A stair covered by murder holes in the north wall rises to a passage in the east wall giving access to the hall over the vault and to a latrine in the projecting SE corner. This corner contains other latrines higher up and is surmounted by a lookout rising higher than the other corners. The hall fireplace is blocked and the window embrasures facing north and south are damaged. The windows of the fourth and fifth storeys are also either blocked or damaged. There was a sixth storey attic room with a passage through the east wall, which rises higher than the other walls.

BALLYTORY   T091077

The French family held Ballytory from at least the mid 13th century until the forfeiture of Nicholas French by the Cromwellians in 1654. Incorporated in the existing house is a tower with a pointed-headed doorway, the usual battered base, and two loops.

Barntown Castle

Bawn at Ballyteige

BARGY   T030088

A wooden panel inside the inhabited three storey house measuring 18m by 9m bears the date 1591. It was probably built by the Rossiters, from whom it was confiscated in 1654 and given to the Harvey family. The segmental-arched doorway is surmounted by a hoodmould, an heraldic panel and machicolation. This end of the building rises up one stage higher with a still higher turret facing SW. The two storey south wing with stepped battlements and round bartizans on the SE and NE corners is probably an early 17th century addition. The building was altered in the 19th century when many new windows were inserted.

BARNTOWN   T000216

This ivy-covered tower, which existed by 1562 and was confiscated from Robert Roche in 1654, measures 7.9m by 6.6m and contained a cellar and loft under a vault which has fallen, and three upper storeys once connected by a spiral stair in the SE corner. The third and fourth storey rooms had fireplaces in the west wall, where there is a projecting breast, and latrines in the NW corner. The east facing entrance protected by a machicolation has been rebuilt. The lobby within had a murder-hole.

BARRYSTOWN   S854118

The tower was forfeited by the Barrys in 1654. It measures 8m by 7m and has a pointed-headed entrance and staircase in the west wall. The cellar is well provided with musket-loops and has one covering the entrance lobby, which also has a murder-hole. There is a loft under the vault, above which nothing now survives.

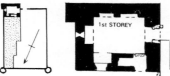

Ballyteige: plans   *Barntown: plan*   *Barrystown: plan*

BORRISHAMON   S962574

A platform 30m by 25m was once enclosed by a wall and a wet moat up to 8m wide. On the NE is the lower part of a small gatehouse with one hinge stone of a drawbridge. The site seems to have already been ruinous by the early 17th century.

BROWNSWOOD   S978355   C

Parts of the east and south walls of a tower of the Brownes of Mulrankin stand three storeys high and include a hidden chamber within what remains of the vault. There are alcoves for gunloops in the SE corner and east wall and windows higher up.

BRYANSTOWN   S820179

Within the house is a small tower built by the Roches, which passed to John Isham in 1546, but which has back in Roche hands by 1640. It has a cellar and loft (with one original window) under a vault and two upper storeys now modified to form one room. There is a blocked staircase in a projecting NE corner turret.

Butlerstown: plans

Castletown: plan

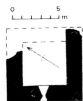

Ballyhire: plan

Doorway at Butlerstown

Butlerstown Castle

Brownswood Castle

BUTLERSTOWN T044088 D

This tower was confiscated from the Butlers in 1654. Recently re-roofed with rebuilt gables, but without a full set of floors, it measures 9.7m by 8.6m over walls averaging 2.3m thick in the cellar, which has one double-splayed loop and embrasures for two more now gone. The north wall contains the round-arched entrance with a portcullis groove and machicolation, and also the stairs, covered at the bottom by a murder hole from a room opening off the loft under the vault. The room above has windows with seats facing west, north and south, a fireplace on the north, and chambers in the SE and SW corners, the latter being a latrine. A stair in the east wall leads up to a room with a similar layout, except that the mural chamber is at the NE corner, since the SE corner contains a spiral stair to the fifth storey, which has a small window in each wall. The stair continues to the wall-walk, ending in a turret with three ogival-headed loops which was originally timber-roofed. One of the east-facing stepped merlons of the parapet has a crossloop.

CASTLEBORO S870370

William Leigh sold this stronghouse to Robert Carew in 1669, although it had belonged to James Butler in 1640. It measures 15m by 9m and has the entrance at the north end. All three storeys have later windows, a stair tower has been added on the east side, and the only fireplaces lie at the south end on the top storey. There was also an attic. The SW corner has a top turret and the SE corner has a turret corbelled out from a lower level. The lowest level was originally vaulted.

CASTLETOWN T112049

Only the cellar and loft under the vault remain of a tower owned by the Codds until 1712. The doorway facing east is lintelled and has an upper hinge socket remaining for the yett. The cellar retains three double-splayed loops.

CLONARD T121199

Now forming part of a cowshed, and lacking the west wall which contained the entrance, is the 7.9m wide tower surviving as high as the vault over the cellar and loft. The loft retains one window. The Suttons of Clonard were forfeited in 1654. See page 168.

Castletown Castle

Clonard Castle

Clonmines Courthouse

CLONMAHON   S933545

Footings of a wall beside a quarry remain of a bawn described in 1610 as having two towers. The castle was granted to Thomas Masterson in the 16th century and was rebuilt in 1625 by Sir George Calvert.

CLONMINES   S844130

The abandoned town of Clonmines on the west bank of the Owenduff river has a remarkable group of embattled buildings. The town was not walled but has traces of a modest ditch isolating its west side. The Black Castle is a tower house 9.8m by 8m probably built by the FitzHenrys. It has a cellar and loft under a vault and three upper levels, the lowest of them reached by a stair in the south wall rising from a west facing doorway protected by an external machicolation and an internal murder-hole. This room and the one above each had a fireplace on the north, a latrine in the NE corner, and a small chamber in the SE corner.

The Augustinian Friary seems to have been fortified with the addition of a bawn north of it, perhaps part of the enlargement by Nicholas FitzNicholas in 1385. Fragments remain of a bawn wall with a wall-walk, off which were reached the upper levels of a tall tower about 4.2m square at the NW corner. The bawn has two west doorways and a south-facing gatehouse with a portcullis groove adjoining the nave west wall. From it there was access to a wall-walk upon the south aisle. South of the friary is a farmhouse incorporating an altered tower 6.4m square on the west side of a walled court. The Suttons occupied this tower until 1849. SE of this building lies the 7m high gable of a Jacobean house of one main storey with bedrooms in the roof. It has remains of a bartizan on the SW corner.

West of the farmhouse and friary is a graveyard containing a ruined church with a west tower with a vaulted lowest level which may have been defensible. The church itself is much ruined but the tower still has two upper rooms. Standing very closeby to the NE is an embattled building 11.4m by 7.7m, which seems to have been a church once fitted with a piscina, although also sometimes described as an ecclesiastical court house. It contains a single room with a rib-vault at the east end and a barrel vault at the west end, where there was a gallery reached by a spiral stair in the NW corner, which is continued up as a turret, adjoining which is a machicolation on pyramidal corbelling protecting a doorway below with a drawbar slot. There is a second unprotected doorway on the north side. There are east and south windows of two lights and two other narrower windows.

Black Castle, Clonmines

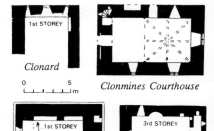

Clonard

Clonmines Courthouse

Black Castle, Clonmines: plans

Clougheast Castle

CLOUGHEAST   T120056   C

This tower built by the Codd family measures 8.7m by 7m and has a cellar with three double-splayed loops and a room in the NE corner. The north wall contains the pointed-headed doorway with a machicolation and portcullis groove. The entrance lobby is commanded by a murder hole from a chamber opening off the loft under the vault. Opening off the embrasure of the loft west window is an L-shaped room in the SW corner. The room above has three rectangular windows with hinge sockets for shutters, a latrine in the north wall, and rooms in the other walls, that on the south having access via hatch to a prison below. A stair in the south wall rises to the fourth storey, which has a latrine on the west side and four windows, that on the east side being of two lights under a square hoodmould. Both these levels had fireplaces in the north wall. The fifth storey only has slit windows. Above there is a gallery in the west wall to give access to the attic room and the northern section of the wall-walk surrounding it. There are pigeon nesting-boxes in the attic gables. There are stepped battlements and a turret over the NW corner.

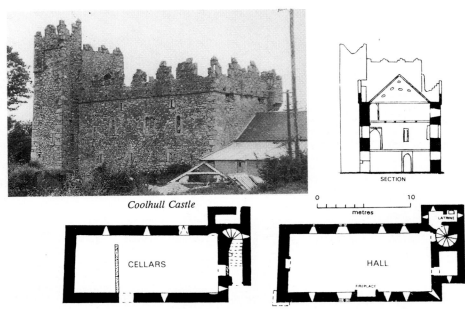

Coolhull Castle

SECTION

CELLARS

HALL

0   10
metres

LATRINE

FIREPLACE

Plans & section of Coolhull Castle

COOLHULL   S885099   C

No history is recorded for this interesting fortified house measuring 17.6m by 8.6m with gunloops in a bartizan on the SW corner. The east end wall is thickened for most of its length to contain the entrance (with a machicolation) in a SW corner re-entrant angle, a spiral stair reached from it, and two small rooms higher up. This part of the building rises high above the stepped battlements of the rest, its battlements being reached by a secondary SE corner stair, and it has an even higher extension beyond the north wall to contain latrines. The main block contained a hall nearest the stair and a private room beyond, set over dark cellars, and having low and poorly lighted bedrooms above. The hall has five loops, including one in the SE corner covering the approach to the entrance, a fireplace on the south side, and a pair of windows opposite each other with pairs of round-arched lights. The private room has a small fireplace but only two small windows.

COURTHOYLE   S820249

In 1654 Nicholas Devereux held this tower probably built by the Walshes. The entrance was probably in the destroyed east wall. The vault has collapsed and nothing remains of the upper levels. The cellar has several long loops, the loft has one window, and the destroyed spiral stair in the SE corner retains one crossloop.

CULLENSTOWN   S876086   D

An earth bank marks the west and north sides of a bawn 64m by over 40m around a tower measuring 8.6m by 7m built by the Cullen family which has been modified into a house, everything over the room over the vault having been destroyed. The north wall contains the entrance and stairs up to a loft with two windows. A NE corner spiral stair then led to the upper levels and a passage in the east wall to a latrine. The room over the vault has a fireplace on the south and windows with seats on the south and west.

DANES CASTLE S865116

The name is derived from the Denne family, owners in
the 13th century, although the existing building may be
the work of the Cheevers family. The tower measures
8.3m by 6.2m and has a north doorway with a
machicolation and an east doorway with a murder-hole.
The other sides of the cellar have double-splayed loops.
From the east entrance lobby stairs covered by murder-
holes rise in the east and north walls to a loft with two
windows and onto the hall over the vault. This room has
a latrine in the NW corner, windows with seats facing
east, south and west, and a fireplace in the north wall,
which also contains a spiral stair to the fourth storey.

Deeps Castle

That level has a windows facing east and west and a fireplace on the west, plus a latrine.
The fifth storey has windows facing east and west. There seems to have been a turret
over the top of the stairs in the NW corner but the battlements have been destroyed.

DEEPS S981272

On the east bank of the River Slaney is a ruined stronghouse probably built by the
Devereux family in the early 17th century. It measures 14.7m by 11m over walls 1.6m
thick, except that the SE wall is thickened to 2m to contain stairs rising from a doorway
with a drawbar slot at the south end of it. There were originally vaults over two rooms at
ground level and the one served by this entrance may perhaps have been a kitchen since
it has a deep fireplace in a projecting breast surmounted by high chimney stacks. The
other lower room had its own separate entrance, later converted into a loop, and access
to a spiral stair rising the full height of the building in a turret projecting from the NE wall
at the east corner. The hall above has a central fireplace in the NW wall, flanked on either
side by large mullioned windows , one blocked and the other damaged by the destruction
of the north corner, which is now closed off by a modern wall. The level above had several
large windows and possibly three latrines. It was probably divided into three rooms,
perhaps with a SE corridor.

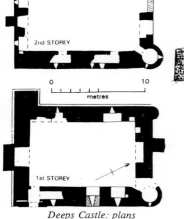

Deeps Castle

Deeps Castle: plans

Danes Castle

DUNBRODY   S713149   E

Three (out of an original four) gables with projecting chimneys remain of a stronghouse of two storeys and an attic begun by John Etchingham but probably left unfinished when the 1641 rebellion broke out. The house lay in the east end of a bawn 33m long by 13.5m wide with round corner towers with gunloops. A brick outbuilding lay along the west and south sides of the bawn. The crossing and chancel of the nearby Cistercian abbey shows signs of having been adapted as a manor house sometime after the dissolution.

DUNCANNON FORT   S728082   E

There are no remains of the original tower house and bawn held by John Etchingham in 1508, originally held by the Whites. Strengthening of the promontory against artillery was mooted in 1552 but not executed until the 1580s and 90s, when outer ramparts with flanking bastions were provided, the original parts repaired, and a barrack block added. The ramparts were widened and stone faced in 1611. The fort withstood a siege by Confederate Catholics from December 1641 to February 1642. The garrison declared its

support for the English Parliament in 1644 and was captured by the Catholics in March 1645 after a two month siege. The fort was attacked by Cromwellian forces late in 1649. It surrendered in August 1650 to Samuel Cooke. James II is said to have left the fort for Kinsale and then fled to France, it being surrendered to the Williamites in July 1690. A new seaward battery was made at the west end in 1724 and most of what remains of the rest is of 18th and 19th century date, a garrison being maintained here until 1857. The buildings were burnt by the IRA in 1921 but were renovated for further occupation by the Irish army during World War II.

Dungulph Castle

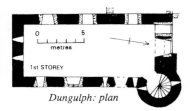

Dungulph: plan

Dunbrody Castle

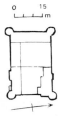

Dunbrody: plan

DUNGULPH   S779075

The three storey fortified house of the Whitty family is still occupied, having been renovated in 1917. The windows are all modern, as are the battlements with a SW corner bartizan, and the only old features are the segmental-arched doorway protected by a machicolation, and the NE corner stair-turret.

ENNISCORTHY   S973398   H

The Kavanaghs held Enniscorthy from 1328 until 1550 and probably had a castle on this site, which was probably fortified as early as the 13th century, but the present building seems to be mostly the work of Sir Henry Wallop in 1588. However, the irregular layout of the north wall, with a turret corbelled out above the acute NE corner suggests work of an earlier date may survive there. The NW corner has a tower 4m in diameter and the southern corners have more boldly projecting round towers 5m in diameter with loops commanding the entrance set between them. The building measures 14.4m by 11.6m and is subdivided by a later crosswall on each of three unvaulted storeys connected by a stair in the SE tower. There is a projecting chimney stack on the east side. The northern extension with another NW corner tower dates from a remodelling of 1903. The castle now houses the Wexford County Museum.

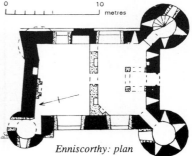

Enniscorthy: plan

Two views of Enniscorthy Castle

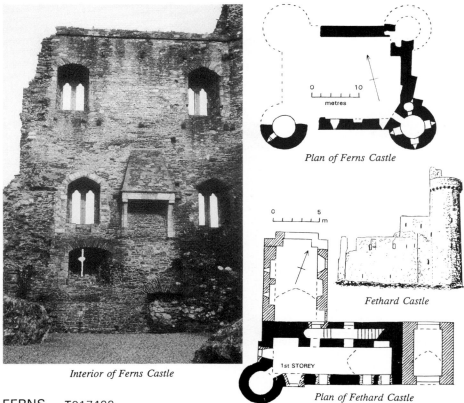

Plan of Ferns Castle

Fethard Castle

Interior of Ferns Castle

1st STOREY

Plan of Fethard Castle

FERNS   T017498

William Marshal had a castle a Ferns and traces of a ringwork have been found, possibly a relic of Dermot MacMurrough's house burnt in 1166. The existing building has upper windows of paired trefoil-headed lights suggesting a mid-13th century date, when Ferns was held by William de Valance, husband of a Marshal heiress. It measures 27m by 23m over walls 2.4m thick above a battered base rising from a rock-cut ditch, part of which was cleared out a few years ago. The internal width is too great to have been floored right across and the probability is that there were three or four ranges with timber-framed inner walls set around a tiny central court acting as a light-well. The lowest level has three crossloops in the south wall. The second storey has a fireplace in the south wall. Of four corner towers 10.5m in diameter the NW one has vanished and not much remains of the NE one, but part of the SW tower stands complete to the top of the parapet, and the SE tower is almost intact, except for the top-coving of the parapet. it contains a rib-vaulted chapel on the third of four storeys connected by a spiral stair.

The castle was captured by the O'Tooles in 1331 but was retaken by Bishop Charnell. It was taken over by the Kavanagh MacMurroughs in 1360 and the surrounding town then quickly declined. John Travers took over the castle for the English crown in 1550, Lord Deputy Grey having captured it during the rebellion of 1536. The Mastersons held the castle from 1583 until it was surrendered to the Cromwellian Sir Charles Coote in 1649. The castle was sold to Thomas Kiernan of Dublin in 1660 and passed to the Donovans, owners until the ruin became an ancient monument in state care.

Ferrycarrig Castle

Ferns Castle

FERRYCARRIG   T014232 & T015232   B

On a cliff above the south bank on the River Slaney, west of the bridge, is a memorial tower within an oval platform 40m by 28m defended on the accessible south side by a rock-cut ditch up to 2m deep and 5m wide. This site is assumed to be that fortified by Robert FitzStephen in 1169, the first Norman castle built in Ireland. Excavations in the 1980s showed that the rampart within the ditch had an internal stone revetment.

Perched on a rock on the north bank of the river, east of the bridge, with its battered base enveloping the crag, is a tower house probably built by the Roche family. It measures 7.3m by 6m and contains a cellar and loft under a vault, and one complete room above with three windows, crossloops at the NW and NE corners, a latrine by the stairs and a fireplace in the south wall. A spiral stair in the NW corner leads to another storey of which only the lower part now remains. The cellar has two double-splayed loops, three gunloops probably inserted later, and a rebuilt south-facing doorway with a murder-hole. Stairs then rise up in the east and north walls.

FETHARD   S794052   B

This building is thought to have been built in the 15th century by the bishop of Ferns. It may have been later held by the Suttons but it was occupied by Nicholas Loftus in 1641, when it was captured by a party of Catholics led by Captain James Downes. It was remodelled in the 19th century and remained occupied into the 20th century. A long block containing a hall 12m long by 4.7m wide over a vaulted cellar adjoins an older gatehouse to the east. A wing, also with a vaulted cellar, extends from the west end of the north wall. A doorway in that wall is protected by a machicolation and gives onto two stairs, one rising direct to the hall. At the SW corner is a 15m high circular tower with a vaulted roof. A spiral stair in a turret rising still higher gives access to the western wall-walk. There was a room over the hall west end. There are ogival-headed windows in the tower and (blocked) in the north wing, which was a slightly later addition with the hall NW latrine destroyed to give access to its upper rooms. To the NE is a motte rising 2m to a top 13m across. There seems to have once been a another stone castle at Fethard, and a turret shown on a map of 1771 may have been a relic of a long-lost town wall.

Hilltown Castle

Kilhile

Kilcloggan

0   3
└──┴──┘ m

Kilmannan

GREATISLAND   S684153

A ditch and rampart isolating the east side of a headland above the River Barrow may go back to the time of Harvey de Montmorrisco in the late 12th century. Old maps show sites of two castles within the 250m by 200m enclosure. One was an early stone castle repaired in 1286. The second castle is mentioned in 1607.

HILLTOWN   S884149

William Esmond owned this fortified house in 1640 but it may be sixty years older than that. It has a three storey main block 12.8m long by 7.5m wide with a round bartizan at the SW corner, although the parapets have been destroyed. There are no latrines or stairs but there are four rectangular windows (two of two lights) with square hoodmoulds in the middle storey and several blocked two-light windows on the top storey, which has projecting chimney flues on the west and south. The middle storey has a fireplace backing onto the four storey tower at the north end which is still embattled and set so as to project beyond the east wall, but leave a re-entrant angle at the NW corner. The original entrance probably lay there, as in the similar building at Coolhull.

HOOK HEAD   X733973

The lighthouse on the headland near which Raymond le Gros landed in 1169 (see Baginbun on page 189) is a 22m high circular keep which existed by 1245. After a period of disuse it was restored in the 1650s. With 19th century modifications it still serves as a lighthouse, being painted externally with bands of white and black. The tower measures 12m in diameter and has three rib-vaulted storeys, all with blocked fireplaces, and connected by stairs curving round within the wall thickness. The upper levels each have three mural chambers and the lowest level just one. All the windows have been modernised (although they are still small) and a railing has replaced the parapet.

KILCAVAN   S879132   C

The north and east walls of a tower of the Fitzhenrys stand four storeys high with a window in each wall at each level. There may have been a top vault but the cellar was not vaulted. The hood-mouldings on the house adjoining are probably 17th century work reset from a destroyed larger building, the scar of the roof of which survives against the tower.

KILCLOGGAN   S760047

A jamb of a bawn gateway and a doorway to its former wall-walk adjoin the north corner of a 17m high tower measuring 6.1m by 5.7m which belonged to the Knights Hospitallers and later passed to the Loftus family. The rebuilt entrance in the SE wall is protected by a machicolation opening off the stepped parapet. Stairs lead round the east corner up to the second storey which has a fireplace on the SW side and two blocked windows. Projecting turrets rising up as lookout platforms clasp the north and west corners, one to contain spiral stairs and the other to contain latrines on two levels and a chamber at the top level. The third and fourth storeys have ogival-headed windows facing SW and NE.

KILHILE   S714118   D

The 6.3m long north wall and parts of the east and west walls stand to wall-walk level, but the southern half has gone. The north wall contains the entrance, protected by a machicolation from the fifth storey and by a murder hole, and a stair up to the loft, at which level there is a latrine in the NE corner and a room in the haunch of the fallen vault. The third and fourth storeys had fireplaces in the west wall. In the early 17th century the tower was held by John Etchingham as part of the Dunbrody estate.

Kilhile Castle

Ferrycarrig: plan

Hook Lighthouse

Kilcloggan Castle

KILLESK   S745159   C

Nothing survives of the castle of the Barrons of Burnchurch first mentioned in 1568 but there is an interesting fortified church, first mentioned in 1370, containing a single chamber 10.8m long by 4.6m wide lighted only by three narrow loops. The western part has thicker walls to support a vault and above (reached by a stair in the SW corner) is a priest's chamber with a murder-hole protecting the doorway on the south side. See p21.

KILLIANE   T059166   H

A house now used as a hotel has replaced one side of a quadrangular bawn 35m long by 26m wide. The 1.4m thick and 8m high wall is otherwise fairly complete and has a round-arched west gateway with a machicolation, a turret corbelled out at the SW corner, and a 3.5m diameter round tower at the SE corner. A rectangular structure with one double-splayed opening at the NE corner forms part of the house. The southern wall-walk has a plain parapet with three gunloops probably of later date. The west wall-walk is reached by a stair rising from beside the tower house projecting west from the NW corner.

The tower house measures 12m by 8.3m and has several recesses with double-splayed loops in the lowest level, a vaulted loft above, and an entrance facing the house. It and the lowest of several flights of stairs in the east wall are commanded by murder holes. The third and fifth storeys windows have been altered but original windows, including one with two ogival-headed lights, remain on the fourth storey. The third and fourth storeys have fireplaces in the north wall and latrines in the NW corner. There are turrets on all four corners and stepped crenellations between them. The SE corner turret has a bellcote.

The castle was probably built c1500 by the Hays, but had passed by 1543 to the Cheevers family, who were forfeited by the Cromwellians in 1654.

Mackmine: plans   *Plan of Lady's Island Castle*

Lady's Island Castle   *Killiane Castle*

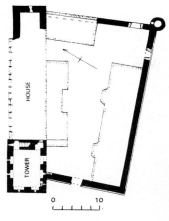

Plan of Killiane Castle

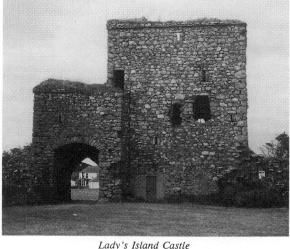

Lady's Island Castle

LADY'S ISLAND   T107075   B

A headland with a ruined medieval church is isolated by a 1m thick and 70m long curtain wall with a tower house measuring 9.1m by 7m set in the middle of it. The tower has a cellar with east and west double-splayed windows and a loft under a vault, and three upper rooms, the lower two of which are linked by a spiral stair in the SW corner and have remains of fireplaces in the north wall and latrines in the NE corner. A modern shrine adjoins the tower north wall and immediately west of it is a gatehouse 6m wide by 3.2m deep with a drawbar socket for securing a two-leaved gate. A dramatically leaning tower 4.8m by 3.5m with evidence of three storeys, one with a crossloop, is all that remains of an outer wall 70m in front of the main wall. The site seems to have originally belonged to an Augustinian community and was held by the Bishop of Ferns after the Suppression. It was leased to the Brownes of Mulrankin who had obtained ownership of it by 1654.

LINGSTOWN   T037078

Just a pile of rubble now remains of a tower which collapsed in 1985. It had a north-facing pointed-arch entrance with a machicolation, murder-hole, and possibly a portcullis. A straight stair in the north wall led up to a spiral stair in the NE corner which led to the third and fourth storeys and wall-walk. Over this upper stair was a lookout platform. There was a chimney stack on the north side. The tower was built either by the Synott or the Lambert families.

MACKMINE CASTLE   S972322   D

From the outside the ruined mansion appears entirely 19th century since the medieval tower at the SE corner is disguised with rendering, new windows, and a slightly projecting added fifth storey surmounted by battlements with round corner turrets rising above the rest. The tower measures 9m by 7.5m at third storey level, above the battered base containing a cellar and loft under a vault. The third and fourth storeys are linked by a spiral stair in the SE corner and have original fireplaces with smaller 19th century fireplaces set into them. A straight stair in the east wall leads down to the lower levels. The east-facing entrance lies above where the original entrance must have been. See page 180.

Mountgarrett Castle

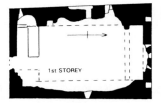

Mackmine Castle

Mulrankin: plan   *Mountgarrett: plan*

MOUNTGARRETT   S725294   G

Only a scarp marks out a bawn 60m by 35m but part of the four-storey tower house still stands to wall-walk level. It measures 15.2m by 10m and has a pointed-arched entrance in the south wall. The interior is badly defaced but shows evidence of a guardroom east of the entrance, over which was a tier of chambers, while to the west a stair led up to a spiral stair in the SW corner. There are gunloops and a fine third storey mullioned and transomed window with a square hoodmould in the north end wall, which also contains two latrine chutes. The tower is said to have been built by Patrick Barrett, Bishop of Ferns in the early 15th century but its features suggest that it was rebuilt or remodelled in the late 16th or early 17th century, when it was held by the Butlers.

MULRANKIN   S997101

The Brownes held Mulrankin from at least the 13th century until William Browne was forfeited in 1654. First mentioned in the early 16th century, the castle was captured and plundered by the Kavanaghs of Ballyanne in 1572. The tower measures 9m by 7.2m and has an entrance facing west, from which a stair in the south wall rises past a doorway to the loft under the vault and onto the third storey, which has ogival-headed windows facing east and north, a damaged fireplace on the west, and a latrine in the NE corner beside an opening which may originally have been a doorway onto a bawn wall-walk. The fourth storey reached by another stair in the east wall has blocked north and south windows. There is a lookout over the stair in the NE corner but the main parapet is fragmentary.

Jamb of town gateway, New Ross

Mulrankin Castle

NEWCASTLE S980144

A house adjoins the east wall of a tower measuring 6m by 5.5m which contains the blocked original entrance and staircase. The lowest level has two double-splayed loops, a chamber in the SE corner, and an inserted north doorway. The loft under the vault has one window and the room above has three, whilst little remains of the level above. No fireplaces or latrines remain. The castle is assumed to have been built by the Rossiters of Rathmacknee but was held by Richard Jennings in 1640.

NEW ROSS S722278 A

Just one side of the Fair (or Maiden) Gate of the town walls remains with a portcullis groove and traces of rib-vaulting. Nothing remains of the North Gate, the South (or Priory) Gate, or the Three Bullet Gate across Neville Street, but a small fragment of the wall remains in William Street and a D-shaped tower 6m high of two storeys lies in Nunnery Lane. The wall was probably built in the late 14th century and protected the north, east and south sides of an enclosure sloping steeply down to the River Barrow on the west.

POULMARL or TAGHMON S918197

This tower measuring 10.8m by 10.3m has a basement and loft under a vault and three upper storeys, each of which had a latrine in the SW corner and a fireplace in either the south or east walls. The castle is first mentioned in 1549, when held by William Hore. The east-facing doorway was closed by a portcullis and covered by a machicolation and a murder-hole opening from a room reached from the loft. The basement has double-splayed loops facing west and north and a gunloop. The battlements reached by spiral stair in the NW corner have gone but bartizans remain on the NW and SE corners. The two upper storeys have chambers in the north wall, the lower chamber being reached from the upper.

RATHLANNON   T019165

This tower measuring 9m by 7.6m stands complete with stepped battlements but the pointed-headed entrance with a machicolation and murder-hole operated from the third storey is the only original feature, apart from the spiral stair to the battlements. The interior has been refaced in brick and the vault torn out. The tower belonged to the Esmonds. They had another tower at Johnston nearby to the NE, where a later extension remains in use and the Irish Agricultural Museum is located in farm buildings nearby, although the tower house there was destroyed c1945.

RATHMACKNEE   T031140   B

Rathmacknee was a Rossiter seat from the 14th century until confiscated in 1654. A five storey tower 8.9m by 7.9m lies in the SE corner of a bawn enclosed by a wall 1.2m thick and 5.3m high to the wall-walk, which is complete except for a 9m gap on the south. Immediately north of the tower are the gateway defended by a machicolation and a stair to the wall-walk. There is a round bartizan on the bawn NE corner. The SW corner is chamfered off. Within the western part of the bawn is a modern house.

The tower west wall contains the entrance with a drawbar-slot and a stair. The cellar has one double-splayed loop commanding the bawn entrance and there is a loft under the vault. The room above has three windows (one is blocked), a loop and fireplace on the south, a latrine in a turret projecting south from the SE corner and a chamber in the north wall with a hatch down into another room below. Stairs in the north wall lead to a fourth storey with a similar layout, and another stair leads to a fifth storey with three windows with seats and two mural chambers. There are stepped battlements and lookouts on all the corners except that to the NW. A gap in the parapet suggests a former machicolation (possibly of wood) over the entrance.

Rathmacknee Castle

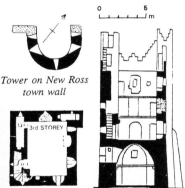

Tower on New Ross town wall

3rd STOREY

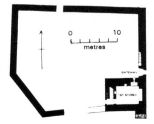

Rathmacknee: plans & section

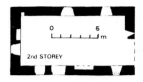

Rathshillane: plans

Rathshillane Castle

RATHRONAN   S985109

A derelict farmhouse incorporates the vaulted cellar and two upper storeys of a tower which belonged in the 17th century to the Brownes of Mulrankin. No original features have survived a later cutting-down and remodelling of the building.

RATHSHILLANE   T093068   C

The first mention of this fortified house is in 1616, when it was held by Robert French. Of three storeys without vaults, it measures 13.1m by 7.4m over walls 1m thick. The entrance at the south end of the east wall is segmental-headed, has a drawbar slot and machicolation, and there is a recess above for a plaque. The lowest level has musket loops set just either side of the NW and SE corners and there were several others which are now blocked. The middle storey has a large fireplace on the west and a smaller one at the north end, where a private room was probably partitioned off between the windows of two and three lights in the west wall. The third storey also has two fireplaces, several blocked two-light windows, and a latrine at the SW corner. There are corbels to support the floor of this storey. There was probably an internal stair of wood at the south end. There are stepped battlements with round bartizans with machicolations on the SW and NE corners.

Rathronan Castle

Bawn at Rathmacknee

Bartizan, Rathshillane

Rathumney Castle

RATHUMNEY   S768165   A

Possibly erected by John Barry in the early 15th century, and held in the 17th century by John Allen, this 25m long by 8.6m wide building lay on one side of a bawn and contained a central hall with a kitchen with a chamber over at the north end and a two storey chamber block at the south end with fireplaces, and latrines and stairs at its east end. The hall and kitchen each have separate entrances with drawbar slots facing west and the hall entrance led to a screens passage also with a west doorway. The hall has tall windows and the rooms at each end have double-splayed loops.

RICHFIELD   S950074

A farmyard occupies a moated platform 90m by 70 with an inner rampart, the moat being 10m wide on the east but narrower elsewhere, and interrupted by farm entrances. The house is a much-altered tower 11.4m by 7m with two barrel-vaulted cellars and an entrance on the south side, but no other original features remain. This castle was originally called Ballymagir and was an important Devereaux seat.

Sigginstown: plan

ROSEGARLAND   S859153

Only the vaulted cellar (with unusually tall loops) and part of one upper storey remain of a tower 12.7m by 8.5m with an entrance in the east wall and a latrine turret projecting west from the NW corner. The staircase lies in the north wall. The castle was probably built by the Nevilles, from whom the estate was confiscated in 1536. The castle was held by the Synot family from 1605 until confiscated by Cromwell's government in 1654.

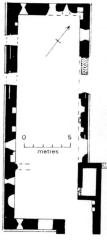

Rathumney: plan

Rathumney Castle

SCAR S938123 D

This tower of the Bryan family measures 8.9m by 7.2m and has a lintelled east-facing doorway with a murder hole. Both the cellar and the loft between it and vault have blocked doorways towards an added house about 7m wide which extended 16.5m to the south, although only fragments of it, including a chimney on the south, now remain. The room over the vault is reached by a stair in the north wall and has a latrine in the NW corner, a slop-stone facing west, a fireplace on the east, and three windows, all blocked or much damaged. Another stair in the north wall rises to a fourth storey with several blocked or damaged windows, and to the former wall-walk.

SIGINSHAGGARD S939189 D

A tower measuring 6.6m by 6.1m lies at the east corner of a bawn 28m square marked by a bank and ditch. The pointed-arched entrance facing SW retains a machicolation but the internal murder-hole has been destroyed along with most of the lobby. The cellar has three double-splayed loops and several gunloops making a mid 16th century date likely. There are further gunloops in the loft below the vault and others opening off the spiral stair in the west corner and off each of the three upper rooms. The third storey has a latrine in the east corner and a fireplace on the NE side. The wall-walk and parapet has not survived. The tower was described as ruinous in 1640, when it belonged to Philip Siggin.

SIGGINSTOWN T062070 C

The north wall of this tower which was confiscated from the Siggins family in 1654 faces towards a ruined brick house of much later date. This wall contains the blocked pointed-headed entrance with a portcullis groove, machicolation, and a covering crossloop. There are other crossloops at third storey level lighting a latrine in the SW corner and a spiral stair in the NE corner, reached from the entrance by a straight stair in the north wall. The fourth storey also has a latrine in the SW corner, whilst the SE corner contains a chamber with another crossloop reached from the embrasure of an east-facing window. Both these levels have fireplaces in the south wall. The stair rises to a fifth storey with windows on all four sides and then ends under a lookout platform. Most of the parapet has fallen.

SLADE   S746844   B

The castle of the Laffan family by the harbour consists of a stronghouse 13m by 7m with its SW corner adjoining an older and higher tower 5.4m square. The pointed-headed tower entrance faces south, away from the stronghouse and is protected by a machicolation and murder-hole. A adjacent stair leads to a passage in the east wall to the loft under a vault and, via a SE corner spiral stair, to the third storey, which has a fireplace on the west, a latrine on the east, and windows facing north and south. There are two further storeys, without fireplaces or latrines, and then another vault, above which are stepped battlements. The south end of the tower rises one stage higher with a lookout post above.

The stronghouse dating from the late 16th century has its own round-headed entrance with a murder-hole in the south wall just west of the tower. It admits to a lobby from which there is access to the westernmost of three vaulted rooms, which was a kitchen with a fireplace with a projecting breast in the end wall. There is also access to the middle room, and, via a stair, to the middle of three rooms on the upper level. This was a hall with a fireplace on the east. West of it was a chamber with four windows, some of two lights with ogival heads. Another chamber to the east has a third storey room above it reached by a continuation of the staircase. The stepped battlements must have been reached from this upper room. A block was later built in the NW re-entrant angle between the tower and house to provide second storey level access between them.

SLEVOY   S877175

This tower measuring 6.5m by 5.6m has a lintelled entrance in the north wall and a stair rising in the west wall past a doorway to the loft under the vault to the room above, little of which remains, although there is a fireplace and large window on the north and a latrine in the SE corner. The cellar has one double-splayed loop. No bawn now survives, but one is mentioned in the 1650s, when the castle belonged to Alexander Rossiter.

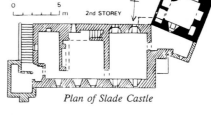

Plan of Slade Castle

Tellarought Castle

Stokestown Castle

Slade Castle

0   3
L__L__J m

Tellarought: plan

1st STOREY

3rd STOREY

1st STOREY

Taylorstown: plans & section

Taylorstown Castle

STOKESTOWN   S694236

The only original features of this much-altered tower measuring 7m by 6.6m are several blocked loops and a large blocked mullioned and transomed window with square hoodmouldings at third storey level. In 1582 the castle passed from the Prendergasts to George Dormer, a merchant of New Ross.

TAYLORSTOWN   S818143   C

This tower about 7.8m square belonged to James Rochfort in the 17th century. The lowest storey has recesses with horizontal gunloops on the SE and SW sides, a lintelled doorway on the NW, and a later doorway cut through the NE wall. Under the stair in the NW wall is a chamber reached from a hatch in the floor of the landing outside the doorway to the loft under the vault. On the opposite side of the landing is a doorway to the house later added beside the tower, little of which remains. The room over the vault has a fireplace on the SW, two gunloops in the east corner, and latrine off the spiral stair in the north corner leading to a former fourth storey which has been destroyed.

TELLAROUGHT   S756214   G

Most of the south wall, which contained the entrance, has been destroyed of this tower measuring 7.3m square which was probably built by the Suttons, although it had passed to Matthew Forde by 1640. The cellar has four recesses but no surviving openings. Stairs rise up through the west and north walls to a loft under the vault and then to the third storey, which had a fireplace on the north and windows on each side. A spiral stair in the NE corner then led up past the fourth storey, which has two windows, one with seats, to the destroyed battlements.

TINTERN   S794100   E

In the 1560s Anthony Colclough remodelled the already-embattled chancel of the Cistercian abbey church into a three storey fortified house, providing it with new windows, and the crossing became a four storey tower with battlements stepped up at the corners. Another wing was built over the vaulted chapels east of the destroyed south transept. The nave only seems to have been made habitable in the 18th century. West of where the cloister lay is a gatehouse later made into a stable-block, now the monument office.

TRACYSTOWN   S888195

This tower measuring 7.8m by 7m has been destroyed above the level of the vault over the cellar and loft. It has a rough doorway protected by a murder hole in the south wall. Stairs then rise up in the west wall. The tower belonged to William Hore in the 1650s.

West Gate, Wexford

WEXFORD   T051214

An 18th century barracks lies on the site of a castle which existed by 1221 and is assumed to have been built by King John. It is said to have been a rectangular keep with four corner towers like those of Carlow, Ferns and Lea. The names of the constables from 1310 to 1390 are known. The castle was surrendered to Cromwell's forces in 1649.

Considerable lengths remain of the early 14th century town walls following the line of a rampart of the Viking period. The gunloops here and there must be 16th century. A rectangular tower remains west of Mallon Street, and there is a round tower on the section between George Street and West Gate. Another round tower remains west of Abbey Street. The West Gate remains in use as a visitor centre. It has three upper rooms with fireplaces and latrines over a vaulted passage. There were turrets on the outer corners. The third storey has a doorway to the wall-walk of the main wall. Castle Gate, St Bride's Gate, St Peter's Gate, Rabby's Gate across Mary Street, and St John's Gate have all been destroyed. St Selskar's Abbey also has an embattled tower at the east end of the south nave, but it contains no fireplaces or latrines to indicate a possible habitation.

Town Walls, Wexford

West Gate, Wexford

Tintern Abbey

OTHER CASTLES REMAINS IN COUNTY WEXFORD

AUGHNAGAN S938161 Defaced lowest stage of tower 6m by 5.8m with double-splayed loop. A Hore possession from mid 16th century to mid 17th century.

BAGINBUN S800031 Rampart and ditch 230m long cutting off 22 acre promontory. Raymond le Gros camped here in 1170 but the earthworks may be somewhat older.

BALLYBRENNAN BIG T069133 House may incorporate walling from a castle of the Synott family, owners since the 13th century.

BALLYHIRE T141105 Ivy-covered lowest part of tower 8.5m square with one double-splayed loop. Belonged to the Lambert family.

BALLYMACANE T072075 Stone on site has date 1612 and initials of three members of Stafford family. Old photograph shows ruined house of two storeys and an attic.

BALLYMACAR S744254 Traces of building about 20m by 6m within platform 35m by 23m enclosed by narrow ditch with remains of inner rampart on east.

BALLYSHELIN S956167 Oval platform with possible ditch on west with traces of some stonework at the north end. Belonged to the Hore family.

BUTTERMILK S695123 6m square base remains of three storey tower protecting fishing weirs of Dunbrody Abbey. Held by John Etchingham in 1654.

CASTLE ANNESLEY T185415. Two storey D-shaped flanker 5m diameter remains of the bawn and house built 1618-21 by Sir Francis Annesley.

DUNCORMICK S918092 D-shaped platform 50m by 40m with ditch on south. The lofty tower which once stood here has now gone.

DUNGEER S906217 Gunloops in one complete wall with returns of two others remaining of T-plan stronghouse occupied by Thomas Roche as a tenant of the Suttons.

DURRA or DIRR S960158 Held by Meyler family in 1585. Main tower gone but a two storey 6m diameter flanker with gunloops remains of the bawn.

GORTINS S972138 Low fragment of 1.2m thick walling of tower of Prendergasts confiscated in 1654. Stones from doorway lying nearby.

HILLCASTLE S092106 U-shaped wet moated platform at farm. Mansion demolished c1960 incorporated a tower of the Hay family mentioned in late 16th century.

HOUSELAND S760012 Footings of 5.8m square tower held by Redmonds in 1561, and by Nicholas Loftus in 1640. Evidence of north-facing entrance.

KILMANNAN S970152 Tower 5.7m by 5.4m with doorway towards former church to east. Stair rises over recess in NE corner. Vaulted cellar and two upper levels.

LIMERICK T149660 One round tower with gunloops remains of a bawn with a pair of houses of two storeys with attics built c1615 by Sir Laurence Esmond.

LONGGRAIGUE S841183 The house incorporates the battered base of a tower which was held in the early 17th century by the Bryan family.

MACMURROUGH'S S729302 Excavated traces of small 17th century house.

MILL LANDS T027303 Remains of moated platform 40m square. Possible site of moated house built by Sir Adam Loftus c1619-21 but ruined by 1654.

MULLINDERRY S812162 Still-occupied stronghouse of the Hore family. Measures 23m by 7.5m and has two storeys and an attic. Corbels remain of NW corner bartizan.

NEWBAWN S826222 NE wall 6m high with two double-splayed loops and pointed-arched entrance with murder hole remains of 7m square tower of the Browns of Mulrankin.

NEWBAY T013205 Battered wall in stable block may be remnant of castle held by St Selskar's Priory in 1540. It had passed to the Roches by 1654.

PEPPARDS T195451 Thick old walls of the Peppards' tower remain in a house.

TACUMSHIN T070067 Buried in vegetation is the 2m high base of a tower 8m square which belonged to the Hays until the 17th century.

TOMHAGGARD T030080 6m high fragment of 7.5m long SE wall with the cellar filled in and a small chapel built on the filling beside a road.

CASTLE SITES IN COUNTY WEXFORD

ARDENAGH S897168 Vanished tower belonging to Hore family in 1640s.

ARNESTOWN S741262 No remains of tower mentioned in 1650s.

BALLINDONEY S809360 No remains of tower marked as site on old maps.

BALLINESKER T116288 Remains of tower said to have stood until c1825.

BALLYBRENNAN S916317 Modern mound on site marked on old maps.

BALLYCARNEY S969487 A pair of three storey rectangular towers still stood in 1840 as remnants of the now-vanished stronghouse built by Sir James Carroll c1617.

BALLYCONNICK S946138 Held by the de Boscos in the 13th century, the Boshers in the 15th century and the Bushens in the 17th century. No remains.

BALLYGARVAN S786186 In 1654 Sir Caesar Colclough held the decayed castle of the Rossiters of Slevoy. Ruin shown on Gill's map of 1811 has since disappeared.

BALLYGERRY T125119 Site of castle of Synnotts shown on old maps.

BALLYHOGE S983295 16th century house destroyed in 1922 replaced FitzHenry castle.

BALLYLANE EAST S742233 No remains of castle shown on 1841 map.

BALLYLEIGH S760333 No remains, rather doubtful, but site marked on 1924 map.

BALLYRANE T054121 Site of vanished tower once described as being 18m high.

BALLYSESKIN T002069 Tower and house of Cheevers family passed to Colonel Bunbury in 1654. Had two towers. Last standing part collapsed in 1886.

BALLYTRAMON T052257 Site of stronghouse of Synotts of Ballybrennan which fell down in 1940. Probably Z-planned, with two round corner towers.

BANNOW S825071. Chimney stack survived near church until 19th century.

BATTLESTOWN S771094 Site of tower held by John Etchingham in 17th century.

BERKELEY S759298 Site of tower shown complete on 1841 map.

BOLEY S798168 Site of 8m by 6.6m five storey tower destroyed c1903 near 32m wide moated platform. A Tintern Abbey possession granted 1566 to Sir Anthony Colclough.

BRIDESWELL S978121 Just two corbels with faces remain of a castle which was confiscated from Nicholas Devereaux in 1654.

BRIDGETOWN S988096 Site of castle of Brownes of Mulrankin demolished c1835.

BROWNSCASTLE S915218 Later ruin on site of David Synnott's stronghouse.

CARRIGMANNON S976261 Site of castle on strong site above River Slaney sold by the Furlongs to the Devereaux family in 1638.

CASTLEPALISER T116064 Castle of Codd family destroyed c1810. No remains.

CLERISTOWN S958141 A rather doubtful site, not mentioned in any records.

CULLENTRA T004229 Probable stronghouse site. Mentioned in 1666 when granted to Philip Hore. Lands previously held by Roches of Drinagh.

DRINAGH T057186 Site of seat of Roches from mid 16th century.

FORT CHICHESTER T184676 Nothing remains of a fort established in 1610 under the command of Captain Denis Dale. It was captured by the rebels in 1641.

HARPERSTOWN S931168 Farm on site of castle of Harper family mentioned 1526.

JOHNSTOWN T020168 See entry in main gazetteer for Rathlannon (p182).

KILCOWAN S959097 Site of castle of Keating family destroyed c1825.

LACKEN S766282 Site marked on 1841 and 1926 6" Ordnance Survey maps.

LATIMERSTOWN T038189 Site marked on 1841 map.

MOUNTFIN S965497 17th century stronghouse with four corner towers perhaps built by the O'Breine family and demolished c1970.

MORRIS T185422 Last wall of Murphy (or O'Morchoe) castle quarried away 1936.

NEWCASTLE T007247 Site of Roches' castle, noted as in decay in 1654.

NEWTOWN S842093 Last part of probable Prendergast castle recently removed.

NEWTOWN T189703 Site of probable stronghouse with rear stair turret begun by Sir Richard Cooke being granted estate in 1612. Still incomplete in 1621.

OLDCOURT S708222 Depression on site of castle of Suttons.

POLEHORE S980237 No remains of castle owned by Hores until 1883, but burnt in 1798 rebellion. 1841 map shows a second castle site nearby to NW.

PRIESTHAGGARD S702175 Remains of tower held by Walter Meyler of Duncormack in 1570 removed a few years ago. Had murder-hole over entrance.

PROSPECT T199600 Site of stronghouse and bawn (both with flankers) and walled garden built by Sir Edward Fisher between 1612 and 1621. "Decayed" in 1654.

RATHASPICK T024182 Georgian house may retain part of castle of Codd family.

REDMOND'S HALL S 746001 Loftus Hall of 1870 stands on site of castle of the Redmond family which was granted to Sir Nicholas Loftus in 1666.

ROSSLARE T112214 Nothing remains of a late 16th century fort remodelled by the Confederate Catholics after they took it over in 1642. Captured by Cromwell in 1649.

RYLAND S929547 Featureless wall removed c1980. Held by Kavanaghs in early 17th century but passed to Lord Annesley in 1650s.

WARREN'S CASTLE S773343 No remains, but marked on old maps.

WILTON S943350 1840 house on site of William Alock's house of c1695, replacing a castle held by Stephen Furlong in 1376, and Pierce Butler in 1654.

The exact locations of possible early 17th century stronghouses at Ballyvodock, Monaseed, Tomduff and Wingfield are unknown.

MOTTES AND RINGWORKS IN COUNTY WEXFORD

Ballinamorragh T086264,   Ballingowan T124377,   Ballyhoge S976285,   Ballymore T099507, Ballymoty T045404, Ballyorley T071452, Castlesow T028287, Doonooney S896279, Duncormick S918094, Glascarrig T214496, Hooks S959096, Inch T129325 Killegny S842347, Kilmuckridge T165405, Kiltrisk T174451, Loggan T078699, Middletown T198547, Morabeg S979377, Newcastle S836194, Old Ross S794276, Pallis T139680. See also the entries for Ferns, Ferrycarrig, and Fethard, etc.

CASTLES OF COUNTY WICKLOW

ARKLOW CASTLE   T242735   C

Beside the council offices is a 25m long curving length of wall, probably 13th century in date, extending from the main road to an ivy-mantled three storey round tower above a ravine. Near the tower are two loops and a window in the curtain wall. The Butlers had a seat here by the 1190s. It was captured in 1331 by rebel Irish but recaptured in 1332 by Justiciar Lucy. The Kavanagh MacMurroughs took the castle in 1452 and held it until 1530, when it was returned to the Butlers. The castle was repaired in 1571 and was captured by the Confederate Catholics in 1642. It was burnt by them in 1649 to prevent it being taken and occupied by Cromwell's forces. Ramparts with ditches, palisades and gates were erected around the town c1571-6.

BALLINTRUER   S909931

On the SE side of an oval enclosure 45m long by 33m wide are the footings of a tower 8.5m square with walls up to 1.5m thick. The east end of the south wall stands 3m high. Footings of the south wall of a bawn continue west from this wall.

BALLYVOLAN CASTLE   T288017

Footings and two higher fragments on the north (one with putlog holes) of a wall from 1m to 1.5m thick are set on ringwork 55m across now occupied by house and garden of 1959. There is a surrounding ditch 2m deep and 13m wide with an outer bank.

BLACK CASTLE, WICKLOW   T323940   A

There is a tree covered motte 6m high above the river north of Wicklow. This must have been quickly superseded by the stone fortress some way east of the town known as Black Castle. Low walls on the north and SW sides and higher fragments at the east and south corners remain of a fan-shaped court about 25m across, the NE side being curved, and the SE side having traces of a range of buildings. The court was isolated by a deep rock-cut ditch from an outer bailey to the west, the rampart of which has vanished.

A castle at Wicklow (probably the motte) is mentioned in a grant of Henry II to Richard de Clare in 1174. The stone castle was taken over by Edward III in 1350. The town does not seem to have been walled until an earth rampart and palisade were provided in the 1570s, and was always vulnerable to attacks by the O'Byrnes. They came to an agreement with Henry VIII in 1542 but destroyed both the castle and town in 1580. The castle was regarrisoned for Elizabeth I in 1581. It was seized by a Confederate Catholic force under Luke O'Toole, but later recaptured by Sir Charles Coote.

Black Castle, Wicklow

Killincarrig: plan

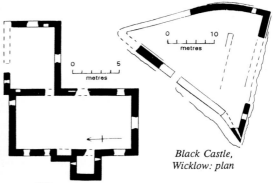

Black Castle, Wicklow: plan

Fassaroe Castle

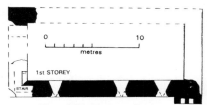

Plan of Kindlestown Castle

Kindlestown Castle

CARNEW CASTLE   T014630

The still inhabited 18th century house incorporates a 16th century tower of four storeys with a wing flanking the original pointed-headed entrance doorway commanded by a machicolation from the third storey. The tower has a NW corner turret and latrine chutes remain, but the windows are of later date.

CASTLE KEVIN   T183985   D

Henry de Londres, Archbishop of Dublin, founded this castle c1214. It was later remodelled as a bastion against the O'Tooles, who eventually obtained a grant of the site. The castle seems to have been destroyed in the early 17th century and not rebuilt. Part of a gatehouse and footings of a NE corner of another structure remain on the east side of a motte with a summit roughly 35m square rising 6m from a ditch 2m deep with an outer bank on the south and north sides. The latter also flanks a bailey platform 65m wide which extends 140m to the east from the motte ditch.

FASSAROE CASTLE   T243174   D

The west and south walls containing embrasures and aumbries remain of a tower built in 1535 by William Brabazon, Treasurer of Ireland, together with footings of the other two sides. Part of a vault over the second storey still remains.

KILLINCARRIG CASTLE   T287112   D

A kitchen wing projects NE from a stronghouse measuring 14.3m by 7.6m built in the early 17th century, probably by Henry Walsh. There is a recess for a plaque over where the entrance doorway on the east side was torn out in the 1940s, and a stair turret projects from the middle of the west side. There are large chimney stacks on the north and south gables. The ruin is much obscured with ivy.

KINDLESTOWN CASTLE   T279118

Within the east end of a ditched enclosure 50m by 20m stand the north wall and SE corner of an early 14th century hall-house probably built by the Archbold family. It measures 20.6m by 9.7m over walls up to 1.9m thick and had a vaulted basement and a hall above probably with a private chamber divided off at the west end, since latrines were provided in a slight projection northwards from the NW corner. A third latrine chute discharged below a squinch arch between this projection and the main wall higher up. The north wall contains three loops below the vault and four windows above which are not much bigger, and there is a west facing crossloop in the latrine chamber in the NW corner. There are traces of a stair in the NE corner. See illustrations on page 193.

KNOCKROE CASTLE   S940053

On top of a ridge in a valley south of Hollywood is a motte rising up to 6m to a summit 15m across. The 2.5m deep ditch has an outer bank on the west and south and is crossed by a causeway from the bailey platform measuring 50m by 45 on the north. There are fallen masonry fragments of uncertain date on the motte slopes.

NEWCASTLE MCKYNEGAN   T293042   C

King John is thought to have had a castle built here c1210-13. On the west side of a circular platform 60m across is a gatehouse now measuring 14.6m by 8.6m. with niches for armoral plaques on the west side. The castle was captured several times by the O'Byrnes and was destroyed by them in 1405. Probably dating from c1280-1300, the gatehouse was mostly rebuilt after this district was recovered for the Crown in the 1540s and the upper storeys were then laid out with public rooms to the north and private withdrawing rooms with large windows and brick fireplaces at the mostly destroyed southern end. The vaulted entrance passage was flanked by guard rooms, and there was space at least on the northern side for a mezzanine storey with a big fireplace, but in the 13th century layout the side rooms were of one storey and projected further west into a pair of D-shaped towers about 6m in diameter.

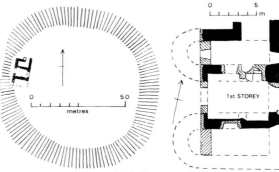

Oldcourt Castle   Newcastle McKynegan: plans

OLDCOURT CASTLE T260175

A platform on a knoll above a stream bears traces of a bawn with a gateway between two round towers, the eastern one of which still stands 2.5m high. Projecting from the NE corner is a tower 7.8m by 5m with vaults over the lowest two of four storeys, the lowest level having no direct access from outside. A NW corner spiral stair once linked the upper levels. The third storey has ogival-headed windows facing east and south. The tower may always have been intended to be part of a larger structure and it bears on the west side the roof mark of a 17th century house.

POWERSCOURT CASTLE T211164

The castle built in the late 15th century by the 8th Earl of Kildare probably in the same position as the 19th century house (possibly with older parts) which was destroyed by fire in 1974. The conifer covered platform 50m by 40m on slight ridge to the NW may be the site of the castle in Balyteny built in 1316 which was ruinous by 1355. The Kildare stronghold was wrecked by the O'Tooles in 1535, repaired the same year, and later handed over to them. The building was again destroyed in 1650.

THREECASTLES T011156

Of the three castles from which the townland takes its name only the eastern part of one of them remains, measuring 9.8m by 6.4m, and having a vault over the uppermost of three storeys. The crosswall towards the destroyed part contains pointed doorways at the two lowest levels. The lowest storey has double-splayed windows facing east and north. The room above has a two light window with a square hoodmould facing south, a fireplace, and a latrine beside a staircase in a turret projecting east from the NE corner. One of the other castles here lay 300m to the east. In this vicinity an English force in alliance with Brian O'Toole defeated the rebel FitzGeralds in 1547.

Newcastle McKynegan

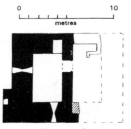

Threecastles

Tower at Threecastles

OTHER CASTLES IN COUNTY WICKLOW

BALLINTRUER S909931 Footings of tower 8.5m square and 3m high fragment of 1.5m thick south wall lie on SE side of oval enclosure 45m by 33m with traces of wall.

BALTINGLASS S868888 Footings with trace of possible SE tower remain of abbot's residence (tower and later house), demolished for materials in 1882.

BURGAGE S976123 Blessington Reservoir waters caused collapse in 1950s. North wall and west wall with entrance of tower stand 8m high beside lake.

CARYSFORT T123827 Fragment by St Brigid's church possibly of fort built by Viceroy William Cary c1628, and abandoned after capture in 1641 by Catholics.

CASTLE MACADAM T200791 Small fragment of wall on spur above Avoca River.

CASTLEQUARTER S935905 Stone-lined moat around platform 50m across. An old map suggests that there was once a stronghouse on rocky platform on SE side.

GRANGECON S842959 Fragment of tower with chimney stack NE of house. Datestone of 1610 with initials HH. Second datestone of 1625 now missing.

MACDERMOT'S T273914 Undated and defaced vaulted gateway passage at south end of platform 37m by 30m within ditch up to 10m wide with outer bank.

STUMP OF THE CASTLE T196905 Remains in garden of 13.5m square building with corner turrets 3m in diameter standing in SE corner of 50m square moated platform.

TALBOTSTOWN S920875 Ditch 8m wide with inner face stone lined around court 50m by 45. Turrets face west, NW and north, possible fourth at NE.

SITES OF CASTLES IN COUNTY WICKLOW

BRAY T262187 Site of tower possibly on site of castle built before 1225 by Walter de Ridelesford.

CASTLE LAURENCE T085810 Barn on site of stronghouse of Sir Laurence Esmond.

CASTLESALLAGH S923935 No remains. Tower & extension shown on 1650 survey.

DUNRAN T273022 The ruin with corner turrets at the top may be a folly, since it contains no old features or vaults. Old castle probably stood opposite side of road.

KILPIPE T102760 Enclosure marked on old map. No remains now visible.

KNOCKRATH T153926 Two large terraces on site of an O'Byrne castle said to have had a tower 8.7m square with round NE corner tower.

OLDCOURT T021150 No remains. Described as tower with later house by NW corner.

PHELIM'S T131874 Supposed site of Philim McFeagh O'Byrne's stronghouse.

RATHDOWN T289137 Former platform 43m square with 6m wide ditch and outworks. Sewage works on site of stone building alongside.

RAYMOND'S T069731 Traditionally said to be the site of castle.

SESKIN S973939 Platform 50m square is said to be site of Colonel Percy's 17th century stronghouse.

Marked as castle sites on 1838 O.S. maps: Aghrim   T123803,   Clogh S873864, Kilballyowen T096774, and Kilpipe T103760.

Possible motte site: Athdown T067140

MOTTES AND RINGWORKS

Ardoyne S882707, Ballycore S814940, Boleylug   S904884,   Castleruddery S919939, Donard S930975, Killamoat S978853, Kilpipe T111772, Mount Kennedy T262071, Rathdangan S969855, Rath Turtle Moat S964152.

Black Castle, Wicklow

INDEX OF CASTLES

FOLLY PUBLICATIONS BOOKS   by Mike Salter

Folly Cottage, 151 West Malvern Rd, Malvern, Worcs WR14 4AY, England

IRISH CASTLES TITLES - Five volumes covering all of Ireland
CONNACHT   2004   104 pages, 365 illustrations
ULSTER   2004   72 pages, 200 illustrations
SOUTH MUNSTER 2004   128 pages, 340 illustrations
LEINSTER   2004   200 pages,   640 illustrations.
NORTH MUNSTER   due out late 2004 or in 2005. No details yet available.

SCOTTISH CASTLES TITLES - Five volumes covering all of Scotland
SOUTH WEST SCOTLAND   1993   152 pages, 347 illustrations.
HEARTLAND OF SCOTLAND 1994   140 pages, 299 illustrations.
LOTHIAN AND BORDERS   1994   168 pages, 338 illustrations.
GRAMPIAN AND ANGUS   1995   200 pages, 370 illustrations.
WESTERN AND NORTHERN SCOTLAND 1995 152 pages, 200 illustrations.

WELSH CASTLES TITLES - Four volumes covering all of Wales
GWENT, GLAMORGAN & GOWER   2003 edition 112 pages, 250 illustrations
MID WALES 2001 edition 72 pages, 95 illustrations.
SOUTH-WEST WALES 1996 88 pages, 130 illustrations.
NORTH WALES 1997 88 pages, 125 illustrations.

ENGLISH CASTLES TITLES - Eighteen volume set, plus separate index volume
SHROPSHIRE   2001 edition 88 pages,   146 illustrations.
STAFFORDSHIRE   1997 edition   64 pages,   85 illustrations.
WARWICKSHIRE   1992   56 pages,   87 illustrations.
HEREFORDSHIRE & WORCESTERSHIRE 2000 edition 88 pages, 120 illustrations
NORTHUMBERLAND 1997 1997   120 pages,   210 illustrations.
CUMBRIA   1998   104 pages, 210 illustrations.
DEVON & CORNWALL   1999   88 pages, 146 illustrations.
SUSSEX   2000   72 pages,   100 illustrations.
KENT   2000   88 pages, 120 illustrations.
EAST ANGLIA   2001   88 pages, 130 illustrations.
SURREY   2001   24 pages, 32 illustrations.
YORKSHIRE   2001   120 pages, 215 illustrations.
LANCASHIRE & CHESHIRE 2001   40 pages, 60 illustrations.
WESSEX   2002   104 pages, 180 illustrations.
GLOUCESTERSHIRE & BRISTOL 2002   40 pages, 57 illustrations.
DURHAM   2002   64 pages, 100 illustrations.
EAST MIDLANDS   2002   100 pages, 160 illustrations.
THAMES VALLEY & THE CHILTERNS 2002   80 pages, 118 illustrations.

Also available in a similar format are books about medieval parish churches in:
Scotland (single volume), Wales (4 volumes), England (14 volumes for various counties).
Books about the Isle of Man and the Channel Islands cover both castles and churches.

WEB SITE   www.follypublications.co.uk

See the web site for prices, details of forthcoming titles, availability of existing titles, and
how to order. The web site will eventually include updated and corrected information for
the Irish volumes, together with any extra plans and photographs that become available.